The Cat Who
Went to Paris
&
A Cat Abroad

Also by Peter Gethers

The Dandy
Getting Blue
The Cat Who'll Live Forever

Written as Russell Andrews
Gideon
Icarus

Co-authored with Norman Stiles and Norton
Historical Cats

The Cat Who Went to Paris

&

A Cat Abroad

Two Volumes in One

Peter Gethers

BARNES
&NOBLE
BOOKS
NEW YORK

Contents

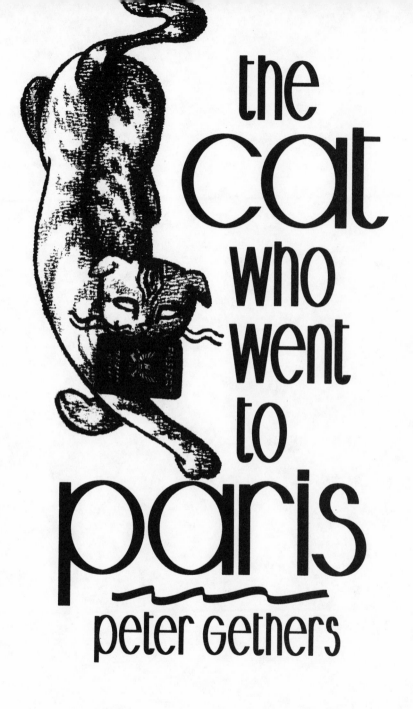

the cat who went to paris

peter gethers

To Dad. You're missed.

To Mom. You're appreciated.

To Janis. I can't believe you let me do this.

To Norton. What can I say? You'll be hand-fed Pounce as long as I'm around.

contents

Acknowledgments

First and foremost, thanks to Leona Nevler. All she did was come up with the idea for the book, think of the title, have confidence that I could write it, then come up with all the right suggestions to fix it. That's a good definition of a great editor.

Esther Newberg deserves a line or two (or a hundred) for convincing me that this was a good idea and, just generally, being the perfect agent.

Kathleen Moloney went through the manuscript word by word, as a favor. That was invaluable.

I wouldn't have Norton if it weren't for my brother, Eric. There's no way to even *try* to thank him for that.

Also thanks to everyone who let me write about them (whether they knew it or not).

Foreword

A few weeks ago, I made out my first-ever will. At thirty-six, it left me feeling slightly melancholy, more than slightly middle-aged, and somewhat sentimental. Looking to share my sentiment, I mentioned to my mother that I had—quite magnanimously, I thought—left my New York City apartment to my brother Eric's one-year-old son, Morgan. Instead of the expected motherly glow of affection and pride, she looked at me as if I were an insane person.

"Can you do that?!" she asked.

I didn't understand her wide-eyed confusion, especially since, on the scale of human accomplishment, my mother ranks her small grandchild somewhere between Mahatma Gandhi, Thomas Jefferson, and Bo Jackson.

"Why not?" I said, just a tad confused. "I mean, I hope he doesn't get to use it for another forty or fifty years, but if he does, it'll go to Eric first and he can—"

"Did you say Morgan?" she interrupted.

"Yeah. Who else?"

"I thought you said Norton," *dear old Mom told me.*

"My cat? *You thought I left my apartment to my* cat?"

"Well," she said, *in a particularly wise moment, and* shrugged, *"with Norton, you never know."*

Before the cat who went to paris

This is a book about an extraordinary cat. However, the extraordinary thing about *any* cat is the effect it has on its owner. Owning a cat, especially from kittenhood, is a lot like having a child. You feed him, do your best to educate him, talk to him as if he understands you—and, in exchange, you want him to love you. He can drive you mad with his independence. He can, just as surely as a child, create a tremendous desire to protect him from anything bad. He is small, vulnerable, wonderful to hold—when he lets you. And he throws up on just about the same regular schedule.

Like children, cats exist on a separate and probably higher plane than we do, and like children, they must be at least partially defined by their relationship with their parents. And though they can do all sorts of amazing things such as hiding in the tiniest room imaginable and refusing to be found no matter *how* late you are for wherever it is you have to take them, they cannot write their autobiographies. That is left to humans. So this, as it must be, is also a book about people. And thus about relationships. And all sorts of other things cats have no business being involved with but can't seem to help themselves.

My involvement with a cat was strictly accidental. In fact, I had to be dragged into it kicking and screaming.

By way of example, a little over seven years ago, someone asked me to name ten things that I believed were truly self-revealing, deeply heartfelt, and absolutely irrevocable. This person, a woman I was going out with, asked me to do this, I believe, because she thought I was a person without much emotion, without a lot of passion. She had, I also believe, been through way too many years of Upper East Side New York therapy in which she had made way too many lists like this. The fact of the matter was that I had plenty of emotion and plenty of passion. I just didn't have much for her. People often seem to fall into this trap in their relationships. They seem to feel that if someone doesn't do what he is expected to do, then there must be something *wrong* with him. This is a much easier way of getting through life, I suppose, than having to think there might be something wrong with the expectations or oneself or the world. Or life.

I did, finally and over my better instincts, make a list of ten things I believed were true about myself. This is another trap that people fall into in their relationships (which cats *never* fall into): we do a lot of stupid things just so we don't have to be alone.

Anyway, this is the list that appeared:

1. I will never vote Republican.
2. Love does not usually hold up to close inspection . . .
3. . . . except for baseball. I *love* baseball—watching it, listening to it on the radio, talking about it, reading box scores. I am a baseball junkie.
4. Life is basically a sad thing, with an even sadder ending, so anything that brightens up a moment along the way is okay. Especially if it's funny.
5. I don't like being a part of anything—a religion, a regular softball game, a corporation, a government, you name it. As soon as some*one* becomes some*thing,* I tend to think he or she is lost.
6. Friendship must be earned. It is too important to fritter away on someone who doesn't want it, won't reciprocate it, or isn't worthy of it. As near as I can tell, people don't have all that much inherent value, but friends sure do.
7. There's very little cause for cruelty.
8. On the other hand, I'll pick entertaining and intelligent over nice any day of the week.
9. I don't care what anyone says: I think Meryl Streep's a lousy actress.
10. I hate cats.

In the years that have passed, a few of these irrevocable items have actually remained steadfast. Several have been altered somewhat, some bordering on the brink of unrecognizability. And there is one of the above that is so ludicrous it now seems inconceivable that it ever crossed my mind, much less made it through my mouth or found its way onto paper.

Numbers 1, 3, 6, and 7 remain absolutely unchanged.

Number 4 is basically sound, although I cannot be nearly so definite about the word "anything." There are terrifying things I did not conceive of when I made my initial list: oat bran, crack, *People* magazine cover stories on recovering alcoholic celebrities, wilding, sequels, and Abe Rosenthal's "On My Mind" column in the *New York Times.*

Numbers 8 and 9 are a little tricky. 8 now depends more and more on my mood and how hard my day was. And Meryl Streep's Australian accent really is astonishing.

Number 5 has changed somewhat. I have found something I am willing to join.

Number 2 clearly relates to Number 5, which will become much clearer as this book continues, and they both, amazingly enough, have changed because of Number 10.

Ah yes, Number 10 . . .

Well, now we've come to the youthful folly, a statement made in such ignorance it boggles the mind . . .

I, of course, have a cat now. Norton.

I treat this cat as very few animals—or people, for that matter—have ever been treated.

If he is asleep in the middle of the bed when it's time for my day to end, I sleep curled up in a corner of the mattress, happily braving stiff necks and bad backs so he remains undisturbed.

I take Norton everywhere I go. He's been skiing in Vermont, to a writers conference in San Diego, to the best restaurant in Amsterdam, back and forth on a regular basis to Paris. At one of that city's premier hotels, the Tremoille, when my assistant calls to make a reservation for Mr. Gethers, the desk clerk knows to ask: *"Avec son chat?"*

I bought a house in Sag Harbor, a real-life Bedford Falls of a town near the tip of Long Island, and though there were many other mitigating circumstances, the secret and overriding reason for the purchase was because my cat *loves* to run around in a yard.

I've had one girlfriend break up with me because she believed I liked Norton better than I liked her (which I did). And I once didn't go on a vacation with another girlfriend to my favorite resort hotel in America because they wouldn't accept small, very well-behaved felines.

I worry about him, I talk about him (and *to* him, I have to add) to the point of idiocy, and if he doesn't sleep within a crooked arm's reach of my pillow—which he doesn't about one day a week—then I don't sleep very well. I actually worry that I've done something to offend him.

I sometimes—and this is a particularly tough one to admit publicly—let him eat off my spoon. Usually ice cream or yogurt. Chocolate's his favorite flavor, and it's a pretty funny thing to watch when he decides it's time to lick that sucker clean.

It is hardly a one-way street, however. He does all sorts of things for me that are pretty wonderful for a cat.

He goes for walks with me. No leash. On a beach with no cars around to disturb him, he's gone up to two miles, walking anywhere and everywhere from ten feet behind me to three feet in front of me. His record in traffic is three blocks, which he does most Sunday mornings when I stroll to Sean's Murray Hill market in Sag Harbor.

Norton will wait for me anywhere, no matter where I

leave him. If I'm at a hotel, I can dump him outside by the pool or in the garden, and let him play there all day or night long. When I go to get him, he will be nowhere in sight, but when I call or whistle for him, he'll meow exactly once, then leap out of his hiding place to rush to join me. I honestly believe I could drop him in the heart of an African jungle, leave him for a year, reappear, and as long as I could find the bush he was last seen scurrying under, he'd be there waiting for me.

He likes to roughhouse. His favorite game is to pounce on my hand when it's moving tauntingly under a sheet, wrestle it, and try to eat it—but he will *never* bite or scratch any part of me that he recognizes as mine. If sometimes he gets carried away in the heat of battle and a claw accidentally isn't pulled in in time when my hand comes out from the linen, he will freeze at the sound of my yelp, put his paws over his eyes, and bury his nose under the pillow in shame until I pat him on the head and assure him I'm okay.

He sits on the side of the tub when I take a bath.

If I, as I sometimes forgetfully do, close the door to a room, leaving Norton on the other side, he will howl and meow as if possessed until I open the door. He does not like to be left outside of anything I am inside.

He trusts me.

He is quite a comfort when I'm sad and makes being happy much more fun.

He has seen me through broken hearts and illness and death.

I love my cat, if you haven't gotten the drift yet.

He actually forced me to change my list of irrevocable self-realizations.

In doing so, he changed my life.

When a small gray animal does a little thing like that for you, how can you *not* let him sleep in the middle of the bed when he's tired?

The cat who came to New York

Have you ever seen a Scottish Fold?

One cat book I read dared refer to the breed as a "mutation." What they are, in fact, are incredibly handsome cats whose ears fold over in half, forward and then down, giving them a vaguely owl-like look. Their heads tend to be rounder than regular cat heads, and their bodies, at least all the ones I've seen, seem to be short, firm, and trim. Officially they are a shorthaired cat, but I would unofficially place them somewhere in-between a long- and a shorthair. They feel particularly soft and nice. Their temperaments range from sweet to sweeter. All of the ones I've met and spent time with are intelligent, though of course none have risen to the heights of brilliance that mine has.

They actually do come from Scotland. Apparently, the first one was discovered in 1961 at a farm near Dundee, by some people named William and Mary Ross. All of the fold-ear cats running around today can trace their pedigree back to Susie, which is what the Rosses named the first one they discovered.

The first time I ever heard of a Scottish Fold was when I got a phone call from my brother, Eric, who lives in Los Angeles. We talked about life (it seemed fine), work (since he's a screenwriter, it was hard, nasty, and full of deceitful intrigue), women (they were getting younger), and our health (we were getting older). The conversation seemed to have run its course when he dropped the bombshell.

"Oh, yeah," he said. "Did I tell you I got a cat?"

If this were a screenplay, the words *Long Pause* would now appear in parentheses, because there was a long one. A real long one. In that long pause my eyes rolled back in my head, my mouth dropped open as far as it could stretch, and I was certain the world had gone mad.

"You hate cats," I reminded him when I was finally able to speak.

"I know," was his response. "But this one's different."

I then heard the description of my first Scottish Fold, whom he'd named Henry. I have to say, I wasn't convinced.

"But you hate cats," I repeated. "We both hate cats. We loathe and despise them. We always have and we always will." By this time I think I was starting to whine. "We like *dogs.*"

I could tell, even from three thousand miles away, that my brother was smiling that annoying superior smile he has when he thinks I'm saying something idiotic.

"You'll see," he said again. "This one's different."

I have to sidetrack here.

At the time, my girlfriend's name was Cindy Wayburn. We'd been going together for three years or so, having quite a nice time. At one point, about six months earlier, Cindy had casually mentioned to me that she was thinking of getting a cat. I, just as casually, mentioned that if she did she might think about spending her nights in someone's apartment other than mine.

We argued, we discussed, we argued some more. She cajoled. I brought up my "cats don't fetch" premise and we argued even more. She even took the tack that it would be good for *me* to have a pet. I'd made the mistake of mentioning to her once that I missed having an animal around the house, that it felt lonely without one.

"A pet, yes," I said. "A cat, no."

"But you travel so much," was her comeback. "You couldn't have a dog. It would die in about two weeks."

"I know," I said. "That's why I *don't* have a dog. But that still isn't convincing me that a cat is a good idea. A cat would die in about two weeks, too—because I'd kill it."

"You've never even been around cats. You'd like them once you got to know one. And it would be good for you. You spend a lot of time at the beach house—you could have company. You wouldn't have to spend so much time talking to the old ladies who hang out at the grocery store."

"How do *you* know I spend so much time talking to the old ladies? Who told you?" I thought this had been a well-kept secret. Every summer I spent a solid month writing at a beach house I rented in Fair Harbor, Fire Island. Cindy, during the years it was Cindy, would come out on weekends, and I'd toil alone during the week, insisting that I loved the solitude. But after three days of slaving away over the typewriter (this was before I dared to punch away at a laptop), I'd begin to miss human companionship. I'd start to make a few more phone calls than usual, beginning around ten-thirty in the morning. After six days, my friends would start to keep their phone machines on since most of them didn't have the time to spend helping me avoid doing my work. At the ten-day point, I'd finally break down and start making three trips a day to the Fair Harbor market. It was only two blocks from my house, and there was usually a group of elderly housewives hanging out there, gossiping with the butcher and with each other. By my third season at the beach, I'd become a regular at the market. I knew everything there was to know about hundreds of people I'd never met. And best of all, I wasn't at the typewriter for half-hour stretches, three times a day.

"Have you ever lived with a kitten?" Cindy demanded, ignoring my pleas to reveal the Fire Island squealer.

"I've never lived with a snake, either. And I don't want to. I don't like them. Was it Frank, the butcher? Was he the one who told you?"

We went around in this adultlike manner for a reasonable amount of time—about seven hours—until eventually she decided that getting a cat for herself or for me wasn't going to be a plus in our relationship. To my great relief, our arguing ended and things went back on an even keel.

Until Cindy went to Los Angeles to visit her mother.

She wasn't particularly looking forward to the trip, since

she didn't much care for her mother. Once a year, however, filial guilt won out over common sense and Cindy would go west and pay a visit. Mrs. Wayburn—and I'll try to be as fair and objective as I can here—was an absolutely horrid woman who lived in some part of the outskirts of L.A. I'd never actually heard of, in a delightful little community called La Mobile Home Cité. If they'd had a slogan, it would have been "Come Spend a Few Depressing Years with Us Before Your Internal Organs Start to Fail." All in all, it was a great place to spend time if you didn't care about air, space, or ever looking at anything attractive.

This visit was worse than usual. After the second day, they had a huge fight. Cindy wanted to take her mother out to a fancy dinner, simply to be nice. Mom, in her typical upbeat way, said that all food tasted the same to her—like a lump of decaying, cold, gray clay—so there was no point in throwing money away on something as unpleasant as eating well. Cindy thought this was an unhealthy attitude, mentioned this to her mom, and the battle ensued. An hour after that, she was in my brother's house, crying and eating a delicious *tarte tatin* (my brother happens to be an excellent cook).

Eric was extremely nice to her, really cheered her up, and by the time she called me to say good night, she was in a terrific mood. Much better than could have been expected. So good, in fact, I should have been suspicious. She told me she was going to spend the next morning shopping with my brother, then would be on a mid-afternoon plane home. She'd decided she didn't want to see her mother anymore, and with no mother responsibilities, she didn't want to stay in L.A. The last thing she said before she hung up was,

"You won't believe how cute Eric's cat is. Wait till you see him."

I hung up, deciding I could wait a pretty long time.

At eleven-ten the next night, my phone rang.

"I'm at the baggage claim," Cindy announced. "Are you awake?" Her voice had that special singsong quality it had when she was feeling particularly affectionate toward me.

"I'm awake," I said, in much the same tone.

"I'll be there in thirty minutes."

"I can't wait," I told her. And, in truth, I couldn't.

Cindy had a key to my apartment and could bypass the various security buzzers and phones and TV cameras most people had to go through to get into my building. So thirty minutes later, I heard my front door open. When I came out of the bedroom, Cindy was standing by the door, grinning happily.

I went to kiss her.

"No," she ordered. "Stop."

I stopped.

"I have something to show you."

"You do?"

She nodded.

"Do I have to go to the hallway to see it?"

"No," she said, still with the biggest grin I'd ever seen on her face. "Stay there. Close your eyes. I'll tell you when."

I stayed, I closed my eyes. I heard her "when" and opened them.

Cindy was holding a little ball of fur in her hand. One

hand. It was so small, for a moment I thought she'd brought an extremely well-behaved mouse back from California.

But it wasn't a mouse.

It was a tiny, tiny gray kitten with a round head and funny-looking ears that folded forward and down. The kitten was sitting up in her palm, boldly swiveling his head around, gazing at all the sights in my loft apartment.

"You got yourself a cat?" I stammered weakly.

The kitten stopped swiveling his head, now stared directly into my eyes, and mewed. A quiet little mew right at me. And to this day I swear that he smiled.

"No," Cindy said. "He's not for me."

"Who's he for?" I asked quietly.

When she didn't answer, I said, again quite softly, "Cindy? Who's the cat for?"

When she burst out crying, I had a vague suspicion I knew the answer to my question.

I'd known for years that if I ever had a pet—I assumed a dog—I'd name him Norton. There wasn't even a close second choice.

My favorite name for an animal—and my favorite animal up to that point—was Yossarian, my brother's dog. Yossarian was, in my opinion, not just an incredibly cute cockapoo, which, for those of you who are strictly cat lovers, is half cocker spaniel and half poodle. He was also a genius.

He was never on a leash, not even in New York City. He would walk with you to the corner, stop, wait for you to cross the street, then trot along beside you. He would wait outside of stores for you while you shopped. He was also extremely friendly and just generally had a kind of existential, world-weary air to him that made you believe he was capable of carrying on a very interesting drawing room conversation. In French.

I got to take care of Yossarian once, for a stretch of about six months, when Eric was living in Spain. I was living in a fifth-floor walk-up in the West Village, a divey little apartment, and Yossarian moved in with me. It didn't take long for me to realize that Yos wasn't wild about climbing up and down the five flights of stairs whenever he had to go for a walk. He especially wasn't wild about it in winter, when the snow and ice were already tough enough on his L.A.-tenderized paws.

I'd had him perhaps all of a week when, to my horror, the little guy started limping. I noticed it as we were strolling down Greenwich Street. His right front paw was definitely curled up in front of him, and he was favoring it. I went over to him, picked him up, and checked him out. I couldn't find anything wrong, but he was looking at me in such a pathetic way, clearly the dog was in great pain. I set him down just long enough for him to do his thing, then scooped him back up, carried him back to my building and up the five flights to my apartment.

I decided not to panic. I figured I'd give it a few days, then if the limping continued, I'd take him to the vet.

Yos seemed fine in the apartment, perhaps moving around just a bit slower than usual. Once he'd get outside, though, the limping would start up. I'd have to carry him around, set him down when he had to relieve himself, then pick him back up and return to my apartment with the dog cradled in my arms.

On the third day of this routine—he was now limping slightly even in the apartment and I was caringly carrying him up and down the stairs three times a day—we went for our afternoon stroll. I set Yosie down on the snow, and since I was with a woman friend, she and I walked on ahead to give him some privacy. After about half a block, I turned back to see how my ward was doing. He was doing just fine. In fact, he was doing so well, he was racing around the sidewalk in front of my building, playing with another dog. I couldn't believe it. I mean, this dog was *moving.* Full weight on that right front paw.

"Yossarian!" I called.

The dog froze. Didn't move an inch. Then he looked down at the snow on the ground, looked at me, looked back down at his paw, which was resting on the snow, one more look at me, and his paw shot up in the air in a desperate attempt to replicate the pathetic position he kept it in when he was feigning his limp.

"Forget it," I said. "The free ride is over."

If dogs can shrug, Yossarian shrugged, put his paw back down, and resumed his frolic with his playmate. That was the end of the limp.

I wasn't the only one who felt that Yossarian was far more human than the normal quadruped, by the way. A few years ago, when he was thirteen years old and getting sickly, my brother had a "roast" for him. About twenty people showed up with presents for the dog, Eric served food and drink, and everyone proceeded to tell their favorite Yossarian stories. I called from New York just to make sure that someone told my "limping" story, which was by then part of the Yossarian legend.

When, about a year after that, Yos died, I promise you, everyone who was there that day was truly happy that they'd gotten to tell him how much he'd meant to them over the years.

Ever since Eric had taken the *Catch-22* name for this brilliant little dog, I'd been trying to come up with a comparable name for my future pet, which I always assumed would also be a dog. Dunbar was a consideration, but it came from the same book, so I discarded it. McMurphy was a possibility, but then the movie version of *Cuckoo's Nest* came out and I hated it, so that was the end of McMurphy. I went further back in the annals of literature and quickly rejected everything from Falstaff to Tristram to Verloc, then moved on and rejected Malloy, Zorba, and finally even Snoopy.

I considered Steed (or Emma, if it was a female) from "The Avengers," but somehow those just didn't stay with me. Travis stuck around for about six months—that being the name of the character played by Malcolm McDowell in *If . . .* and *O Lucky Man!*—but then a friend of mine got a dog and named him Travis as in Travis McGee.

I switched to the sports field in a move of anti-intellectual desperation.

I couldn't name a pet Willie. What if some poor oaf thought I was naming it after Willie Davis or Willie Wilson or some other inferior imitation of the godlike Mays? I couldn't risk it. None of my other idols' names really lent themselves to being repeated over and over again while trying to coax a four-legged animal out from under the bed. Muhammad? Julius? Roger "the Dodger" Staubach? No.

Jim Brown? Forget it. I'd wind up with a pet who'd periodically throw me off a balcony. I was just about to settle for Clyde, figuring I would have a very cool pet who would never panic under pressure and would play great D, when, about two years before Cindy walked into my apartment with a cat, the name came to me.

I'm a television baby. I always watched it, I always liked it, when I grew up I even wrote for it. Sitcoms were always my fave (once "Bronco Lane" and "Sugarfoot" went off the air). From an aficionado's lofty view, there are only a handful of sitcoms that deserve the label "great." I'm not talking about campy "Gilligan's Island"-type garbage. I'm talking great writing, great acting, great characters. "Bilko" has to be near the top. Same with "The Mary Tyler Moore Show" and "The Dick Van Dyke Show" and, later, "Barney Miller" and "Taxi." But there's one that's in a class by itself. The others aren't even close. Best characters, best fat jokes, best sets, best straight man (or woman, actually), best Grand High Exalted Wizard, and the two best performances in TV sitcom history. Obviously, I'm talking about "The Honeymooners," and like a flash, I had visions of one day—and then every day for years and years—being able to come home from a hard day's work, call out, "Norton, pal o' mine, I'm home!" and see a little furry guy come leaping toward me, licking my face in a frenzy of joy.

As soon as this little cat mewed up at me from Cindy's hand, I knew that Norton had finally arrived.

I knew one other thing, too. And this came in just as much of a flash as the name.

It was love at first sight.

It doesn't make sense. There's no explanation. It's never happened to me before or since with man, woman, or beast, and I don't know if it ever will again.

I started to get angry at Cindy. I wanted to yell. I began to sputter and to say things like "How could you do this!" I was all set to pace and wave my arms around in the air like a lunatic. But I wasn't able to do any of those things. I didn't have the opportunity. Cindy was busy doing her impersonation of Lucy when Ricky comes home after finding out she disguised herself as a painter to get an audition at the club. "I thought you'd like him . . . *sniff* . . . Eric said you'd like him . . . *sniff* . . . I'm sorry . . . I thought . . . *sniff* . . . *Unaughhhhwaaaaaaaaa* . . ." I knew I wasn't going to get anywhere in that direction, so I turned to you-know-who. With my mouth still open, I looked into the little cat's eyes and I melted. Just dead away, gone, total mush.

Cindy, now switching to her Laura Petrie mode, trying not to cry but letting me know she might start again any moment, held out her hand, and I took the kitten from her. Having absolutely no experience with babies of any species—human or four-legged—I held him kind of awkwardly. Cupping him in my right palm, which I supported with my left, I brought him closer to me, raising him up to my face until we were nose to nose. I don't think he could have been more than six inches long or weighed more than two pounds. He was a light, soft gray with irregular patches of dark gray circling his body. Bits of white spread across the top of his paws and ringed around his little black-and-orange nose. Three startling lines of black began right between his eyes and streaked all the way down his back, broadening by his tail so that his back half was darker than his front. His tail, even then, was very bushy, with black rings around it. It looked like a tail that could have belonged to a raccoon. His eyes were huge, twice too big for his head, oval and green. I had absolutely never in my life seen anything that was so cute, so independent, so smart, or anything that had ever looked quite so much as if it belonged to me. He never flinched or shifted his gaze away from me. He simply mewed once more and licked me more or less on my right eyelid with a sandpaperlike tongue the size of a small bristle on a paintbrush.

"He's six weeks old," Cindy said in a little bit of a hushed tone, drying her eyes. "And there's something very special about him. I don't think he's just a normal cat."

I switched him to my left hand and ran my right hand lightly over him, from his head to his tail, the first time I'd ever petted a feline.

"Of course he's not just a normal cat," I said. "How could he be? He's mine."

The shopping Cindy had done with my brother, of course, was to go out and buy this little cat, Norton. When she had seen what a Scottish Fold looked like, she flipped. She told Eric all about how she wanted to get a cat and how I wanted a pet but refused to consider a cat, and he, having known me for a much longer time than she had and knowing how I'd react when I saw a Fold, told her they'd go looking the next morning.

They drove out to the Valley, to the breeder where Eric had gotten Henry. The breed was, at the time, relatively unknown but already on the expensive side. Eric had paid three hundred dollars for his. (Now, believe it or not, a good Scottish Fold will cost you up to fifteen hundred smackers.) He was a big believer in the theory that if you're going out to buy something, it's much better to spend as much money as possible and be as impractical as you can.

As luck would have it, the breeder had recently ushered in a new litter of Folds. She had too many Folds. Because they were so expensive, she didn't think she could sell them all before they got so big that they'd get underfoot. She knew Eric, she took a liking to Cindy, so she gave them one for seventy-five dollars, with the simple promise that they'd give the kitten the best possible home.

"Here, I'll give you my favorite," she told them.

She picked a six-week-old cat out of a cardboard box and handed him over. Along with his breeding papers, she gave them an article that had appeared the week before in the *San Fernando Valley Register.* The story was on exotic breeds of cats, and as an example of the exotic Scottish Fold, there was a photograph of the cat Cindy was holding. For the use of the article, the kitten had been named Baby, and the caption under his photo said, "Unlike some deceptively named feline families—Himalayans, for example, have no tie to the mountains—Scottish Folds like this kitten, 'Baby,' actually originated in Scotland."

"He's a star," the breeder said.

"I sure hope so," Cindy told her.

He certainly acted like a star on the trip home. Cindy was a bit nervous taking such a young animal on the airplane. She wasn't sure how he'd react, what he'd do to go to the bathroom, whether such a long flight would make him neurotic the rest of his nine lives. She quickly found out he wasn't the neurotic type. She had him in a little box, but minutes into the flight, she lifted him onto her tray table just to check him out. He yawned, lay down, and immediately went to sleep. She figured she'd leave him there until either the cat or the stewardesses started to freak out. Neither happened. The cat sat or slept on the tray, happy as could be, for the entire trip. The dread bathroom problem never came up. (As Norton has proved on many a flight since, he either has an abnormally strong bladder or an equally dominant sense of decorum. On this initial trip and on hundreds to come, he simply waited until proper facilities presented themselves.) Occasionally he would stretch, look around, then sit back down. He meowed only twice. Both times Cindy cooed at him and stroked him—and he made it very clear that that was exactly why he'd bothered to speak. The stewardesses fussed over him delightedly, brought him milk, even picked him up to show him off to various passengers. Through it all, the little kitten acted as if he'd logged as many miles as Chuck Yeager.

In the taxi from the airport to my apartment, he scrambled on the backseat over to the door handle, which he stood on, stretching up to peer out the window as the car drove him into Manhattan.

"It was weird," Cindy said, as I held him in my hand. "Not only did he have absolutely no fear, he acted like he knew where he was going—*and was looking forward to getting there.*"

The cat now wiggled a little bit in my palm, so I gingerly set him down on the floor.

"He'll be scared now," Cindy told me. "Kittens are always scared of new surroundings. This place'll seem huge to him and that's frightening to a cat."

Uh-huh.

My frightened kitten meandered over to a couch in my living room. Then he strolled over to the couch opposite it. Then he went back, halfway between the two, plopped down on the rag rug, and went to sleep.

I watched his little chest moving up and down while he slept. I'd never seen anything conk out quite so quickly. I knew I had an imbecilic grin on my face, but I couldn't help it.

"Norton," I called to him softly. "Norton . . ."

The kitten's eyes opened slowly. First they were just a slit, then they held at half-open, then his head tilted and he was looking up at me.

I smiled at Cindy.

"Look," I said. "He already knows his name."

The cat who went to Fire Island

3

Most people think that owning a cat is a lot less of a responsibility than owning a dog.

They're wrong.

They're especially wrong if a particular owner happens to decide that a particular cat is so sensitive, intelligent, and aware of what's happening that he has to be treated on a higher level than the owner's fellow human beings.

There actually is a certain logic to this. After all, people have *choices.* They do not have to be friends with someone they don't like or who mistreats them. They do not have to be alone if they choose not to be. (This is a general classification, remember: it does not necessarily apply to those people who don't use deodorant in the summer, think Sandra Bernhard is funny, or who idolize the Robert De Niro character in *Taxi Driver.*) They do not have to eat only when someone remembers to feed them. And, most of all, if the person they live with comes home late, most people do not have to worry that that person has been eaten by a predator.

Cindy thought I was going a little overboard with this last comparison, but *she* was the one who gave me a book called *The Natural Cat.*

She gave it to me because it was rather immediately apparent that Norton was not only breaking down my resistance to *him,* he was breaking down a lifetime resistance to his entire species.

First of all, it's very difficult to resist anything that is so vulnerable. And there are very few things more vulnerable than a six-week-old kitten. Second of all, he didn't *act* vulnerable, which is even harder to resist. He scrambled, he clawed, he nudged; he took over my apartment is what he did. Third of all, he took over *me.*

His first sneak attack in this regard came in the middle of the night.

Cindy and I had a very particular sleeping order. I always slept on the left side of my bed, she on the right. I slept on my side; she curled around my back with her arms wrapped around me.

We weren't sure whether Norton should sleep on the bed. We didn't know if he'd wriggle around all night, keeping us awake, a prospect which didn't much excite me. We also didn't know if he'd even *want* to sleep with us. Maybe we were too huge and frightening. So we decided to leave it up to him.

His first night, we heard him sliding around the living room floor as we were falling off to sleep. It seemed as if he'd made his choice—he'd find his own bed. Fine with me. No problem. Everyone knew cats weren't as affectionate as dogs, anyway. He could sleep wherever he damn pleased.

I awoke in the morning, as usual a few minutes before Cindy. With my eyes half open, I listened for the sounds of a small cat at play. Nothing. A bit worried, I strained to listen more carefully. It seemed natural that a newborn kitten should be awake causing trouble. Still nothing.

Then I felt a very light stirring from my pillow, and I rolled my eyes down to get a look.

What I saw was a small, gray ball of fluff, comfortably resting under my cheek and neck. He was awake, his eyes wide open, but he wasn't moving. Not an inch. He was staring straight at me, waiting for me to make the first move.

Without lifting my head, I slowly twisted my left arm, bringing it up so I could pet him. With two fingers, I stroked the top of his head, rubbing between his eyes down to his nose. He shifted, ever so slightly, stretching his neck so I could scratch under his chin. We stayed like that for several minutes, the cat stretched out luxuriously, the owner scratching away.

I felt pretty good.

He'd chosen me to sleep with. Not just the bed. Me. Not Cindy. *Me.*

It was *embarrassing* how good it felt.

I swiveled around to glance at Cindy. She was awake now, too, watching us and smiling.

Thus began a whole *new* sleeping arrangement. When Cindy spent the night, Norton would stay in the living room until we fell asleep. But every morning, when I awoke he'd be scrunched against my neck, partly under my cheek, absolutely wide awake, waiting for me to scratch under his chin.

If it was just the two of us—me and the cat, not me and Cindy—Norton would take Cindy's place before the lights went out. He'd lie in her spot on the bed, head on her pillow, body stretched out like a person, usually under the covers. I'd turn my back to him, and he'd snuggle up there, exactly as Cindy did. In the morning he'd still be on her pillow, wide awake, staring straight at me, waiting for me to rise and shine. When I'd open my eyes, he'd move a few inches to me, lick my eyes or my forehead, then move to his under-the-cheek-and-neck position for five minutes of petting and scratching.

He never, ever woke me up. Never, ever meowed for breakfast. *A deux* or *ménage à trois*, he would stay quietly in bed until I was awake, wait until his morning petting, then he'd get up and join me for breakfast in the kitchen—one black coffee, one chicken and kidney in cream sauce deluxe.

His next sneaky little way of worming himself into my life was my own fault.

I wanted to show him off. (I knew that was a bad sign, but there you have it; there was nothing I could do about it.) So I started taking him places. Not far away. Just to friends' apartments. He was, needless to point out, quite a hit, proving to be as fearless in these apartments as he was in mine, prowling and hopping around from room to room. Some of these friends had cats of their own and were a bit worried about possible confrontations. I couldn't imagine how anything—even a rival cat—could object to Norton, and as it turned out, I was right. Most of the time, the cat whose turf we were invading would immediately hiss and circle Norton, whom I'd have plopped down in the middle of the living room. Norton would peer over at the tough king of the castle, give him a look as if to say, "Who are you kidding?"; then he'd roll over on the ground and look as cute as an animal could look. The grown cat would, more or less, have no choice but to come over and be friendly. Otherwise he'd look like a warmongering idiot in front of his owner.

It seemed like too much of a bother, on these goodwill tours, to lug his carrier around the city, especially when he was so tiny, so I'd simply put on a windbreaker or a raincoat and stick Norton in the pocket. Walking a few blocks was no problem. He'd sit calmly, occasionally sticking his head out over the pocket's rim to peer around, then retreat back inside. He actually got pretty good at this form of transportation. Even on long subway rides to the Upper West Side. The noise didn't seem to frighten him; rather it intrigued him. The sudden jarring stops and starts struck him as something of a fun game. The only drawbacks were (1) the bums who, thinking they might be hallucinating, would want to touch him to make sure he wasn't the step before the pink elephants, and (2) the garrulous strangers who were positive that a cat in one's pocket was an open invitation to tell life stories, tales of woe, or worst of all, adorable pet anecdotes of their own.

On Saturdays, I started to get into the habit of taking him with me on my errands. He never squawked about this; in fact, I think he liked it. Most shops were happy to see his little head pop out and swivel around. In my local bakery he came away with quite a few scraps of cookies and sweet rolls and he developed a serious taste for jelly doughnuts;

in the local grocery store he often lucked into pieces of cheese and the occasional chicken part. He'd even stay quiet—in an oversized pocket—for a relaxing brunch in a Village restaurant on a Sunday afternoon. A few waiters and waitresses wondered why I always ordered a glass of milk—a short, round glass if at all possible; if not, a tall glass and an empty saucer on the side—to go with my Mimosa or Bloody Mary, but no one ever said anything. To this day, I'm sure there are several maître d's and busboys who talk about the bearded fellow who always left little puddles of milk under his seat. You'll just have to take my word for it that I was actually quite neat. Norton, however, is one of the sloppiest lappers I've ever seen. When he's thirsty, his tongue reminds me of nothing so much as one of those machines that swirls paint around, nearly at the speed of light, on small canvases so kindergartners can create instant works of abstract art.

I got used to keeping my hand inside my coat on my travels about town, and constantly stroking this soft little cat. He got used to these hour- or two-hour-long adventures. When I'd leave the house without him—as I was forced to do far more often than I liked—he would look way too sad. As a result, it was taking me longer and longer to get out the door. (Have you ever spent five minutes explaining to a cat about your day's agenda and how it just wouldn't work if he came on your important meetings with you? Have you ever tried it when you have company? A word of advice: Don't.) Norton clearly didn't like being left behind. He much preferred being carried around in a pocket to spending the day dozing on the windowsill.

My only problem other than my five- and ten-minute

out-the-door soliloquies, was that summer was coming up. Even for Norton I didn't think I could wear an overcoat in the New York summer.

Meanwhile, since it was immediately apparent that Norton and I were joined at the hip (or the pocket, as the case may be), Cindy did two things. First, she got a cat of her own, a normal full-eared cat for whom she paid Bide-a-Wee five dollars. She named him Marlowe, as in Chandler and *The Big Sleep*, not the sixteenth century and *Tamburlaine*. I couldn't really object. I mean, here I was with my own cat who was sleeping on my head and for whom, twice in the first two weeks of our relationship, I'd stayed home from work so I could get to know him better. I no longer had a leg to stand on as far as cat-prevention was concerned. Besides, I liked Marlowe quite a bit. He was just as sweet as Norton. (In fact, in some ways, sweeter; it was clear from the beginning that Norton had a touch of the rebel in him. He liked to test me. Little things like scratching at the couch. To be perfectly honest, my attitude was that if scratching the couch gave him so much pleasure, let him scratch. It wasn't that big a deal to get a new couch every so often. But a horrified Cindy insisted that was no way to raise a kitten, so whenever Norton scratched, I would tell him "no!" just the way Cindy told me I was supposed to. He was definitely smart enough to realize he was doing something wrong and would immediately respond to my warning. He would stop scratching at once and move about three feet away from the leg of the couch. Then, watching me all the way, he would, inch by inch, slink back to the leg, stick his paw out, and give the thing one or two good rakes. I would clap my hands, say "no!" again, and he would scamper those three feet away. I'd turn my back and, two minutes later, hear the familiar scritching of claws on canvas. I must admit I was proud of this James Dean–like adventurous streak and secretly encouraged it, whereas Cindy loved the fact that *her* cat wouldn't *dream* of doing anything to upset her.) Marlowe was quite handsome in his own way, too, a beautiful dark coat streaked through with black and brown, though even Cindy had to admit he wasn't in my guy's league. He was also a much better jumper than Norton. Marlowe could do something that never failed to amaze me. He could jump from the floor to the top of an open door and balance himself there. Norton used to eye this physical agility with some envy, I believe, though he soon realized his own limitations and comfortably settled for intellect over brawn. Overall, though, as truly nice as Marlowe was, he was *normal.* He was a cat. Norton was something more.

The second thing Cindy did was buy me the aforementioned book, *The Natural Cat,* so I could actually learn something about my animal. It's a wonderful little book, and I quickly studied up on such things as how cats clean themselves and how they adjust to litter boxes and all the things cat owners around the world already know and don't need to read about here. To me, it was all fascinating, much like discovering a whole new culture. I had never heard anything purr before, and I thought it was very possibly the most wonderful, soothing noise I'd ever listened to. I liked nothing better than having Norton stretch out on the bed or couch with me lying on top of him, the full weight of my head plunked down right in the middle of his body. He would purr and purr and purr in delight. I soon realized I was passing up reruns of "The Rockford Files" in order to spend an hour listening to this motorboat sound.

I had also never seen fur on anything's back stand straight up or claws that retracted. I was particularly fascinated by his claws because, as much as he loved to scratch, his claws *never* came out when we were roughhousing. He made it quite clear that such a thing was unthinkable, and I found myself touched and moved by his instinctive gentleness. In general, I was extremely interested in reading about the whys and wherefores and history of all such behavior and physical reactions.

In the last chapter of *The Natural Cat,* the psychology of the feline is discussed. At some point in the chapter, it says to watch and notice: if you come home from work every day at six o'clock, when you arrive at the regular hour, your cat will be dozing contentedly in some comfortable spot. He will be relaxed and calm when he lifts his head up to welcome you home. HOWEVER: if you usually come home at six o'clock, and then you don't come home until eleven or so, when you walk in the door your cat will be pacing up and down, nervously wondering if you've deserted and abandoned him. This is because his fifty million years of jungle instinct will have taken over, and the cat is sure that you've been eaten by a predator. He has no idea you went for a drink with a co-worker, then hit a ballgame with a pal. The only thing he can conceive of is that you were minding your own business, lapping up some water from a lagoon, and some tusked animal weighing over two tons came along and bit you in half.

I started worrying about this. Not obsessively, not day in and day out. I wasn't that far gone. But if Cindy and I were out to dinner and it got past nine o'clock, I would start to get a little edgy.

"What's the matter?" she'd say.

"Nothing," I'd respond. Then I'd glance at my watch nervously.

"What *is* it?" she'd want to know. "You're wriggling. You only wriggle when there's something wrong."

"It's nothing. Really. I'm just a little tired."

"Do you want to go?"

"No, no," I'd say. "Absolutely not. I'm fine. Let's stay."

Five minutes would pass and I'd nudge her under the table. "Maybe we should go *now*," I'd whisper. And we would, much to Cindy's confusion and annoyance.

When we got to my place, Norton would be standing by the front door, looking, I was sure, incredibly stressed out. I'd pick him up, pet him for a while, reassure him that his dad had survived another day in the nasty jungle, tell him what a great dinner he was in store for, then sigh with relief and exhaustion that a crisis had been averted.

After a couple of weeks of this, Cindy figured out what was going on. She took *The Natural Cat* off my bookshelf and threw it away. She also forbid me to read anything or learn anything more about cats. She decided it was too dangerous.

The germ had already been forming, but this whole predator business put it over the top. I was beginning to think that, whenever and wherever possible, I should just take Norton with me. I would be a lot more relaxed, and I was pretty sure he'd enjoy tagging along with his dad rather than sitting around my apartment all day. The short pocket trips worked okay. Why not the more major excursions?

Cindy wasn't as supportive as I'd hoped. She told me I was crazy.

"You can't just take your cat on trips all over the place," she informed me.

I didn't understand why not. "He likes me. He's pretty calm. He goes to your house okay. What's the big deal?"

"The big deal is he's a *cat.* Cats don't like things like that."

"He does."

"He's a kitten. He'll go along with anything. When he gets bigger, he's going to hate it."

"I don't think so," I said. "I think he'll go for it."

"It just doesn't work that way," she said, shaking her head.

"Well, I'm gonna try it," I told her. "I like him. I like being with him. I don't see why he won't like being with me."

In fact, I had a place in mind I knew he would love to visit.

Fire Island is about an hour's drive or train ride from Manhattan. As mentioned, I rented a house there every summer, in the town of Fair Harbor. It was a wonderful little guest house, painted a deep sky blue; one room, comfortably furnished, with a Pullman kitchen and a sleeping loft. It had a cozy deck, which, even though the beach was only fifty feet away, I could rarely bring myself to leave. The entire island is approximately twenty-six miles long and about two blocks wide from bay to beach. There are many different little communities, each with distinctly separate rules and equally separate lifestyles. The rules range from *No Eating in Public* in one particularly crowded community to *No Campfires on the Beach* in a particularly cautious community to *No Rich People's Seaplanes Landing Here or We'll Blow Your Head Off* in one particularly blue-collar community. The lifestyles range from *Wild-Divorced-Heterosexual-Manhattanites-Discoing-the-Night-Away-in-Desperate-Search-of-a-New-Year's-Eve-Date* to *Boring-Please-Don't-Give-My-House-a-Funny-Name-I'm-Here-to-Relax-Not-Talk-to-Strangers* to *If-You're-Not-Gay-and-Haven't-Rented-*Can't-Stop-the-Music-*at-Least-Three-Times-Don't-Even-Bother-to-Step-Off-the-Boat.* I was in one of the Boring-Please-etc.-etc. communities and I liked it fine. In fact, I thought it was pretty close to heaven. There was one restaurant, which I dined in once a summer, a little grocery store, which, as mentioned, I went to a little too often, and a five-and-dime run by a woman who used to be a Rockette. (She was kicking when *The Men,* Brando's first film, played there.) There were a lot of nice families around me with a lot of nice kids. Best of all, cars aren't allowed on Fire Island. If you don't want to walk, you take a bike. If you don't want to do either of those, your only other choice is to sit in the sun and listen to the waves lap up to the shore. It seems like a place, with its wooden boardwalks and water taxis and everybody-knows-everybody-else feel, that time has forgotten. Above all, it is safe. Fire Island makes you feel that nothing bad can happen there, certainly nothing worse than, if you're a kid, falling down and skinning your knee, or if you're an adult, having too much to drink at a cocktail party and winding up in bed with a fat woman named Naomi. Which is why I thought it was the perfect place for Norton to make his first excursion.

Once Cindy understood I was quite serious and that there was no way I was leaving my cat home alone for a whole weekend, she decided to give it a try with Marlowe. She didn't want him to grow up feeling like the neglected stepchild.

For our first trip *en famille,* we took Tommy's Taxi, a van service that picks you (and a lot of other yuppified weekenders anxious—and loud about it—to leave the city) up in Manhattan and drops you off at the Fire Island ferry. We bought a regular pet carrying case, a plastic one with metal bars on the top. Since both cats were so little, we figured one case would be plenty big enough.

We met the van at Fifty-third and First Avenue, loaded our bags on, then climbed aboard and made ourselves as comfortable as we could amidst the jewelry and designer clothes and exposed body parts. The cat case sat on my lap.

About fifteen minutes into the trip, I decided that it couldn't possibly be very comfortable curled up inside a portable pet prison, so I opened it an inch and stuck my hand in to reassuringly pet both guys. Marlowe didn't respond. His nose was buried in a corner, and he was trying his best to pretend he had been in a coma for about three weeks. Norton, however, scurried over to my fingers and began shoving his nose up against them. I stroked him for a minute, then when Cindy was looking away, staring rather horrifiedly at a pair of dangling gold earrings that spelled out a phone number—three numbers hanging from the left ear, four hanging from the right; I assume the woman wearing them had the area code tattooed someplace I didn't want to know about—I lifted Norton out of the box and quickly shut it back up.

He looked up at me gratefully and meowed. At the sound, Cindy glanced over. When she saw the kitten on my lap, she rolled her eyes.

"I know, I know," I told her and tried to pretend that I sympathized with her hard-hearted approach to pet travel. "But he looked so unhappy in there."

"He wasn't unhappy," she told me. "He's a cat. *You* were unhappy because you weren't holding him."

I glanced down at Norton, who was curled up in a ball on my lap, his head resting on the back of my hand. I nodded at Cindy, acknowledging that her assessment was correct.

"At least move your hand," she told me. "You can't be comfortable sitting like that."

"I'm all right," I told her.

"You're comfortable?"

"Well . . . not exactly. But . . ."

"But what?"

"But *he* looks so comfortable."

"I think," Cindy said, "I may have made a mistake."

The rest of the trip went according to form. Marlowe cowered in the box, doing his best Helen Keller impersonation; Norton wound up inching his way up my arm and perching on my shoulder, watching the countryside slide by as we sped along the L.I.E.

One of the things I liked best about his position on my

shoulder was that it didn't ever seem to occur to him that he couldn't just push me out of the way or take up whatever space he wanted to take up. That's where he wanted to be, so that's where he belonged. And I had to agree. It only seemed fair. He was little; he was being lugged around not by his own choosing; he had no idea where he was going or why. If he wanted to sit somewhere and at least get a good view, how could I complain? I felt—and I think this is one of those clever things that cats somehow manage to do—*honored* by the fact that he chose me to be his piece of comfortable furniture.

In fact, not only wasn't I complaining, I was mesmerized watching Norton on his first trip in the van. He spent almost the entire hour staring out the window, hunched forward, his neck craning, his nose pressed against the glass. Something fascinated him out there, though I sure couldn't tell what. Every so often he'd turn to look at me and his eyes were full of questions. He'd stare at me until I felt ridiculously ignorant, and I'd whisper, "What? What do you want to know? *What?* Tell me!" When it became plain that I couldn't help him, he'd turn back to the window and continue his vigilant watch.

The thing is, it's not as if he were watching a flickering fire in a fireplace, unfocused and glazed by simple noise and movement. For Norton, this was hardly a vacuous way to pass the time. He wasn't *just* staring. His eyes were alert, constantly moving, his head shifting back and forth as if he were keeping track of a baseline-to-baseline rally at an exciting tennis game.

He was so *interested*. And it made me incredibly curious. I acted like a proud father whose son was about to win a sixth-grade spelling bee. I kept nudging Cindy, not saying anything, just flicking my eyes toward Norton as if to say, "Will you look at him? Is he smart or what?"

Several people on the van actually stopped talking about themselves long enough to notice that there was a kitten perched on my shoulder, a kitten with folded ears who seemed to be unduly interested in the landscape of Long Island.

A couple of them reached over to pet him. Norton took the attention with what I would come to know as his typical laissez-faire reaction to adoring crowds. He didn't shrink away or scurry back into his carrier. Nor did he rub his nose affectionately against unknown palms or offer encouragement in any way. He simply sat there and took the cooing and petting and compliments as stoically as he could. At some point he turned to me, since we were basically at eye level to each other, and the expression on his face said, "It's all right. This is just the price I have to pay for being me."

I nodded at him knowingly, and when the petting stopped, he snuggled a few inches closer, turned away from the strangers, buried his face against my neck, closed his eyes, and went to sleep.

Marlowe, who in the van had certainly been, if not happy, quiescent, did not take well to the twenty-minute ferry ride from mainland Bay Shore to Fair Harbor on the island. He wouldn't move an inch in the carrier, and when Cindy went to pet him reassuringly, he drew away from her touch. I think, if he hadn't been as truly sweet as he was, he might have hissed at her. But things hadn't quite reached that tragic level.

Norton, of course, only made matters worse because he took to the open sea (or, at least, the open bay) as if he were related in some way to the Popeye family.

As in the van, his nose went right to (and through) the metal bars at the top of his carrier, and he made it plain as day he wanted out. So, once again, I reached in, scooped him up, and set him on my lap.

Within a few experimental minutes, we found the position we both liked best: me with my left leg crossed over my right knee at a ninety-degree angle, Norton with his body on my right thigh and his head resting on my left foot. (For him, that's still his favorite traveling position, although as he's gotten older and bigger, his body and head now go from right thigh to left knee. For me, as *I've* gotten older and my joints creakier and creakier, it's less and less comfortable. Of course, I'm too well trained to change. I much prefer creaky joints to a disgruntled traveling companion.)

He also, about ten minutes into the crossing, decided the water was practically as interesting as the highway. With me holding the middle of his body as firmly as I could, he perched himself back on my shoulder, with his front paws resting on the ferry's railing.

Cindy was a little nervous seeing him in such a precarious position, and I must admit so was I. Believe me, I had visions of myself diving overboard in search of a floundering kitten. But I did have hold of him. And even more of a but, I simply had a very strong sense that this particular cat would not do anything as rashly crazy as jump off my shoulder into the freezing bay. I don't know why I had such faith in him, except to say that he more than justified it. I expected him to behave in a certain way right from the beginning, and he almost always did. I've left Norton in cars with the doors open, in airport waiting rooms while I went off to confirm tickets, in restaurant chairs while I went to use their toilets. Not once do I ever remember him running or jumping or hiding.

We got some awfully strange looks on that boat: a boy and his seafaring kitten. Then in twenty minutes we were back on land. We'd been on a taxi, a van, and a ferry. We'd braved rush-hour traffic, the spray of sea salt, and crazed sun-worshippers. The premier leg of Norton's first real journey was complete.

The cat who commuted

4

Norton took to outdoor life immediately. It was a little frightening how easy it was to begin thinking of him as a country squire.

We took both cats into the little beach house and flipped open the carrier. Marlowe—poor guy; I hope no one ever reads this to him because he's going to get one hell of a serious inferiority complex—wouldn't come out. If I hadn't spent many more months in his company and *seen* him out and around, I'd venture to say he might *still* be in that box. Norton, on the other hand, had his new pad all checked out in a matter of minutes. He was the second coming of Tony Bill in *Come Blow Your Horn*.

He sniffed the miniature house out thoroughly—around the couch, over to the Pullman kitchen, up the ladder stairs to the sleeping loft. After exploring the upstairs, he stuck his head over the edge of the loft to look down at us, and I knew exactly what he had in mind. When we made eye contact I shook my head only once, but firmly—and I'm convinced that's why he took the stairs back down to the living room floor, one little jump at a time instead of one great twelve-foot leap. I knew (and he knew) he could have done it. But I knew (and I'm sure he knew it, too) I probably would have had a heart attack.

Back downstairs, he checked out the bathroom, hopped onto the rim of the tub, slid down inside it. It was vinyl and very smooth, far too slippery for a kitten his size to easily leap back out, so when he began meowing impatiently I had to go fetch him. This became a fairly regular ritual until he grew to a more adult size and could get out of his own scrapes. At least once a day I'd hear a plaintive meowing echoing from the bathroom and have to go to the rescue. I must admit, partly to pay him back for dragging me away from work or fun or bed, partly because it was extremely funny to watch, I'd usually give him three or four tries on his own. He'd see me, try to scamper up the wall of the tub, not make it, and slide back down toward the drain. After a few unsuccessful attempts, he'd meow sharply, just once, to let me know the game was over and he wanted my help—*now.* He was not humiliating himself for my enjoyment any longer.

Norton particularly liked the walls of the beach house, which were covered with a burlap cloth. Quite attractive, no doubt, but also very handy for climbing.

While Cindy and I were doing our best to coax Marlowe out of the carrier, we heard a very quick ripping noise—actually five or six quick ripping noises—and turned around to find Norton up near the ceiling, his claws clinging to the wall fabric.

I, of course, thought this was the greatest thing I'd ever seen. I was ready to rank Norton with Columbus, Tom Sawyer, John Glenn, and the first guy who ever ordered mail-order meat on my list of great adventurers. Cindy, luckily for my bank account, quickly pointed out how expensive it would be to completely refurbish every wall in the house. So we quickly pulled Norton down and tried to discourage this particular excitement, although it, too, became something of a regular occurence.

We next went out of our way to orient our adventurous cat. A litter box was set up in the bathroom, and we carried him to it so he'd be unable to use ignorance as an excuse for any accidents. (It turned out that in three years on Fire Island, he never *once* used a litter box. Outside, one giant sandbox was at his disposal, and I think he took great satisfaction in relieving himself in the freeing manner of his ancestors.) We also put food and water down for him and Marlowe—separate bowls, of course—but we figured Marlowe was *weeks* away from eating. Norton acknowledged the food with a quick bite or two of kibble, but his mind was elsewhere. He wanted the great outdoors.

Although he went straight for the screen door, he was still such a small kitten—not yet three months old—Cindy thought that, for health reasons, we shouldn't really let him loose outside. He was too young to be exposed to all those unknown germs and ticks and other strange things that abound in nature and that I couldn't even bring myself to think about. But he seemed so anxious to take off for parts unknown . . .

I had a solution. It was a perfect summer day, so we quickly changed into our formal Fire Island wear—shorts, no shoes, no shirt for me, tank top for Cindy—made ourselves some iced tea, and began Step One of turning Norton into an outdoor cat. We put a blue collar on him—quite distinguished-looking nestled in his gray fur—and got a long, long string, maybe thirty feet long, from the Rockette lady. We used the string to make an impromptu leash, carried Norton onto the porch, and tied him to the handle of the door.

Minus Marlowe, who still hadn't budged from his portable prison, Cindy and I took our iced teas—by the way, these were nonalcoholic iced teas; this is worth explaining because we'd learned that, for some unknown reason, in bars and restaurants anywhere on Long Island, if you just order iced tea, they give you something with enough alcohol in it to topple an elephant—sprawled into our madras beach chairs, and waited to see what would happen.

We didn't have to wait long.

Norton needed a few seconds to get his bearing. This was a little different from being transplanted into a strange living room. This was like being picked up by Brian Dennehy in *Cocoon* and going for a stroll on a strange planet.

First he went into a crouch. He glanced around nervously, as if waiting for something to pounce on him. Then he relaxed a bit. He took a step forward, still staying fairly alert to the potential for danger. His nose twitched, taking in the hundreds of brand new odors, and his folded ears switched from side to side, hearing all sorts of things, like birds and crickets and bees, that he had had no idea ever existed. Then a great thing happened.

Norton suddenly sprang into the air in a joyous leap. Baryshnikov would have been jealous of his form. He landed on his padded feet and went right back up, this time swatting at the string, which lay stretched out before him. A meow came out of him, but not a normal meow. This one sounded suspiciously like "whooooppeeeee!"

It took maybe thirty seconds for my cat to race exhilaratedly all around the deck. It took me maybe thirty *minutes* to unwind the string—which was now tangled up under a chair, around a square outdoor table, around another chair, twice around Cindy's ankles, over and then back under a third chair, somehow wrapping around the table again before coming to a sudden stop somewhere in the middle of the deck as the leash ran out of slack.

Norton couldn't move an inch. By the time I'd managed to straighten things out, he was raring to go again. And go he did. Another thirty seconds later, I was doing my best to unwrap him from his string straightjacket. Cindy couldn't stop laughing, Norton couldn't stop running, and I couldn't stop unwinding. All three of us were as close to happy as it's possible to get.

Within a couple of weeks, we had the routine down cold.

Thursday evenings, pack one bag each, load each kitten into his own carrier—we'd splurged for comfort's sake; *their* comfort—catch the five-thirty Tommy's Taxi and the seven P.M. ferry to Fair Harbor. Marlowe would hunker down in his carrier, emerging only when he was safely inside our house. Norton would spend the van ride on my shoulder, staring out the window, and the ferry ride on my lap, lean-

ing up against the railing. Once we hit land, he was beginning to squirm and think seriously about jumping out of his
carrier. I knew it wouldn't be long before he'd be prowling
the island on his own.

I'd bought a new travel case, perfect for him, easy for me.
It was really meant for dogs, but he was quite comfortable
in it and seemed to like it better than the old one. It was
a soft cloth shoulder bag with a hard strip underneath it for
support. There was a mesh patch in front so the animal
could breathe and see out. Norton didn't need the mesh to
see or breathe, because I never zipped the thing closed. I
just stuck him in and hung the bag on my left shoulder while
he sat there, head swiveling in every direction, taking in
every single sight, sound, and smell. It wasn't long before
I didn't even have to pick him up and put him inside. When
it was time for us to take a trip, I'd simply lay the bag on
the floor and he'd step right in and settle himself there.

After a month of weekends spent mostly trying to untie
string from every available item on our deck, we decided
it was time to turn the cat loose. My landlord, whose family
shared the front deck with us, was complaining. Their bicycles were so tightly wrapped in string by this point, they
looked as if they were bike mummies excavated from Tut's
Tomb.

On the chosen weekend, Cindy and Marlowe had to stay
in the city. One of Cindy's best friends was in from out of
town, and they decided to have an official GNO (Girls'
Night Out). The whole wild works—non-diet Cokes, oil on
their salads, loud public discussions of bladder infections.
Norton and I were on our own, bacheloring it up.

Friday night, on Tommy's Taxi, I happened upon a startling and, in years to come, useful revelation. It had always struck me as quite odd that none of the reveling weekenders in the van or on the ferry ever paid much attention to the fact that there was an incredibly cute cat on my shoulder, doing incredibly cute things. I didn't expect banners or original songs about "A Cat Named Norton"—

> *Who's the cat with the floppy ears?*
> *Who's the cat who ain't got no fears?*
> *Who's the cat doin' all the cavortin'?*
> *That ain't no cat—that's Norton!*

—or anything like that, but I did expect the occasional "What a cute cat!" or "Is he always this good?" or "What happened to his ears?" No. Usually I got nothing.

Well, this Friday I was riding along as usual, immersed in the *Post* sports section, cat on my shoulder studying the L.I.E. landmarks, when a woman behind me, wearing a sweatshirt that read "Life's a Beach," said, "What kind of cat is that?"

"A Scottish Fold," I explained. "His ears fold in half. See?"

"He's amazing."

Smiling, I went back to the sports section.

"Excuse me," the woman sitting next to me said. She had on a T-shirt that said, "Life's a Beach." "What kind of a cat did you say he was?"

"Scottish Fold," I repeated. "See? His ears fold like this."

"He's beautiful."

"Thank you."

"Is he always this well behaved?"

"Always," I said proudly.

Back to the sports pages.

"Is that a Scottish Fold?" the woman in front of me asked, turning around to smile at me. She *didn't* have on a T-shirt that read "Life's a Beach." But the guy sitting next to her did.

"Uh-huh." I nodded.

" 'Cause his ears fold like this."

"Uh-huh."

"He's so *cute.*"

"I know."

"Is he always this good?"

As a person who's always prided himself on being an acutely sharp observer of human behavior, naturally enough I had absolutely *no* idea why, all of a sudden, Norton's ears were the main topic of the car ride. I had zero concept of what was different from past rides.

It wasn't until I was on the ferry that it hit me.

We were on the upper deck. Norton was peering fixedly at the gulls swooping around the waves. I was munching on a take-out order of fried clams, a specialty of Porky's, the wonderfully divey pub by the ferry.

I was single this trip.

That was the difference.

No one wanted to bother admiring my cat when I was sitting next to an attractive woman I was obviously attached to. But this night there was no Cindy. So all of a sudden, Norton was the perfect conversation starter.

I was mildly stunned. I'd never really seen myself as the object of a van-ful of women's lust and desires. And I'd certainly never viewed Norton as bait to be trolled. Were times so bad that people wouldn't even *talk* to someone unless they wanted something? Like a mate for life? It was amazing. It was . . .

As if on cue, a hand swooped down in front of me and plucked a clam—*my* clam—from the styrofoam plate.

I looked up to see a reasonably attractive woman, late twenties, holding the clam in her fingers. She was wearing—remember, this goes back a few years now—a *Flashdance*-type T-shirt. Over the course of the summer, I was going to become far too familiar with this look. (One of the amazing things about a sleepy little place like Fire Island being so close to Manhattan is the way fads sweep in and take over the entire island. My own personal favorite fad is a game called Kadima. It might also be called The Stupidest Game Ever Invented. It consists of one wooden paddle per player—of which there are usually two or three—and a hard black rubber ball. The object of the game is to stand ape-like on the beach, preferably in the middle of a particularly crowded section, where you can annoy people who are trying to mind their own business and have a good time. One player hits the ball to another person, not letting it touch the sand. There's no net, no out of bounds, no points, no rules other than what I've reported. What there *is* is a really loud, annoying noise that echoes every time ball hits paddle. Sounds like a lot of fun, doesn't it? Believe me, that summer Kadima was good for *hours* of entertainment on the ocean's edge.)

Anyway, back to the clam thief.

Her T-shirt was intentionally torn at the neck, revealing a darkly tanned shoulder (with a lot of flesh to tan) that had a tiny tattoo on it. I had an irrational fear that if I got too close to the tattoo, it would say, in micro letters, "Life's a Beach." So I averted my eyes, or at least refocused them on the clam.

"I knew that anyone with such a cute cat," she began, "wouldn't mind sharing his food. I'm *starving.*"

She showed me all her teeth in the friendliest smile I'd ever been on the receiving end of. It would have been more effective if her gums hadn't gone from her forehead nearly to her knees.

"May I have my clam back, please?" I asked her politely.

Her teeth sparkled again, only this time she popped the little fried sucker right in between the uppers and lowers.

"What kind of cat is that?"

I didn't answer. I was too busy watching her chew.

"How come his ears are down? Is he afraid?"

I shook my head. She swallowed. I watched the little bulge in her throat slide down out of view.

"Did you sedate him? How can he just sit there like that?"

Then she moved. Her bejeweled, tan fingers reached toward my plate again. This time my hand went up to meet hers. To her surprise, our fingers locked for a moment. But she managed that dazzling smile again. The smile faded somewhat when I said the words "Touch another clam and die."

I'm pretty sure she thought I was kidding, because she tried to disentangle her hand and make another go at my dinner.

"I don't want to be rude," I said, in my best quiet Clint Eastwood impersonation, "but I'm extremely hungry. I bought these clams so I could eat every single one of them, except for the ones I give to my cat. I don't mind if he reaches down and takes one because I know him. But I don't know *you*. So if you try to get to them, I'm afraid I'm going to have to find out where you live, sneak over in the middle of the night, and break your thumbs."

I did everything but say, "Are you feeling lucky, punk?" It seemed to do the trick.

She backed away slowly—clearly she'd been flirting with the Ted Bundy of the ferry set—and disappeared into the crowd.

I looked down at the cat draped over my shoulder. He looked back at me and meowed.

"I know what you mean, pal," I told him. "I don't think we're ready for the singles scene."

The next morning was D-Day. Norton was about to hit the shore.

He knew it, too. Don't ask me *how* he knew, but he did. I've come to expect this from him. He always seems to know when a big event is upon us: if I'm going on a trip, if *he's* going on a trip, if something particularly sad has happened, if something particularly festive is about to happen. If I didn't know better, I'd swear he keeps a calendar hidden somewhere in the apartment. Because as he got more and more used to going away to the beach for the weekends, his morning routine even changed. Mondays through Thursdays, we'd go through our wake-up cuddling, and then, as I dragged myself out of bed, Norton would race to the kitchen, jump up on the counter, and wait impatiently for me to feed him. On Fridays, he'd race along the same path—off the bed, through the bedroom door, around the corner, sharp right, cut through the living room, past the front door, into the kitchen—only he'd skid to a sudden stop at the front door and wait there eagerly. On Fridays he didn't even care about breakfast. He just wanted to hit the open road.

On the day of his first outdoor solo expedition, the moment my eyes popped open in the morning, my guy was out of bed, waiting at the front door of the Fire Island house, glancing back repeatedly to see what was keeping me.

Still rubbing sleep out of my eyes, I pulled on a pair of shorts, climbed down the stairs of the loft, and met him at the door. I hesitated. For one brief melancholy moment I had a vision of Norton on the side of an endless road, thumb out, heading far away in search of fame and glory. I composed myself, remembered that he didn't *have* a thumb, then I swung the screen open. Norton *didn't* hesitate. He scooted outside. In the blink of an eye, he was gone, racing across the yard, racing right back, disappearing in a flash under the deck.

I realized I had two choices. I could act like a total lunatic and tail him outside, try to follow him around wherever he went and keep an eye on him. Or I could be a rational, sane man: relax, make myself a pot of strong French Roast coffee with just a dash of cinnamon, get the newspapers, read about the fascinating events of the day, then go for a healthy, invigorating morning swim. It seemed like an obvious choice.

I decided to follow Norton.

He was having the absolute time of his life. Frolicking, chasing birds and squirrels—not catching, just chasing—

crawling through the grass on his belly, chomping on flowers, and generally enjoying his new role of jungle beast on the prowl.

After half an hour or so, I decided he was safe and sound, more than able to cope on his own with the great outdoors, so I went back inside to attend to some people-related chores such as trying to write a book and earn enough money to pay for Norton's summer house.

I never *really* worried. I knew he'd stay fairly close to home or, at least, wouldn't go so far away that he couldn't find his way back. Periodically, I'd step to the front door or back window and call his name, just checking up. I'd hear one crisp meow in response, letting me know all was well, then I'd go back to work.

At lunchtime I decided to head to the market (I'd forgiven them for ratting on me to Cindy). Going for the surprisingly mature route, I didn't even check up on Norton. I figured he wouldn't miss me for the twenty minutes I'd be gone, so why bother him? I didn't want him to think I was an overprotective dad. Feeling as proud as a father whose son has just gotten his driver's license and is driving away on his first date, I made a list of what I needed to buy and took off.

I was three quarters of a block toward the market when I first heard it. A faint growling of a meow, a little whiney in fact. I took another two steps, heard it again. *Brrrrrrmeowwwww.*

I stopped, turned my head. Norton was in the middle of the sidewalk, twenty feet behind me. He was trying to follow, but I was walking too fast.

"What are you doing?" I asked. "Go back to the house."

Again I headed for the store, managing to take all of two steps before hearing a much more insistent meow. When I turned, Norton had scampered a few feet closer.

"Then come on," I called. "Let's go."

And much to my astonishment, he ran up until he was about five feet behind me. Then he stopped. "Come on," I told him. "I'll walk slow." But he wouldn't budge any farther.

I took a few more steps, glanced behind me. He was following—but he stopped when I stopped. I went a few more steps, glanced. He'd kept pace.

I walked the rest of the three blocks to the market, and Norton followed, always staying five feet behind, every few feet meowing to let me know he was still there. Several Fair Harborites passed by and stopped to stare in amazement. I acted as if there were nothing at all unusual about the world's cutest kitten going for a lunchtime promenade with his favorite person.

Twice, people on bikes zoomed past and Norton froze. But he never panicked. Once they were gone, I just had to reassure him that everything was okay, that bikes were only an occasional hazard here in the real world; then he'd resume his faithful trot, taking my word that I was watching out for his best interests.

In a few minutes we were at the entrance to the market, where there were about ten times the number of people Norton had ever seen in his entire life. Kids were racing around playing tag, bikes and skateboards were skidding to and fro, several people with "Life's a Beach" T-shirts were trying to impress several other people with *Flashdance* T-shirts. Even for Norton it was a bit much.

As we approached, I wasn't sure what to do with him. See if he'd stroll inside and peruse the aisles with me? Pick him up and carry him? Ask someone to keep an eye on him while I shopped—a ten-minute cat sitter?

Norton ended my pondering and took matters into his own paws. After sizing up the situation, he darted past the door to the market, sprinted ten feet or so toward the dock, then disappeared into a thick row of bushes.

I had a feeling that most of my afternoon was going to be spent coaxing him out from under the greenery. After twenty minutes of trying, I figured there was nothing to be done about it. I could see him and he clearly wasn't going anywhere, so I decided it was safe to leave him while I shopped. I went into the market, bought the makings for a delicious lunch—two juicy knockwurst, some German potato salad, a dark Heineken, a can of Nine Lives Turkey Giblets—then trooped back outside to assess the cat situation.

The situation was this: the cat was gone.

Standing in front of the bush he'd been hiding in, I called his name. Nothing. Not a sound, not a stirring. I got down on my hands and knees and peered through the thicket, but there was no sign of gray fur anywhere. My throat felt as if I had a two-ton chunk of granite stuck in it; my stomach was flip-flopping to beat the Seven Santini Brothers. I couldn't believe it. How could I have left him alone outside? What was I thinking of? As smart as he was, he wasn't human. He wasn't even a dog. He was just a cat! A cat who'd never been outside on his own before, and I'd deserted him, left him stranded! And now he was either hiding somewhere, shivering in total terror, was hopelessly lost, never to be found again, or had been kidnapped by two brothers named Rick and Mick who had already tied the first firecracker to his tail.

Forcing myself to be calm, I took a deep breath and called Norton's name a second time. There was only a terrible silence. For one long second. Then two seconds . . . then . . . *brrrrrmeowww.*

A gray head with folded ears poked its way out of the bush—exactly where I'd last seen it. The rest of the body followed. Norton stood on the sidewalk, looking up at me with one of his "What's the problem?" looks.

I didn't want him to see that I'd completely lost faith in him and panicked, so I only allowed myself a minute sigh of relief. Then I turned and walked past the market, not stopping until I was on my own front deck. There was no need to look behind me: Norton, of course, had kept pace, trotting briskly five feet behind the entire way.

Over the course of the summer, Norton's little jaunts turned into a wonderfully pleasurable routine. Cindy was having to work more and more on the weekends, so Norton was, every two or three weeks, my only beach companion. He always walked me to the market in the morning, he usually walked me there at lunchtime, and he sometimes deigned to come along at dinnertime. Rarely did he walk by my side. He was most comfortable lagging those five feet behind. He would meow periodically just to let me know he was still tagging along. Once I got used to this, I stopped even bothering to turn around to check on him. I'd simply walk merrily on my way, hear him alert me that all was well, and I'd call back, "Okay, okay, let's try to keep up." I got quite used to, as people passed us by, someone turning to a friend, whose eyes would be bugging out, and saying, "See, I told you."

As we both got comfortable with our walking patterns, he (and I, I suppose) got more adventurous.

My writing partner is named David Handler. We do most of our television and film scripts together; the business is so filled with sharklike monsters whose greatest pleasure is chomping their sharp teeth down on helpless writers that we feel, erroneously no doubt, there's safety in numbers. David and his girlfriend, Diana, had a house four or five blocks north of mine. On the days we worked there, Norton took to accompanying me. He got to know the route well: straight for several blocks, left, then go all the way to the bay. He got to know it so well he began making the excursion on his own. Not infrequently, Cindy and I would be cooking dinner and David would call, saying Norton had been visiting for a couple of hours but he'd just trotted away, so I should expect him home soon. Sure enough, twenty minutes later there'd be a meow at the door, and a certain wandering feline would make it very clear he wouldn't mind eating a can of Cheese and Chicken Chunks and eating it *right now*.

One thing I learned early on is that I never had to worry about losing Norton along the way, no matter how far we traveled. Taking Central Walk—the erratically paved path that went for several miles along the center of the island— to David's, Norton would periodically get distracted or frightened or simply playful. If a squirrel happened to cross his path, Norton would scamper after him, sometimes into the bushes, sometimes under someone's house, sometimes up a tree. If a dog decided to act doglike and bark or growl, Norton was outta there. Same if a bike came clanging along and cruised too close. At first I would simply wait impatiently until he'd reappear, which sometimes took as long as fifteen minutes, or I'd spend the same amount of time crawling around trying to find and catch him. Once, I was in a particular hurry. David and I were to be on the receiving end of a conference call from a producer in L.A. who felt he could just as easily humiliate us over the phone as in person. So I just left Norton where he'd sprinted away to, hidden under someone's deck. I went to my conference call, spent forty-five minutes trying to iron out the intricate plot elements of a super-realistic sitcom episode (involving a college student who broke out in a rash whenever the girl of his dreams kissed him), then convinced David to come and try to look for my kitten. We went to the spot where I'd last seen him, I called his name, and presto, there was Norton, popping out into the sunlight, happy to follow us back to David's, where he could spend the rest of the afternoon playing in the tall reeds by the bay.

It became obvious I could leave Norton anywhere, and for any length of time. Even if we didn't want him, he'd often follow me and Cindy when we left the house. If we were walking over to someone's place for dinner, he'd stay with us until he got bored, meow loud enough so I'd be sure to turn and see where he was, then dash off to have fun on his own. Hours later, after dessert and coffee, I'd make my way back to the spot, call his name, and with one of his *brrrrmeowwwws,* he'd be ready to head back home.

Norton clearly liked the combination of his freedom and

my company as much as I did. It got to the point where it was rarely necessary to stick him into his shoulder bag/ carrying case. He wanted to walk everywhere instead. Leaving for Fire Island from my apartment, he always hopped right into the bag because, even for Norton, asking him to walk on a crowded Manhattan sidewalk was a bit much. Then, when Tommy's Taxi hit the ferry dock, he'd also willingly slip off my lap or shoulder back into the bag— there was too much foot and car traffic, not to mention the general sense of hysteria from the hordes of city dwellers overly anxious to drink frozen daiquiris, get skin cancer, and exchange phone numbers with members of the opposite sex who either owned or looked as if they would soon be able to own a two-bedroom co-op in a doorman building.

But once the ferry was headed across the bay, forget it. Norton was on his own.

As soon as were seated, he was out of the bag and either on my lap or propped up against the railing, checking out the fascinating movement of the waves. He would race to the door the moment we were tied up to shore and hop onto the dock's wooden planks himself. He'd wait impatiently for me and Cindy to make our way through the crowd (Why New Yorkers line up for five minutes—on a boat! Which you can't get off because it's still in the water!—then push and shove so they can get somewhere to *relax,* I'll never know), then race ahead of us toward the house, stopping every ten or twelve feet to make sure we were following. If he was hungry, he'd deign to come inside long enough to chow down, then he'd meow or scratch the screen door until we let him out. I didn't like the idea of his staying out all night—okay, okay, so I had a *touch* of Jim Backus in *Rebel Without a Cause* in me, get off my back— and, to his credit, he always came inside when it was time for me to go to bed. Even having glimpsed the world beyond, he didn't alter our regular sleeping arrangements.

Sunday night or Monday morning, when it was time to head back to the concrete jungle, he would walk with us to the ferry, stopping right before we reached the dock, where he'd hop into the bag and allow me to carry him until we were seated on the boat.

The more comfortable I got traveling with him, the more I realized how much I could trust him.

At the ferry stop was a great divey restaurant/pub, Porky's, whose desirable fried clams were mentioned earlier. Porky's had a take-out window, and I soon got into the habit of leaving Norton's bag—with Norton in it—on one of the benches by the boat while I went to get food before boarding. (I highly recommend their toasted homemade blueberry muffins, washed down with a long-necked bottle of ice-cold Bud.) I wouldn't be gone long, maybe ten minutes, but it would usually be long enough for a small crowd to have gathered round the gray cat with folded ears who was lying nonchalantly on top of his bag, taking a snooze or checking out any interesting fellow passengers.

He was quite relaxed and extraordinarily obedient when told to stay put. Eventually, as his modes of transportation and range of travels broadened, I was able to leave him in airport lounges for as long as twenty minutes while I went magazine or upgrade shopping, and in restaurants, sitting in his own chair while I ate peacefully in mine.

One of my proudest accomplishments, leading to one of

Norton's shining moments, was getting him to walk on the beach. For some reason, cats don't like the sand. Maybe it's too hot for their padded paws; maybe the water scares them; maybe they're put off by all the "Life's a Beach" shirts, umbrellas, and towels. Anyway, Norton was no exception.

Here was Norton walking along the boardwalk *toward* the beach: cocky swagger, confident gleam in the eye, the look of someone who'd been parading around town pointing his finger at a neighbor, saying things like "Howdy, Bill, we missed you at the town hall meeting last night."

Here he was when I'd plop him *in the middle of the beach:* cowering, shaking, racing as far away from the waves as he could get to huddle terrified against the dunes. Picture Jimmy Cagney on his way to the chair in *Angels with Dirty Faces. Norton Dies Yellow!*

I decided this simply wouldn't do.

When a kid takes horseback riding lessons and tumbles off, what's the very first thing he's told? *Get right back on.* I knew I'd never get Norton to go for a horseback ride— well, there's no point in saying *never*—but I couldn't see any reason for him to stay off the sand.

In my own defense, let me say right here and now that I'm not one of those pushy stage parents. I mean, if Ethel Merman were alive, she wouldn't play me in a musical. Although Norton is a show-quality cat, I'd never even *think* of displaying him or training him to do tricks. Those things are for *other* people. This was for me and him. He'd *enjoy* having new areas to roam and explore. Why should he limit himself when he could be frolicking with some beach bunnies down by the water's edge? To end my own defense, let me say that I felt then, and I feel now, a little too much like the parent of a nine-year-old boy who's making the poor lad take piano lessons and says, "Believe me, he'll thank me for this when he's older."

The first few times I let Norton loose in the sand, he was gone the moment I set him down, running for the protective safety of dirt and boardwalk. The next few times, I put him down and held him, letting him get used to the feel. He didn't struggle and he didn't appear too miserable. When I let go, he'd hesitate, realizing that perhaps this whole beach thing wasn't as terrible as he'd assumed—as I'd been telling him repeatedly—but then he'd hunker down and skulk back to real land. Not sprinting exactly but not stopping to admire the view either.

After that it got easier. His instinct was to follow me. I'd never led him astray before; there was no reason for him to believe I was starting now.

Within a week, Norton was walking comfortably on the beach, his usual five steps behind me, meowing a lot more and a lot louder than usual, but he was there. He wouldn't go all the way to the water, but he *would* walk about halfway there, wait while Cindy or I shook loose a towel to lie on, and stick around for half an hour or so, especially if he got to share any of our picnic lunch. I still believe he would have spent more time relaxing there if it wasn't for the constant *thwapp-thwapp-thwapp* of the Kadima balls.

One day, toward the end of August, Cindy and I were invited to a cookout in Seaview, one of the other beach communities. Cindy had a girlfriend who was in a "share" there, a share being when six people share the cost of a three-bedroom house, figuring out such complicated schemes as alternate weekend visits, splitting food costs, and prorating the fee for the largest bedroom or the one with the ocean view or the one closest to the refrigerator.

On this particular weekend, all the sharers were stuffed into the house because it was the weekend of the annual Seaview Clam Bake. Every year, everyone in the small community brought food and drink to the beach—clams, lobsters, burgers, hot dogs, kegs of beer, pitchers of margaritas—dug pits for barbecuing and steaming, and cooked out, drank, and generally made merry. This went on all day and a goodly portion of the night. There was usually music and volleyball games and three-legged races and other Andy Hardyish events; all in all, it was awfully hard to think of a much better way to spend a ninety-degree day in the heart of a New York summer.

Cindy went early to help prepare. She thought it would be fun to be in on the beginning of the festivities. As much as I always enjoyed the Seaview bash, my antisocial theory about large gatherings of human beings always was and is "less is more."

I puttered around until the late morning, did a little work, and, since Cindy wasn't around, caught up on my Rotisserie League stats. Rotisserie League, for those of you in the baseball dark ages, is sometimes called Fantasy Baseball. The game has swept the nation—*USA Today* estimates that 750,000 people now play it—and I'm proud to say I'm one of the cofounders of the original league. The premise is a simple yet immensely gratifying one. You put together a team at an auction, bidding against nine or eleven other "owners," depending on whether you're in the National

League or the American League. The structure of the team is specified: two catchers, three cornermen, five outfielders, nine pitchers, and so on. If you buy Darryl Strawberry—God forbid!—and he hits a home run for the Dodgers, he also hits one for your team. Being a total maniac about the game, I have *two* teams, which makes it nearly impossible to get any real work done during the summer months. My American League team is called the Gethers YeRosebuds, my National League team is the Smoked Fish. (I am respectfully referred to by my National League *compadres* as the Sturgeon General. And believe me, I'd way overpay if there was any way to get Steve Trout on my pitching staff.) I liked to do my stats when Cindy wasn't with me because she thought it was rather scary that a reasonably intelligent person would actually *want* to spend two hours a day totaling up the Hits and Walks Per Inning Pitched ratio for people who toiled in such places as Memorial Stadium and Chavez Ravine.

Satisfied that the Rosebuds were sprouting up for a big stretch run and a little depressed that I saw no end to the Fish's floundering, I decided it was time to head off to the Seaview bash.

Norton was lazily sunning himself on the porch as I stepped outside. His half-ears twitched in idle curiosity when I passed him by. I think he was wondering why anyone would bother leaving such a perfect spot.

"Whaddya say," I asked him. "You up for a stroll?"

Now, Seaview was two miles from where we were in Fair Harbor. The only way to get there in a reasonably straight line was by walking on the beach. Norton had never gone more than about thirty feet on sand. This had the potential for disaster. But I thought Norton would like the cookout once he got there. It seemed worth a shot.

My pal was ready to give it a go. He lifted himself up from his sprawled position and began trotting after me. When it came time, half a block later, to descend to the beach, he meowed loudly.

"Come on," I coaxed gently. "What have you got to lose?"

If I'd been by myself, I probably would have made it to the party in twenty-five minutes. With Norton, I got there in thirty-five. He was perfect—never slowing down, never letting himself be distracted, always keeping pace right behind me, except for when he got frisky and raced ahead of me. He meowed a little more than usual, but he didn't seem to be complaining. He was just feeling gabby.

The way Seaview is set up along the beach, you have to climb up a small incline to get there. When you've climbed, you're standing on a dune overlooking the town's entire stretch of beach. It's not the Grand Canyon or anything, but it's quite nice, especially on a day when there are a couple of hundred people happily cooking and serving and playing.

I climbed, stood there for a moment enjoying the view, and spotted Cindy. She waved; I waved back. I swiveled my head back behind me to check on the walking wonder and said, "Let's do it."

Norton meowed once and followed. Up the incline, down into the laughing hordes. Within moments, the noisiest event of the season was eerily quiet. One by one, heads turned, eating stopped, music ceased. These sophisticated Fire Islanders had seen Frisbee-playing dogs in their midst.

They'd seen a spider monkey with a pail and shovel digging holes in the beach. They'd even once seen a female member of the singles-oriented Kismet community who *wasn't* wearing an ankle bracelet. But they were all staring at the kitten who'd traversed the sandy shores to help them party hearty—Norton of Arabia.

"Where did you come from?" the first person I passed asked.

"Fair Harbor," I told him.

"Your cat walked *two miles* like that?!"

I nodded. By the time I reached Cindy and her friends, I was nodding like a madman, my head bobbing up and down, and I was repeating all the familiar phrases: "Yup, does it all the time . . . Scottish Fold. See the ears? . . . Norton . . . Two miles . . . Fair Harbor . . . Yup . . . See the ears?"

Gradually the cookout went back to normal. The band started up again, backgammon games resumed, shrimps were skewered. Norton, after sampling some grilled tuna, went to play in the grass, away from the sand. I went with him to the steps leading away from the beach, told him I'd come get him in a few hours. I picked him up, kissed the top of his head, then I watched him disappear, knowing he'd be waiting when it was time to go home.

The cat who went to california

My Fire Island landlord was nice enough to extend our summer season until the end of September. But over the Labor Day weekend it hit me: What was I going to do with Norton when I didn't have a summer home where he could frolic the day away? How was he going to adjust to being an indoor cat? Especially—since I had recently learned that the biggest cause of fatalities in New York City cats was their leaping to their deaths out of apartment windows—an indoor cat whose father wouldn't ever again open a window so much as a crack.

By October 1, I hadn't come up with any intelligent solutions. Norton's travels were relegated to going back and forth between Cindy's and my apartment. When she spent the night at mine, Marlowe would come along. He was perfectly comfortable at my place, so it seemed only right that Norton should be their houseguest when the sleeping arrangements were reversed.

I was starting to do a fair amount of business-related traveling. (I should probably explain that the traveling was complicated because my business was complicated. I should say business*es*—and perhaps "confusing" is a better description than "complicated" since I don't actually have one job, I have several, none of which makes all that much sense. One part of me runs a publishing company. That part allows me to make honest-to-goodness grown-up financial decisions, meet anyone interesting I can think of who might like to write a book, and work with very talented and very temperamental authors and personalities. Another part of me writes and produces television and movie scripts. That part allows me to wear sunglasses and hate actors and get really aggravated when producers say things to me like, "I love it! It's perfect! And don't worry, I know exactly how to fix it!"—which actually *was* said by the executive producer of a TV series I worked on. The third and final part of me—probably my favorite part—writes books. This is the part that allows me to sit alone in a room and torture myself trying to invent characters and plots that most people will never read or hear of. It also gives me a chance to create some meaning out of all sorts of otherwise meaningless things. None of these jobs particularly fits together, and I never actually meant to turn into a compulsive workaholic—but somehow it's happened and I kind of like it.) My publishing job—at this point I was helping to start a new imprint within the large and still growing Random House complex—would take me away for a sales conference here and there, a trip to San Francisco to see agents, a quick sojourn with an author to make sure he or she felt loved and appreciated. My writing career was also keeping me busy and on the road. When you live in New York and write for Hollywood, you've constantly got to prove to the networks and studios that living three thousand miles away from the people paying you—and usually paying far too much money to write things that never get made—isn't anything they should worry about. The only proof is visibility, which meant my partner, David, and I had to hop on a plane on a fairly regular basis and show our faces around town.

Norton and Marlowe were great pals; thus it was never a problem figuring out what to do when I went away: Cindy would take him. She was nearly as crazy about my guy as she was about hers, and she truly enjoyed watching the two cats play and stay together for three or four days in a row. All three of them had fun when I was gone.

Everything seemed perfect until this pleasant and easy routine was forced to change. Cindy broke it to me that she was having a little *too* much fun when I was gone.

We had a strange relationship, Cindy and I. I had been smitten the moment I saw her; she had hated me on sight. She thought I was smug, egotistical, and watched too much baseball. But I was persistent—writing, sending flowers, calling, doing everything but watching less baseball—and eventually won her over. We couldn't have been more opposite. She was wary of relationships and hesitant to get involved, positive that she'd be wounded irreparably just at the moment she relaxed enough to decide our particular relationship was a permanent one. Although I didn't believe in or even consider the possibility of permanence, I was an incurable romantic and was more than happy to rush in with my chin jutting and get knocked out with the first straight right hand that came my way. She didn't believe in spending money unwisely and thought it was almost sinful to spend it on one's immediate pleasure and comfort. I believed in spending any money I received as soon as possible—and *only* on things that would bring me pleasure and comfort. She thought she was a terrible human being—which she most certainly was not—while I, on the other hand, couldn't imagine anyone being a better, nicer guy than I. She got depressed all the time; I was almost always happy. She was always cold; I was always hot. She thought it was important to be serious—that times were bad and only serious thought and behavior might improve them. I was of the *Sullivan's Travels* school of behavioral thinking—times *were* bad, so let's laugh it up and try to find amusement in everything. She was searching for meaning. I hoped I'd *never* find meaning in *anything*—or I was in big trouble.

What really brought us together was the fact that we had *one* thing in common—we both wanted to stay independent.

The only thing we could agree on was that we didn't believe in a standard, old-fashioned, monogamous relationship. We didn't believe in marriage. People should stay together because they *want* to stay together—not because a piece of paper tells them they've made a legal commitment. We wanted to be free, unrestricted. If we felt like spending Saturday night together, fine. If we didn't, fine again. No problem. And no ties.

We never actually came out and said the words "I love you." We danced around it with clever phrases like "I really love being with you" and "I love the way we don't have to say 'I love you' and we still know how we feel about each other," but once we realized we liked each other a whole bunch and that we didn't *have* to be in an old-fashioned relationship where we saw each other every Saturday night, we fell into a very comfortable old-fashioned relationship where we saw each other every Saturday night and generally took good care of each other. Neither one of us ever really thought about making more of a commitment than we had to make. In retrospect, it seems obvious that neither Cindy nor I truly understood the nature of commitment. Although, I realize now, I was in the process of learning. It just wasn't with Cindy.

Toward the end of the previous summer, Cindy and I had spent more time apart than usual, but I had attributed that to Cindy's new job and the fact that she was working long and hard hours. It turns out I should have attributed it to the fact that she'd fallen in love with her doctor.

She'd switched to him sometime in the spring. I remembered that she'd mentioned how great he was—and how cute. I also remembered that sometime around the Fourth of July, she'd started saying things like "You know, you really shouldn't eat popcorn. It tends to clog up your intestines" and "Did you know that by the year 2020, the average doctor will spend nearly a million dollars to go to medical school? Doesn't it steam you that people think of doctors as selfish and unfeeling when they have to risk so much to do what they do?"

I'd usually say things like "Oh yeah?" or *"What?"* and then not give it any thought. But I gave it a lot of thought when she told me I was getting dumped for the doc. Especially because it came right after I had invited her to England—the week's vacation was to be a present for her birthday.

"I just can't live a lie anymore," Cindy told me.

I readily agreed that she shouldn't have to live a lie, although I wished she could have lived it until after we'd been to a couple of farmhouse bed-and-breakfasts in Devon. She also wanted me to agree that it was a sad thing that it hadn't worked out between us. I managed to say that I thought it *had* been working out between us.

"No," Cindy said. "I don't know if you're capable of the kind of feelings that I need."

"You mean the kind of feeling where it's okay to dump someone who tries to do incredibly nice things for you like taking you to England?"

"No, I mean abandoning yourself to love. You're an observer," she told me. "I don't know if you're a participant in life."

This stopped me short. I'd always thought I was a good participator. Granted, my idea of a good time was watching *On the Waterfront* for the sixty-second time and then calling Sports Line to find out how the Mets had done, but I'd stack my life experiences with anyone's.

"Oh, you do participate," Cindy now said, "but you hold back. It's as if you're waiting for something."

"For what?"

"I don't know. For something better. Something *different*. Something you don't have. And you're holding back your true self until you find it."

"This *is* my true self," I tried to tell her. "You may not

like it as much as Dr. Polaro's true self, but it's mine."

"You don't understand," she said. And with that I had to agree. I had thought Cindy and I were on the same wavelength. I'd thought we were giving each other what we both needed. I'd thought there was a bond of honesty and trust between us. I'd thought we were finally at the comfortable stage, something men and women have an awfully difficult time reaching together without being in a rest home. Obviously I'd thought wrong.

I didn't stick around for too much longer. For one thing, I was getting awfully sad. For another, I was fairly certain Dr. Polaro's true self would be coming over soon, and I didn't particularly want to be there when it did.

It wasn't easy saying good-bye to Cindy. In a weird way, it was even harder to say good-bye to Marlowe. I'd really gotten to like the little guy. And with Cindy, at least I could hate her a little bit. I knew that wouldn't last, but it was some comfort at the moment. I had no reason to hate Marlowe. He'd never done anything to me but make me laugh and make me feel good. I'd even gotten him finally, on our next-to-last weekend on Fire Island, to go for a short walk with me and Norton. He made it almost all the way to the market. Now I picked him up and scratched his full, standing-up-straight ears. "You can come over anytime," I told him.

Norton was surprised we were leaving so soon. Once I'd lugged him over there, he was prepared to spend the night. He meowed, a tad annoyed, when I put him back into his bag. Cindy didn't pet him or say good-bye to him. In fact, she wouldn't even look at him. I think she felt too guilty.

Or else she thought that *his* true self might ask her what the hell she was doing dropping us for a guy who wouldn't eat popcorn.

The last thing Cindy said to me was, "You won't be sad for long. You don't really love me. You don't know what love is."

The next few weeks were a little rough. I felt funny watching *On the Waterfront* by myself on Saturday night, and Norton didn't understand why (1) he hadn't been out of the apartment at *all,* not even across town to Cindy's, and (2) if he wasn't going to be able to leave, where was his friend Marlowe to keep him company?

Most of my time was taken up working and feeling sorry for myself. I found comfort in little things: I remembered that Cindy once actually told me she thought the ending to *On the Waterfront* was *stupid*—that Brando shouldn't have had to stand up at the end for the men to go back to work; he was risking serious injury (and this was *before* the doctor). I remembered that she liked to sing the theme song to "The Brady Bunch" when she cooked. And I realized, at last, I could now take taxis everywhere without someone trying to make me feel as if I were personally responsible for famine in Pakistan. In fact, within a day, I'd managed to make a list of things about her that so infuriated me, I had almost forgotten about going back to her to beg and plead for a second chance.

Luckily for my sanity (and the sanity of those around me), I was distracted by the need to prepare for a week-long trip to California. I kept busy making appointments, figuring out what I was going to do and say . . . It was only three days before I had to leave that it occurred to me I had to do something with Norton.

I considered calling Cindy to see if she'd still take him. I was fairly certain she would, but I didn't feel it was quite the appropriate thing to do. I didn't like the idea of her knowing I couldn't manage without her. I also had visions of Dr. Polaro, whom I could no longer separate from Son of Sam when trying to imagine what he was really like, performing some strange surgical procedures on Norton's fragile and vulnerable body. So Cindy was out. I called almost everyone else I knew—and not one of them could cat-sit for the week. Either they had a cat of their own and felt it wouldn't work, or their apartment building had a strict no-pet rule, or they were allergic to cats, or they were too nervous because they knew what I'd do to them if anything happened to Norton while he was in their care. By the time I'd run through my phone book, I had two days left to come up with a plan.

The reason I was going to California was that I'd agreed to speak at a writers conference in San Diego. I was going to spend three days there, then go to L.A. for the rest of the week to work, see a few people, have a few meetings, and spend some time with my family. Nothing too hectic, nothing too formal, nothing too intimidating—in other words, absolutely nothing that would preclude taking an extraordinarily well-behaved and well-adjusted cat.

I got on the phone immediately. San Diego was a breeze. The conference had booked all the speakers and would-be writers into a large motel near the UCSD campus. The motel was delighted to have a cat spend a few nights in their care. I had a sudden and brand new appreciation for the laid-back, Southern California lifestyle.

Los Angeles was more difficult, however. My regular hotel wouldn't hear of it. Out of the question. The next five hotels also wouldn't consider having Norton as a customer. But then I struck pay dirt.

The Four Seasons had just built a new hotel in L.A. It was in a very convenient location, was the right price, and was supposed to be terrific. This was their first week open for business.

"How big is he?" they wanted to know.

"Little," I said. "He's very little for a cat."

"Over forty pounds?"

"No. I said he's a *cat,* not a *lion.* I think he weighs *six* pounds.

"Claws?"

"Yes," I said, then realized I should have lied my head off. "But he never scratches anything!" I added immediately. "And if he does, I'll happily pay for any damage." At those last words, I rolled my eyes to the heavens and prayed if there were a god that he hadn't given the Four Seasons a decorator who had a fetish for burlap wallpaper.

"Let me check with the manager. Hold on."

I held on, a wreck, preparing all sorts of arguments for the manager in favor of allowing cats in their rooms. I decided I was even prepared to audition him. "How's this for a deal," I was thinking of saying. "I'll pay for a separate room for Norton for one night, put him in there for an hour. Then you can check him out . . ."

"Hello?"

"I'm still here," I said quietly.

"We'd be pleased to have your cat stay with us," the reservation clerk told me. "What's his name, so I can add him to the guest list?"

That was the first moment I realized I might be able to survive without Cindy. If I was going to marry this wonderful woman on the other end of the phone, I *had* to survive.

The day of the flight, I was totally unprepared. I had no idea how to make a cross-continental airplane trip with a cat, so I was forced to improvise. I assumed that if I were doing anything wrong, some right-thinking airline employee would set me straight.

I was flying with my agent, Esther Newberg, who was also speaking at the conference. Esther happened to have two fears—flying and cats—so when I picked her up at her apartment and she saw Norton, she was ready to call the whole trip off. But Fear Number Two was eradicated by the time we reached the airport. Within thirty minutes, Esther, whose mind is about as easy to change as Attila the Hun's, decided Norton was the greatest animal she'd ever seen. She couldn't get over the way he sat on my lap and peered out the window for the entire drive.

"I'm hoping he does that on the plane, too," I told her.

"What's he done on other flights with you?" she asked.

I decided I wouldn't break it to her. Esther's the nervous type.

When we got to the airport, I put Norton in his bag, slung it over my shoulder, and went to check our bags. At the ticket counter, the woman gave me a boarding pass, tagged my suitcase and sent it slithering along the conveyor belt, then looked Norton right in the eye. She smiled at him, said nothing, and returned my ticket to me.

Next we went to the security checkpoint. Esther went through with no problem. When Norton and I stepped through, I expected alarms to go off to beat the band. But no. I guess those things are a lot more sensitive to steel and explosives than to fur. All that happened was that one of the female guards patted Norton's head when he stuck it out of the bag to check out his surroundings.

When we got to the gate, I began to have serious doubts that anyone was ever going to say anything about my flying with a cat. Perhaps it was a lot more common than I thought.

Boarding, Norton snuggled down into his carrier when I showed my ticket to the stewardess. All she said was "Seat 8C." Not a word about you-know-who.

Esther and I took our seats, and Norton hopped out of his bag and settled onto my lap in his favorite position—lying straight along my crossed legs, head resting on my left foot. I got a blanket and laid it over him, figuring it would make it easier to hold on to him when we took off.

We saw a short film, instructing us how to correctly fasten our seat belts. (I must say, my theory is that if you're a grown-up human being who can't figure out how to fasten your seat belt, the odds are that you wouldn't have been able to make a plane reservation and actually get to the airport, which means you wouldn't be in a position to enjoy this superb cinematic experience.) Then a stewardess passed by, checking to make sure everyone had managed to understand the film and do the fastening correctly. She looked straight at my lap—upon which sat the cat—smiled, said nothing, and passed by to look at the next lap. Still no one had said a word about Norton.

For two hours, Norton sat there, the perfect gentleman, staring out the window, fascinated by his first adult close-up glimpse of clouds. He didn't stir; he didn't make a peep. I began to relax.

Two hours and one minute into the flight, someone finally said the very first thing about the fact that there was a cat on board. It was the head stewardess, a woman of about fifty, who had the delicate good looks of Marie Dressler and the charming personality of Nurse Ratched.

"You've got a cat!" were her exact screaming words.

I looked up from my book. Norton turned away from the window to see who was making so much commotion.

"Get him *out* of here!" she hissed.

I looked over at Esther, glanced back to the stewardess.

"Where would you like him to go?" I asked.

"I don't care!" the woman said. "Just get him out of here!"

"Why don't you open the door," I suggested, "and I'll toss him out over Cleveland."

I didn't have a moment to even admire my own calm and wit, because at this point, things accelerated. The man behind me stood up and said, "Oh, my god! There's a cat! I'm allergic to cats! Get him out of here!" The guy started sneezing like a lunatic.

"The cat's been right here for two hours," I said, trying to be a sane voice in the wilderness. "What the hell are you sneezing *now* for?"

The guy couldn't answer me, unfortunately, because he was too busy sneezing, wheezing, coughing, and struggling to get out of his seat belt so he could escape from the dread cat hair. I thought of suggesting to the stewardess that they should show a short film about how to *un*fasten your seat belt but decided against it.

"Get that cat under the seat!" the woman snapped at me.

"I don't think you want me to do that," I told her.

"Did you hear what I said?!"

"I did. But if you'll just listen for a second—"

"Put him under the seat!!"

I picked Norton—who was responding to the crisis by acting particularly docile and cute—up off my lap and put him on the floor under my seat. When I told him to "stay," the stewardess flew into an absolute rage.

"In his box! Put him in his box!"

Now, I'm not big on public scenes. I'd place them somewhere right below walking on hot coals and sitting through Bette Midler movies on my list of least favorite experiences. But I was starting to get annoyed.

"I *can't* put him in his box. He doesn't *have* a box. That's why I told you you didn't want me to put him under the seat."

This charming woman could not have had a stronger response if I'd said, "I'm carrying a bomb. Give me all your money or this plane's confetti." As far as she was concerned, I was the Salman Rushdie of passengers and she was the Ayatollah.

"What do you *mean* you don't have a box?!" she demanded. At this point I realized there was no way to stop this whole thing from getting completely out of hand, so I figured what the hell and decided to go for it.

"You know those little cages that cats go into? The ones

that fit under the seat? I don't *have* one of those. *That's* what I mean!"

By now, I didn't think it could get any worse. I was wrong. Esther decided to get involved.

"Look," she said—and when Esther says "Look" at the beginning of a sentence, the only thing that comes to mind that *might* be as scary is the moment in *The Godfather II* when Al Pacino hears that Diane Keaton got an abortion— "one of the other stewardesses saw the cat on his lap earlier. She didn't seem to think it was a problem."

"Stewardess?!" The woman was now in an apoplectic fury. *"Stewardess?!!"*

Esther and I looked at each other, not sure what the problem was now. Esther, ever the forceful agent, took a stab at it. "That's right. The other stewardess walked right by and—"

"We are not stewardesses! We are *flight attendants!*"

The next five or ten minutes is a blur. I remember giggling. Then I remember the stewardess . . . er . . . attendant accusing me of smuggling Norton aboard. I have a vague memory of trying to explain that she was mistaken, of her telling me I was breaking the law, of me telling her to go ahead and throw me in airplane jail. I definitely remember Esther rising to Norton's defense and unleashing a string of expletives that would have made John Gotti blush. They didn't seem to have much effect on the Dragon Lady, though.

Other than the fact that there was a wild, untamed jungle beast running free, able at any moment to terrorize the passengers—if you believed what our attendant was saying, the flight was quickly turning into one of those disaster movies starring Helen Hayes and George Kennedy—the biggest problem seemed to be that they were about to serve us some of their scrumptious airplane food. Apparently, health regulations make it illegal on American planes for a pet to be out of his cage during mealtime. Is this a great country or what? We can't lick the homeless problem, but the FAA has made damn sure that we're able to sit in really cramped little chairs and eat microwaved teriyaki chicken in peace and quiet.

We did eventually work out a compromise, which unfortunately didn't involve my being able to staple our attendant's lips together. I simply agreed to forgo the delicious meal, as did my loyal agent. In exchange, I didn't have to toss my cat out and let him parachute his way to safety. He could stay on my lap. The guy behind me could switch seats with another passenger sympathetic to my plight. And our plane could continue on to San Diego without any more hysteria.

Which is exactly what we did. Norton stared out the window, perfectly content, until we landed. Mr. Allergy moved to the back of the plane and spent the rest of the trip breathing clean, cat-free air. Esther was so furious about Nurse Ratched's behavior that she forgot to be afraid of crashing and dying; she even allowed Norton to sit on her lap for a while. The evil stewardess—on principle alone I refuse to call her an attendant—steered clear of us for the rest of the trip, even refusing to bring us coffee or little Wash 'n' Dries.

The final three hours of the trip were calm.

The hysteria didn't begin again until we landed.

By the time we got our bags, rounded up two other publishing people who needed a ride, waited on line at the rental car desk, found our car, and got directions to the conference, we'd been traveling for nine hours. This is the second lesson I learned (after the one about buying a carrier that will fit under one's seat) about transporting a cat across state lines: nine hours is too long to go without a litter box.

Four people and one cat crowded into a shiny Oldsmobile. The people immediately started grumbling about being hungry and hating Southern California. The cat uncharacteristically started meowing like a lunatic. Norton perched himself on the shelf under the rear window and howled. He kept this up for fifteen minutes or so. I think it took that long for him to realize we still had a ways to go to hit the motel. But once the realization set in, he decided to do something about it.

He urinated all over the backseat.

Needless to say, this didn't go over all that well with my traveling companions. Especially because we couldn't get him to stop. I'd never seen an animal—two- or four-legged—pee for quite so long.

I didn't get angry. I couldn't. It was awfully hard to blame Norton. And from the miserable way he looked, he clearly didn't like it any more than we did. He just didn't know what else to do.

As we stopped at a gas station, in a desperate attempt to clean things up, I realized that I was totally unprepared to have a cat with me for the next week. Not only didn't I have a litter box, I didn't have any litter. I also didn't have any cat food, any cat food dishes, or any little cat treats. Basically, I realized that because of my selfishness in wanting him to travel with me, I'd just put my beloved cat through a crash course of Cat Torture 101.

Norton was clearly mortified and humiliated about his public . . . ummm . . . accident. He didn't seem to understand that it wasn't his fault. He hid under the driver's seat until we pulled into the motel. And once I had let my disgruntled passengers out of the car, I took immediate action to rectify my thoughtless ways.

The first thing I did was drive to a market, where I got a large cardboard box. (I've since gotten *much* more sophisticated about this potentially awkward problem. I now stock up on portable, folding litter boxes, twenty at a time. Any pet store sells them; they're sturdy enough to last a week or two, and they easily slip into my briefcase or traveling bag. I can't recommend them highly enough.) I bought some litter. (Again, years later, I've now gotten this all down to a science: two small five-pound bags of litter easily fit into my suitcase. The moment we hit the rental car, I open up the folding litter box, rip open one of the bags, and *voilà*, Norton's got everything he needs, *immediately* laid out on the floor of the backseat. There's no need to torture him for the entire drive to our final destination, and it makes it a lot easier for me to drive him around town for the rest of my stay. Once I get to my room, I take out a second box and tear open the second bag of litter. Not only does Norton appreciate the extra facilities, I'm sure the rental car company and the hotel are a lot happier. I know the bellboys are. The first time I thought to put a litter box in the car,

I didn't have a second one. So when I checked into the hotel, a not-very-happy guy in a uniform had to lug a used cat box up to my room.) I also bought a scooper at the market so I could clean the box out, a week's worth of food, and a container of cat treats.

Back at the motel, I checked in and set Norton up in fine style. Two ashtrays made perfect food and water bowls. I fed him, showed him that I was setting up his litter box next to the sink, then set him on the bed and started petting him, telling him with the utmost sincerity that he was, very possibly, the greatest animal who'd ever lived. It wasn't too long before he was purring. After half an hour, I decided it was safe to unpack. I was pretty sure I'd been forgiven.

Part of the deal with the conference was that I would spend a portion of each day critiquing manuscripts. Any student who wanted my opinion could leave fifteen to twenty-five pages for me to read; then I was to spend several hours sitting by the pool, and each of the students could spend fifteen minutes with me discussing his or her writing ability (or, at least, my educated opinion of his or her writing ability). I always like this part of every writers conference I go to. It's always interesting to see what people are trying to write and to hear what they *think* they're trying to write. Sometimes, however, these sessions can get a bit hostile. Many editors go right for the throat and actually tell the truth. This is not a recommended course of action. Many of the student writers don't take kindly to even the remotest criticism of their precious words. One has to delicately balance truth with encouragement. It's not always easy.

(Imagine trying to critique, without offending the writer, an Oklahoma dentist's true account of the hilarious world of tartar control, called *Open Wide.*) I try to be gentle since, for the most part, I'm not dealing with professionals. With a pro, an editor can actually come out and say, "This paragraph stinks. Cut it." The pro will usually reexamine the paragraph with an open mind and, if it does indeed stink, get rid of it, or at least rewrite it. With an amateur, such a blunt response can produce anything from tears to guns. So I try to look for positives as well as negatives. Basically, I try to give the would-be writers their money's worth.

Along the same lines, I thought I should try to give Norton *his* money's worth. As long as he'd made the trek across country, it seemed foolish to keep him cooped up in the motel room. So the day of my first poolside sessions, I carried Norton with me, set him down by my chair, and told him to have fun for the next few hours.

As soon as he was free to go where he wanted, he took off for the far side of the motel, where there was a lawn and bushes to prowl through. Before he rounded the corner and disappeared from sight, he meowed once, loudly. I looked up, our eyes met (I'm not making this up, I swear), he made sure I took notice of where he was, then he was gone.

A New York editor who was also teaching at the conference came over to me and asked if I knew there was a freeway on the other side of the motel. I told her I wasn't in any hurry to go anywhere, and she then told me she wasn't all that concerned with my travel plans, she was concerned that my cat was going to end up as road kill. I assured her that he was all right, that he did this kind of thing back on Fire Island all the time, and forgot about it.

I began my first session, a critique of what was supposed to be a novel but what was obviously a thinly disguised true story, about a tumultuous love affair between a young Jewish girl and an older Italian man in the 1930s. The book was poetically titled *Matzos and Spaghetti,* and the author was a seventy-year-old woman named Naomi Weinblatt. My helpful comments ("The dialogue is strong, but are you really sure it has a contemporary feel to it?") were interrupted by the worried editor, who stopped by to tell me she'd just been looking for my cat and he had clearly jumped ship. She'd tried calling his name, but he was nowhere to be found. Once again, I told her to relax and went back to my student, who was defending her novel by saying, "But this really happened!"

While I was commenting on the next manuscript, a Civil War novel about a beautiful, tempestuous woman named Scarlett who was in love with a handsome, brutish rogue ("You have a good feel for the era, but it seems a bit derivative"), I heard the editor's voice calling "Norton . . . Norton . . ." I glanced over, and sure enough, she was thrashing through the bushes near where he'd disappeared, trying to coax him out. I shook my head and went on to my next eager writer.

An hour and several manuscripts later (one science fiction novel in which computers that are really human beings create human beings who are really computers; one series of uplifting essays meant to convey the simple pleasures of life, called *Hey, It Doesn't Matter If You're Fat;* one short story by an extremely clean-cut woman named Joy about an extremely clean-cut woman named Jill who's raped by the side of a muddy road, then crawls for miles until she reaches a garbage heap, which she staggers into, buries herself in filth, then dies, wanting only to know the name of her rapist so she can forgive him—my extremely helpful insight: "Write what you know."), my editor friend had organized a little search party. There were now four or five students crawling around the lawn screaming Norton's name, begging him to come home.

By the end of the next hour (a screenplay in which screen time mirrored *real* time—in other words, *nothing* happened; a dozen poems about everyday life, of which the only thing I remember is that the author actually rhymed "June" with "spoon"; and a thriller that had this for an opening line: "The bullet creased his forehead and he felt faint, barely having the energy to remove the pin from the grenade which was hidden in his coat, which he threw at the onrushing Krauts, knocking them to hell and gone, which they deserved." My only comment on this one was "Did he throw the grenade or the coat at the Krauts?"), I couldn't stand watching what had now become a dragnet for Norton. It seemed that most of the San Diego community was searching the grounds for my lost cat. I have to say that although outwardly I was cool, calm, and collected, inwardly I was beginning to get pretty worried. What if Southern California *wasn't* like Fire Island? What if Norton decided to *find* Fire Island and decided the freeway was his best and quickest bet? What if . . .

I decided these musings were getting me nowhere, although I was quite sure one of my students could turn the situation into a bad prose poem. I decided to find out for myself if my faith in Norton had been misplaced.

Never showing my fear, I strode over to where I'd last

seen him meow and called his name once. Without even a moment's hesitation, my little gray cat leaped from the bushes and meowed excitedly, happy I'd come to rescue him from all this noise. I petted him proudly, then turned on my heels and headed up the stairs toward our second-floor room. There was nothing but silence from around the pool as Norton trotted after me, ready for his pre-cocktail nap. When I opened the door to usher him inside the building, there was a spontaneous burst of applause.

As Norton scampered inside, I wondered if it would be possible to teach him how to bow. I decided it was probably worth spending a few minutes working on it.

The rest of the conference went smoothly. Norton, depending on his mood, spent part of each day in the room snoozing and part of each day by the pool prowling. He did attend one of my seminars, spending most of it asleep on the podium, directly on top of my notes.

When the readings and seminars and lectures and poolside sessions were over, reaction to my participation was decidedly mixed. Some people thought I was too harsh; some thought I was a welcome dose of publishing reality. I judged my chances of being invited back the following year at about fifty-fifty. The response to Norton was far more one-sided. It was quite clear he was welcome back whenever he wanted to come.

Before he could return to San Diego, however, Norton had to be introduced to the unique town of Los Angeles.

He, Esther, and I got back into our rental car and headed up the coast. Our only stop was at the first market we came to before we hit the freeway. I explained to the manager why I needed two empty boxes, and he was nice enough to oblige without charging me. The trip went quickly, memorable only because Norton decided to spend half of it perched on my shoulder with his head sticking out the open front window and because Esther decided to spend *all* of it complaining about the fact that the car still smelled decidedly from our last trip with Norton.

I dropped Esther off at the Beverly Hills Hotel, and I went on to the Four Seasons. The Beverly Hills is just a little too show-bizzy for my taste. It's extremely difficult to walk through the lobby or make it through a meal without hearing such charming words and phrases as "fuck *them* if they think I'll go for a step deal" and "the idea is great, but the concept is way off" and "sure, I can get it to Dusty, but is he right for it?" All these things are usually uttered by people who would, in fact, kill for a step deal, have no idea what a great idea actually is and would be terrified if they actually heard one because then they'd have to make a decision, and could only get something to Dusty if they bumped into him on the street and began the conversation with the words, "Excuse me, Mr. Hoffman, you don't know me but . . ."

I dropped Esther off at Show Biz Central and went on over to my hotel. Still a little wary from my encounter with our flight attendant, I was much relieved to hear the desk clerk say to me, with a huge smile on her face, "And this must be Norton."

While he sat on the registration counter, we got checked in quickly and easily, and then we were shown to our room.

I was happy and, as soon as I'd set up the litter box and ashtrays for food and water, so was my cat.

Norton quickly took a liking to L.A. His only problem was at my parents' house. I should say his only problem*s*.

The first problem was an unsolvable one. My parents' house was up in the hills above Coldwater Canyon, and they had coyotes roaming the countryside. Once, when the folks came home from a dinner party around midnight, two coyotes were actually standing in the driveway right in front of the garage. Luckily, the beasts were as frightened of my parents as my parents were of the beasts, and nobody was eaten. But a lot of little animals in the area *had* been eaten. The people who lived next door to my folks had an adorable little poodle. They wouldn't let the dog out at night, fearful that the coyotes would attack under the cover of darkness. But they figured it was all right to let the dog romp around during the day. One morning they let the pooch outside at ten A.M. At noon, they went to find him— and all that was left was the head and the four paws. It was pretty gruesome.

It's difficult to feel sorry for coyotes, as they're unattractive and unappealing animals, but one has to, just a bit. There's so much construction and upheaval around Los Angeles that the coyotes have basically been displaced. Their land is gone and they have nowhere to live or hunt. They are left with little choice but to hang out around rich people's homes and go after their garbage and their pets. I tried explaining all this to Norton, but it didn't go over too well. He didn't care much about the plight of the coyotes. He only cared that he wasn't allowed to venture into the backyard, which looked incredibly inviting to him. But I decided better he be frustrated indoors than coyote food outside.

The second problem was that my parents had two golden retrievers who had the size and intelligence of dinosaurs. Dolly and Rewrite are as sweet as dogs can be. But being around them is like being around two of the Three Stooges. They wag their tails, and expensive crystal goes crashing to the floor. They jump up to greet you, and white linen suits are covered with muddy paw prints. Go to pet them and you spend the next ten minutes trying to wash several gallons of dog slobber from your hands, arms, and even your neck. My parents were wild about these dogs. My father had taken to calling them his "children," and when I called from New York to say hello, if I didn't ask about them, I was severely chastised. I was fairly sure that, by this point, Dolly and Rewrite stood to come out a little ahead of me and my brother in the will.

While I will admit to liking my four-legged "brother" and "sister," it was difficult for Norton to warm up to them—mostly because their favorite activity was chasing him at full speed up the steps, cornering him under my bed, and barking as loud as they could possibly bark, which is about as loud as anything I've ever heard outside of a Who concert I went to in 1972.

Norton got along with the few dogs he encountered on Fire Island. He was usually cautious around them but would give them the benefit of the doubt. I wouldn't say he had any dogs as his best friends, but I had seen him on more than one occasion in my backyard, lying peacefully right next to one of my Fire Island neighbor's dogs. Dolly and

Rewrite, however, were another matter. There was no peace at all when the three of them were in the same house.

The matter settled itself fairly easily. When Dolly and Rewrite were outside (the coyotes willingly stayed away when these two lummoxes were running and jumping about), Norton would come downstairs and poke around the kitchen, the den, and the living room. When the dogs were let in, a gate went up, blocking them off from the upstairs part of the house. Norton would lie on the steps just above the gate, secure in the knowledge that they couldn't get to him and enjoying the fact that his presence there nearly drove them mad.

The third problem was a little more delicate.

My father absolutely loathed, hated, and despised cats.

I tried everything I could think of for his first meeting with Norton. "Don't bring him to the house," he said. I went through my explanation that my guy was different from normal cats, that he was incredibly smart, that he wouldn't bother my father, that at some point in my life, I, too, thought that I didn't like cats, but when I met Norton that all changed. This had about as much effect on my dad as it would have had on a slab of marble. He was unmoved and simply repeated his instructions: "Don't bring him to the house."

I have to say a few words about my father here. He was as perfect a dad as he could have been. We were terrific pals, and I don't think I could have had more respect for him. For years he was one of the top television writers in L.A., and then he became, in his late fifties, one of the top television directors as well. He was a bear of a person, dominating a room with both his looks and his personality.

His shtick was to be gruff and cynical, and on the surface he sure was, but in fact he was the most caring and generous man I ever met in my life. He solved problems and gave advice and was usually just strict enough and unbending enough to provide the right kind of fatherly support. He certainly made plenty of mistakes in his life and his career, but his correct choices more than made up for them. Cindy, who for the first two years she knew him was totally intimidated by him, once said he was the first person she ever met who was larger than life. I always thought he was funny and smart and talented and exceedingly moral, and I enjoyed being with him and my mother as much as I enjoyed being with my closest friends. But he was still my dad and I was still his son—and as such we could, without much provocation, drive each other completely crazy.

As I was taking Norton up to the house for the first time, I had a funny feeling he was going to be another one of those crazy-driving provocations.

The only thing I can really add to the picture, as Norton is about to be introduced to the family, is a brief description of my mother, who happens to be the perfect mom. While my dad tended to bluster, my mom would stay quiet and, behind the scenes, make certain everything was really all right. She has always been the quiet strength behind the family, although she always made sure that everyone else always got all the credit.

My mother, by the time she reached the age of fifty-five, had never officially worked a day in her life. One afternoon, she was in a very "in" restaurant—at the time—Ma Maison. She had decided that she wanted to learn how to be an expert French cook, so she asked the owner, Patrick, how

she should go about it. I think she had something dilettant-
ish in mind, such as going to France for a few weeks and
taking cooking classes. Instead, Patrick told her she should
go to work in the restaurant three times a week—without
pay—and that in six months she'd be a great cook. That's
exactly what she did. She started going in three times a
week as an unpaid apprentice, and within a year, not only
was she a terrific chef, she had started and was running a Ma
Maison cooking school. In the twelve or so years since, she's
become a queen of the L.A. cooking mafia, writing several
respected cookbooks, working intimately with people like
Wolfgang Puck, and befriending people like Julia Child and
Maida Heatter. The only drawback to this is that my mother
is now slightly obsessed with food. I can call up and say,
"Mom, I'm a little down—I got fired from my job and my
girlfriend left me and I was just run over by a truck." The
odds are Mom will sympathize for a minute or so and then
say, "Did I tell you about the crème brûlée I made last
night? It was wonderful. I added some lemon and . . ." And
she'll be off giving me instructions on how to make the
perfect custard.

My mom is fairly unflappable. Nothing much seems to
bother her, and especially as she's gotten more secure over
the years, she always seems to take the long view and the
sane view of things. A good way to illustrate the difference
between the two parents is their reaction when they saw my
first New York City apartment.

I suppose everyone who ever had pretentions of being an
artist and who moved to New York has at one time lived
in an apartment similar to mine. But, to be honest, that
seems almost impossible. I think it's safe to assume that my

apartment was the worst apartment ever built in New York City. It was on Perry Street near Seventh Avenue, right in the heart of Greenwich Village. It was a basement. I don't mean a basement apartment—I mean a basement. A good chunk of what was supposed to be the living room had no floor. It was just dirt and, without working too hard, you could poke around in it and peek down to the subway. When I took the place, there was no kitchen, no bathroom, not even a shower. There was also no light. The only two windows faced the street but were blocked by the building's enormous garbage cans. It also wasn't too well constructed. On particularly rainy or snowy nights, there was usually a pretty good chance that the elements would blow through the cracks in the walls. There is no feeling quite like coming home from a Greenwich Village bar at two A.M. on a snowy, icy, winter morn, crawling into bed—and finding that your sheets have been soaked through and through by snow that has been drifting into your apartment all night.

In my apartment's defense, however, it did have a great painted tin ceiling and a brick wall and a great wooden floor (the parts of it that *had* a floor). Also, it was right in the heart of the Village. *And* it was only $105 a month. Even I knew, however, that it wasn't the kind of apartment that parents love to see their child living in.

I had tried, at the time, to prepare my folks for what they were going to see when they visited New York. I found out later that for weeks beforehand, my mother had driven my father nearly mad saying things like, "Now, remember, when you see Pete's apartment, no matter what you think about it, tell him you love it." Nearly every minute of the day, according to my father, was taken up with her lectures about how important it was to me for them to support my lifestyle and my taste. Finally my father promised he would be on his best behavior and tell me he approved of where I was living—no matter what it was really like.

When it came time for them to actually see it for themselves, my mother spent the entire taxi ride downtown repeating the rules to my dad. "Tell him it's great . . . Tell him you love it . . . Try to remember what it was like when you were young . . ." She'd been psyching herself up for so long that when I finally heard their knock at the door and opened it to let them in, before I could say a word my mother gushed, "Oh my god! It's lovely! It's perfect! Isn't it perfect? What a great apartment!" I had the presence of mind to say, "Mom, don't you want to come in and *see* it first before you decide if you like it?" Embarrassed, she stepped inside. My father followed. After a two-second pause, my father, looking around in wonder, blew his promise to my mother and said, "Holy shit. What a craphouse!"

The best description of my parents—and the difference between them—came from a director named Bill Persky, who, in a toast at one of their anniversary parties, said it was like "Adolf Hitler being married to Julie Andrews."

Adolf, Julie . . . meet Norton.

I came up to the house for dinner, Norton contentedly hanging from my shoulder in his usual bag. I knew my father had told me not to bring him, but I was sure he didn't really mean it.

My mother made an appropriate fuss when she saw him. Not a cat lover herself, she appreciated the two things that were immediately apparent—he was great looking and so

sweet natured. She petted him delicately, not used to being
around a feline. She relaxed when Norton nuzzled her hand
with his nose. As he was nuzzling, my dad called down from
upstairs, "Is that *cat* with you?" When I called up that yes,
indeed, he was, the next roar was, "Well, make sure I don't
see him when I come downstairs!"

After a little bit of confusion and a bit more arguing, we
all finally agreed that it was impossible for me to arrange for
my father never even to *see* Norton, but I did agree to try
to keep him out of the way. First I tried to get my dad to
understand how special this particular cat was, but he
seemed to be the very first person able to resist Norton's
charms.

Norton stared at him with his cutest look. He rolled over
on his back, paws up in the air, inviting my father to scratch
his belly. He tried rubbing up against my dad's leg. He
tried snuggling up to him. Forget it. The man was ice. He
truly didn't like cats, and Norton was a cat. There was no
way this was ever going to be anything but an uneven truce
between man and animal.

I dealt with this as best I could, although I was extremely
disappointed. I felt bad that my dad couldn't open himself
up to the special pleasures that Norton brought me. But
clearly he couldn't.

After dinner, I took Norton back to the hotel, making
sure he knew that it wasn't his fault my father didn't appreciate him. The next few days, I made my L.A. rounds,
seeing agents, writers, film and TV people—a lot of people who called me "babe," told me they loved me like
family, and let me know I was "hot." Luckily, one agent
kept me from getting a swelled head by explaining to me

that it was "easy to *get* hot. The hard part is *staying* hot."

Sometimes Norton came in the car with me, sometimes he hung out at the hotel. When he was in the car, his new idea of fun, begun on the ride from San Diego, was to perch himself on my shoulder while I was driving and hang his head out my open window. By this time I had no fear that he might jump out. That just wasn't something Norton would do. Even in L.A., where people are used to just about everything, I got a few interesting double takes as we were cruising around.

All in all, I decided that taking Norton from coast to coast was a simple thing to do, bound to get simpler as we both got more experienced. And just as I decided I could see no drawbacks to it, a major drawback occurred.

I got a call from my office. We were publishing a celebrity's autobiography. As is so often the case, the celebrity didn't really write the book; he just talked into a tape recorder and with a writer who was supposed to turn out a book that seemed as if it could only have been written by the celebrity himself. This is fairly common practice, as most celebrities, at least most actors and athletes, have a lot of trouble writing anything other than the words "I," "me," "mine," or "more." I had thought that this particular celebrity's book was under control. The ghost writer had done a terrific job, the book was entertaining, and the timing was right—this lucky celebrity had managed to *stay* hot. But as so often happens, this famous man had gotten cold feet. When he read over his book one last time before we were to go to the printer, he decided that, even though he'd assured us every step of the way that he loved the book that bore his name, he couldn't *really* say all those things for the record. We'd have to cut and rewrite and drastically change things—or he wouldn't let us publish. If we tried to publish anyway, he wouldn't do any publicity, which would effectively kill any chance of selling the damn thing.

This charmer lived in Santa Barbara, just a couple of hours' drive from L.A. Since I was already close by, the powers that be had decided I should get in my car, head immediately up the coast, and get to work. I had five whole days to completely rewrite the book so we could meet our promised publication date.

No problem.

Scratch that . . . one problem.

Since our celebrity was already bordering on hysteria, and since I was going to be staying in his home—another minor problem was that since this guy drank so much, it was thought I should be next to him twenty-four hours a day or we'd *never* get finished—I didn't know what the hell to do with Norton. My author was so deranged he could claim he was allergic to cats and throw me out of his house, killing any chance for my mission to be a success.

I could think of only one thing to do.

My mother gulped but agreed to let Norton stay in their house for the five days I was to be in Santa Barbara.

"Do you want to . . . ummm . . . check with Dad?" I asked weakly. "Just to be sure?"

"No," my courageous mother said. "I think it's better if we surprise him."

I had to agree. So, since my dad was off at a meeting, I drove Norton over to the house as quickly as possible, left even quicker, and went out to spend what I was sure would be the worst five days of my life—but which would *still* be better than being around my father when he found out he had to live with Norton for a week.

I was right. When I checked in that night, Mom told me it hadn't gone as well as she'd hoped. For my mother to make an admission like that meant that their house on Hazen Drive must have been something like Nagasaki the day of the bomb. She assured me, however, that Norton was still there—and was still welcome to stay.

When I called in the second night, the report was that Norton had spent some time on the couch in my parents' bedroom and that my father hadn't thrown him out.

The third night, I had been mentally beaten into a near stupor by the aggrieved author, so I was sure I hadn't understood correctly when I heard my mother say the words "Your father told me he thought Norton was quite handsome—for a cat."

The fourth night, I figured I must be getting delirious trying to rewrite fifty pages a day, because I was positive my mother told me, "Norton slept with us last night."

The fifth night, I was too exhausted to even call home. I finished my rewrites somewhere around five in the morning, loaded the manuscript into my suitcase, and ran straight for my car. I arrived back in L.A. at seven A.M.

My mother, who usually is out of bed by six every day, was already up. I kissed her hello and nervously asked after my cat. She smiled, motioned for me to be quiet, and led me up the stairs to her and my father's bedroom. There I saw one of the greatest sights I had ever been privy to.

On the bed, sound asleep under the covers, was my father. On his chest, on top of the covers, was Norton, also sound asleep. My father's arm was curled around the top of the blanket, his hand resting gently on Norton's back.

We tiptoed out of the room, and my mother told me that, during the course of each day, Norton kept trying to get closer and closer to my dad. At first my dad shooed him away. Then, as Norton refused to give up, he began to be intrigued. As soon as the poor guy weakened, Norton went in for the kill. By their fifth night together, he had my dad petting him for hours while he sat directly on his chest. They fell asleep like that. My mom told me that my dad actually kissed Norton good night.

I had a cup of coffee and waited for the two pals to wake up. Norton was glad to see me, although not nearly as glad as he should have been. All my dad talked about was what an amazing thing it was to listen to Norton purr. "He must be happy here," he kept saying. "He purred the whole time."

"I do think he likes it here," my mother acknowledged.

The last words my dad said to me, before I drove to the airport, were, "When are you coming out here again?"

"I guess in a month or so," I told him. "Why?"

He caressed Norton. "Are you sure you don't want to leave him here until you get back?"

The cat who went on dates

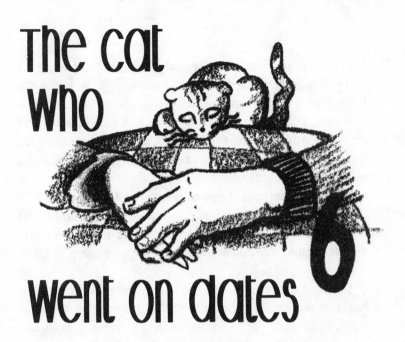

When I returned from California, two significant—and not unrelated—events occurred: Norton discovered Pounce. And I rediscovered the nearly forgotten, rather distasteful yet undeniably exciting ritual of modern dating.

Pounce, for those of you who are ignorant of this nectar of the cat gods, is bite-sized morsels, perhaps the size of a Cheerio. It is serious junk food, the Reeses Peanut Butter Cup for the discerning feline. Pounce comes in small cardboard cans, each can a different color depending on the chicken, liver, shrimp, or beef flavor. I saw them sitting on a supermarket shelf one afternoon and, always on the lookout for a pleasurable experience for my gray companion, decided to bring one can home and try it out.

That night, before I went to bed, I gave two Pounce (Pounces? Pince??) to Norton, then put the can inside a kitchen cupboard. I got undressed and did some reading for work. After half an hour or so, I was ready to turn out the light. Norton wasn't in his usual position on the pillow next to me, so I called his name. As usual, he came running and jumped onto the bed. But he didn't, as usual, settle right down to go to sleep. Instead he scurried and prowled and nuzzled his nose into my face until I realized he was trying to tell me something. I felt as if I were in the middle of a "Lassie" segment, except when I finally got up and agreed to follow Norton, he wasn't trying to tell me that Timmy was in trouble. He was trying to tell me he wanted another Pounce.

I obligingly opened the cupboard, gave him one, told him that this would not be acceptable behavior on a regular basis, then went back to bed. In the morning, I woke up, stretched, felt for a familiar chin to scratch—but there was nothing there. Somehow—I'm sure I should be a tad nervous about how closely Norton and I are attuned to the same wavelength—I knew where he was. My instinct was confirmed when I got out of bed: Norton was sitting on my kitchen counter, staring hungrily up at the cupboard that held the Pounce, scratching pathetically at the cabinet door.

I gave him two more of the biscuits and thus began a daily ritual that goes on to this day. Every morning, before I head off to work, my last deed before I go out the door is to give Norton two or three Pounce. Every night, right before I go to bed, he gets two or three more. I have no idea what makes this stuff so appealing to him, unless it's the scrumptious-sounding pregelatinized wheat feed flour or the equally delicious ferrous sulfate. But I do know that the thought of eating them drives my cat wild with desire. In between his morning and late-night snacks, Norton seems to spend an awful lot of time attempting to tunnel his way through my kitchen cabinet, trying to get to the Pounce on his own. Judging by the scratch marks on the pine, he's just about ready to give the Count of Monte Cristo a run for his money. I expect a major break-through in another few months, when he should either reach the cans of Pounce or the apartment on the other side of the hall.

In case you haven't yet come up with the connection between Norton's snacking habits and the title of this chap-ter, just start thinking of women, during this period of my life, as my Pounce.

For the first time in several years, I was unattached. It was a very strange feeling. As much as Cindy and I had fought against the concept of coupledom, there was no denying that we had been a full-fledged couple—and had been for a long time. As such, we'd fallen into our own routines and been included in the routines of others.

Our deal was that although we were not required to include the other in every little social occasion, there *were* situations that qualified as command performances. If any-thing particularly good or interesting came up that I knew she would enjoy (or, of course, vice versa), she (or I) had first dibs. The same if anything important, horrendously boring, or terrible popped onto our social calendars, a situa-tion where one of us needed the other's support. On the other hand, if either one of us had a normal, everyday, run-of-the-mill occasion to attend, we were not stuck—ei-ther doing the inviting or being the invitee. If I had tickets to the opening of the new Sondheim musical, Cindy *had* to be my date. If I was invited by an actor friend who was appearing in a summer stock revival of *Six Rms Rv View,* I was free to take anyone I wanted. If Cindy had a dreadful wedding to go to that involved driving two-and-a-half hours into New Jersey, I was there. If she had her semi-boring monthly dinner with her uncle who always insisted—loudly—that people were constantly coming up to him on the street and mistaking him for Rouben Mamoulian, she was appreciative if I went, but I didn't *have* to go. It made sense at the time, and it seemed to work for us, for a while at least. (I actually went to dinner a surprising number of times with Uncle Max, but no one, while I was there anyway, ever came up to him and called him Mr. Mamoulian. He liked me because I was the only person he'd ever met, other than all these alleged strangers on the street, who actually knew what Rouben Mamoulian looked like. In case you're wondering, yes, he was the spitting image.) When it *stopped* working, one of the first things to get used to, if I didn't want to go alone, was finding a partner for special occasions. As much as Norton would have appreciated the opening night of *Cats,* I don't think he could have handled most theatrical events or very many charity dinners.

I think I handled the breakup with Cindy fairly well. The night that it happened, I went back to my apartment and had a decent cry. Norton hung out on the bed and let me pet him and hug him to my heart's content. He kept looking up at me, concerned, trying to figure out what could possibly be wrong. I guess I can't say that he ever truly figured it out, but he did purr particularly loudly for a stretch, an open invitation for me to collapse, put my head on his stomach, and use him for a pillow, which I did gratefully for quite a long while.

When I finally felt like talking to a human, I called my oldest friend, Paul Eagle, in Los Angeles. Paul wasn't there, however, so I had to settle for his phone machine. I left a message, something subtle along the lines of "Hi, it's me. Just checking in. How 'bout those Giants, huh? Rams stink. Oh, by the way, Cindy dumped me and I'm suicidal. Give me a call."

Next on my list was my brother, Eric, also in L.A. The message I left on *his* phone machine was a bit more rational: "Hey. Just calling to say I hate women. Talk to you later."

Between the crying, the soothing purring, and the emotional trauma of the day's events, I was now ready to go to sleep. In fact, I was looking forward to a night of lying in the dark for several hours, gazing ahead with a ghostly stare, contemplating the meaninglessness of life, followed by a fitful period of tortured dreams. That was actually starting to seem like fun. So I turned off the lights, gave Norton one last hug and kiss, and began my suffering.

I had suffered for about a minute and a half when the phone rang. I turned on the light and picked up the receiver. It was Eric, my brother, who had cleverly detected the hysteria in my message and wanted to know what was wrong. I told him. The whole story. Repeating the thing out loud, rather than just inside my head, brought a few more tears. When I was done, Eric began to be supportive.

Now . . . understand this: My brother is a great guy and we've been close all our lives. But he lives in L.A. And he's a screenwriter. *And* he's been through therapy (and, worse, acting classes). Add it all up and you get someone who *loves* to be supportive. He likes to hug and share his feelings and tell people he loves them.

Which is all very nice, I must say, except that I am *not* like this. I don't particularly like to hug anyone unless there's a chance we're going to exchange bodily fluids. I don't actually think my feelings are particularly interesting; sharing them usually is about as appealing to me as the idea of sharing Leon Spinks's dentures. Another reason I'm not wild about all this feeling sharing is that I've found most people don't really want you to share your feelings. They want to share *their* feelings and then have you tell them you feel exactly the same way. In general, when it comes to feelings, I much prefer showing to telling.

Nonetheless, I was in no position to complain about my brother's support. I'd just poured my heart out to him. I could clearly take a little genuine emotional contact in return. So Eric told me he was there for me. He told me he loved me. He told me he was sorry the whole thing with Cindy had happened, but at the same time, he was glad because it gave him the opportunity to tell me he loved me, which he didn't get to do often enough. I, in turn, appreciated all the sentiments, except perhaps the last one, which I thought was going a bit far, and told him I loved him, too, which I certainly did.

After half an hour of such talk, we hung up.

I was now exhausted. All that sharing had taken a lot out of me.

The light went off, my head hit the pillow, my eyes closed. Sleep was very near.

But not near enough. The phone rang again.

It was Eric. He asked if I wanted him to come east. For support. I was genuinely touched by the offer, but I told him it wasn't necessary. I had plenty of people to share feelings with in New York if I really felt the need.

"I love you," he said.

"I know," I said before hanging up. "Thanks again."

I think I actually dozed off for a good thirty or forty seconds before the phone began ringing. It was now after two A.M.

"What?" I sighed into the phone.

"Pete," Eric said, "I just hope you understand that I'm here for you, totally and absolutely."

"I understand," I said. "Totally and absolutely."

"I'm just so concerned. You don't sound good."

"Well, I'm pretty tired right now. I'll sound a lot better in the morning. After I get some sleep."

"Are you sure?"

"Pretty sure. Sleep is what's important now."

"I love you," Eric said. "I really do."

"Good night," I said.

This time I didn't even bother to try to fake it. I sat up in bed, lights on, stiff as a board, waiting. I didn't have long to wait.

"Yup," I said into the phone.

It was Paul this time. He'd just gotten my message. He was surprised how awful I sounded and wanted to know exactly what had happened. Well, by this time, I was too exhausted and too cranky to go into much detail. Also, I'd already poured my heart out once; twice in one day was near impossible. So I told him he'd have to settle for the abbreviated version and then get the full rundown the next morning. He understood, and I gave him a short take on the breakup with Cindy: unsuspecting me, trip-to-England birthday present, evil doctor, crying, crying, purring and crying, phone call, phone call, phone call, I love you, I'm there for you, I love you, tired, the end.

Paul sympathized exactly the right amount—about fifteen seconds' worth—then said good-bye. Before I could hang up the phone, though, he managed to get in one quick "I love you."

I sat in bed for a minute, light still on, waiting. I knew my friend Paul. This would be a hard situation for him to resist. After all, this was a person who, when I once called him from New York, long distance, to see if he had the number of an L.A. florist so I could send some Mother's Day flowers to my mother, made a big deal out of finding the right number, keeping me on hold for several minutes, then gave me the number of a pet store. When I called him back, demanding the real number and yelling at him for making me look like an idiot trying to order roses from Phil of Phil's Pet Parlor, he apologized for his sophomoric sense of humor, thumbed through the yellow pages, and gave me another number—which turned out to be a bowling alley. Running up a huge phone bill now, I called him a third time, screamed, and he swore he'd do it right—and gave me the number of a Korean massage parlor. So I was fairly certain he'd be unable to resist a follow-up call now in my moment of despair. It was too good an opportunity to waste.

I was right. In two minutes, the phone rang. Wearily, I answered it.

"Are you calling to tell me you love me?" I asked.

"How'd you know?" a woman's voice answered.

"Who is this?" I asked.

"Laurie."

Paul's wife. She loved me as much as Eric did, she said. But not as much as the next person, an old college friend Paul had called the moment he'd hung up on me. And that old friend didn't love me nearly as much as the next three old friends who called. When Paul finally called back to tell me that the more he thought about it, he *liked* me but *loved* Cindy, I decided that my period of mourning for Cindy was pretty much over.

I realize it seems fairly brief—one night of mourning after several years of love—but I have to say that despite the emotional upheaval, there was a certain sense of relief when the relationship ended. It was a little like being reborn, although, granted, it was like being born with an enveloping sense of sadness. To fight off that sadness, I immediately began to indulge all my single-man fantasies: I bought several boxes of Sugar Pops and Cocoa Puffs and ate bowls of the stuff for dinner—with *no* vegetables on the side. I never went *near* the public television channel on my TV dial and watched sports practically every waking minute. (I realized I had gone slightly over the edge when I was starting to care—deeply—about which woman was going to win the Dinah Shore Open golf tournament.) I didn't make my bed. And I left all the little post-shaving hair particles on the sink—for days on end.

Of course, eventually, other fantasies and yearnings came into play. It wasn't too long before I began scratching at the cabinet door for women.

I wasn't really looking for anything serious or substantial at this point. I was much more interested in shallow, superficial, and, preferably, sweaty.

I wasn't much of a dater. People of my generation never really dated. We hung out, we did stuff, we burned banks, we took psychedelic drugs and rolled around on water beds together, but we didn't really date. This was a whole new experience, and I was determined to make the most of it.

The first thing I learned was that attractive women (and here I'm going with the following somewhat limited definition: models, actresses, and any woman who drives her own jeep who isn't named Gutty, Rocky, or Gertie) like to go out with writers. Not all of them, mind you. A lot of them like to go out with investment bankers or very ugly rock stars or photographers who only have first or last names, not both, but on the whole, they think writers are smart and they're attracted to smarts. This works out well because I've also observed that most writers like to go out with attractive women. In fact, going out on a limb, my own theory is that, deep down, male writers, with the possible exception of Vaclav Havel and Oscar Wilde, write *only* so they can impress women. Otherwise, why go through the sheer agony of lonely, torturous days trying to create, not to mention entire lifetimes of poverty and often ridicule? It's all done in the hope of an Ophelia, an Emma, a Daisy coming up to you in a bar and saying, "Excuse me, aren't you Fyodor Dostoyevski? I just *loved The Brothers Karamazov.* That Alyosha was the *sexiest* man. Is it true that writers create characters based on their true selves?"

Models go for smarts, I believe, because they don't respect their own beauty. How could they? They're around women all day who are even *more* beautiful than they are. Where I see perfection, they see hair that's not as thick as Paulina's. I see sculpted grace, they see skin that's not as tight as Christie's. Their beauty has no mystery for them, no allure, because they see it as something they have no control over. It's an external, artificial attribute. Writers, on the other hand, worship beauty above all. This is partly because most of us are ugly little rodents with bad posture and ailing gums whose sole sense of worth comes from what we can produce from within. And it's partly because we spend most of our lives stooped over a word processor trying desperately to *create* beauty—and we know how difficult, how near-impossible and absolutely hellish that is to do.

So . . . it's established that writers go for attractive women and that attractive women go for writers. But there's one other thing that women tend to go for and fuss over and melt at the sight of.

Riiigghhhttt.

Cute gray cats with round heads and folded ears.

Hallelujah.

~~~

The first step in restructuring my social life was to decide what to do about a place for the summer. The little blue house in Fair Harbor had never been *my* house as much as it had been *our* house. Cindy and I had found it together and enjoyed it together. It didn't seem right for Norton and me to go back without her and Marlowe.

Enter Norm Stiles, a man destined to go down in the Fire Island Hall of Fame.

A friend for several years, Norm had been out to the house to visit us a few times over the various summers. Now he'd decided it was time to take the plunge and begin regular weekend visits. He asked if I wanted to share a house.

The more I thought about this, the better it seemed. It would be fun to have a big place instead of the blue dollhouse. It would be great to have a regular tennis partner. We could have parties—actual people coming over to Pete and Norm's for fun and recreation. Plus, I liked to cook and Norm said he liked to clean up.

Done.

We not only took a bigger house, we took over a familiar one. David, my writing partner, and Diana had decided it was time to settle in Connecticut, so we moved into their place. Norton certainly appreciated the convenience of this resettling, since he already knew how to get to the house from all points. His only reservation about the spot was one particular bluejay who lived around there. This bird had a thing for my cat and would fly around him, mocking him loudly, occasionally swooping down and pecking at Norton's head. Norton *hated* this bird. I used to try to explain to him that *he* was the cat, he was supposed to be able to take a bird one on one, but my pep talks never took hold. Until the day we left Fire Island, Norton was totally intimidated by the bluejay.

My initial instincts about the move had been correct. Having a bigger house was a nice luxury. Norm and I played combative tennis. I learned to make a mean grilled chicken and Norm turned out to be the best dishwasher stacker I ever saw. (I swear, it seemed that he could cram most of the house, including the living room couch, into that thing.) But the one thing I had to get used to was people.

I'd been a summer resident of Fair Harbor for four years. In that time, I hadn't met one single person other than the two guys who ran the market, the Rockette Lady, and my excuse for not writing—the coffee klatch. A good part of this is due, as I'm sure you've realized by now, to the fact that I welcome new, close relationships into my life about as warmly as the eighteenth century welcomed lepers. Norm, on the other hand, had been a weekender for about a minute and a half before he knew every single person who had a home in the community, most of their regular guests, and all of their personal habits. Walking down the street with Norm was an amazing experience. His level of popularity was such that I nicknamed him "the Mayor," as in "the Mayor of Fair Harbor." Thinking of Norm as the Ed Koch of the beach set was not so farfetched.

"Hey, Norm! How's it hangin'?"

I couldn't get over the fact that near total strangers would just stop and pat him on the back. Women flocked around him. Norm happens to be the head writer for "Sesame Street," which, in addition to being the best job in the world, means that women automatically think he's intelligent, sensitive, and funny. He actually is all of those things—although if you ever meet him, ask him what he was doing with those binoculars on the porch that night.

"Norman, you were a wild man last night! Are you discoing tonight?"

I had to stop at this one and ask him where the hell one discoed in Fair Harbor. Norm told me they turned the restaurant into a club at eleven P.M. Shocked, I wondered when they'd started doing that, a week or two ago? No, Norm told me—four years ago.

Oh, well. So I wasn't big on staying up past ten o'clock during the summer.

One little guy who obviously *had* been out and around, however, was a certain debonair Scottish Fold.

Norton usually tagged along on my strolls with Norm to the tennis court or the market or the bay. It was unbelievable how many Fair Harborites knew him. It seemed that every other person we passed would first say hello to Norm, then give Norton a warm greeting—by name—then look at me and stare quizzically, as if to say, "Hmmm, this guy looks vaguely familiar. Oh, well, maybe not."

Sometimes I'd initiate the conversation and ask how they knew my cat. A common response was "Oh, he comes over and visits with us all the time."

When people would speak to me directly, I'd usually get "Oh, you're the guy Norm told us about. Is it true you refuse to ever leave your porch?" or, my favorite, "Ohhh, you're Norton's dad!" It wasn't until *many* people had greeted Norton on our strolls that it occurred to me he never wore a name tag. Which meant that unless he *spoke* to my neighbors when he went visiting, they couldn't possibly know his name.

I decided not to pursue this line of thinking any further. It didn't seem healthy.

"Normie, meet you at the sixish ce soir?"

Now this is something that deserves to be discussed.

There was a strange and eerie Stephen Kingish ritual that took place in Fair Harbor every Friday and Saturday evening. As I'd sit on my porch sipping a beer, shoes off, relaxing, I'd see scores of people, dressed as if for the ballet—or, at worst, a "Miami Vice" audition—parading by, heading toward the dock. Most of the women had on enough makeup to make the National Kabuki Theater of Japan proud. Most of the men had on shirts that revealed enough hair on their chests, shoulders, and backs to re-sod a good-sized minor league baseball stadium. They all had drinks in one hand, and their arms were all cocked at forty-five-degree angles, I suppose the best possible angle to prevent spillage.

It wasn't until Norm was there to explain the mysteries of Fire Island that I truly understood what I was witnessing.

The dock was the best place in town from which to watch the beautiful sunsets. So all the townspeople would gather there under the pretense of enjoying nature's spectacle but, in reality, they would be desperately trying to pick up any member of the opposite sex who didn't have sun poisoning and spend the night with him or her. These gatherings regularly started around six in the evening, thus the endearing word "sixish" was born into our vocabulary.

There were regular sixishes and special sixishes (like July Fourth, when there were not only fireworks but local artisans peddling their photographs, jewelry, T-shirts, and personalized Kadima paddles), and there were theme sixishes. There was something awe-inspiring when, come the annual *Animal House* sixish, fairly successful lawyers, publishers, realtors, what have you, would stand around in togas, sipping their drinks, swiveling their heads in search of amiable companionship, and chanting, "Par-*ty* . . . par-*ty.*"

Norm took me to a sixish, against my better judgment. I didn't really like mingling with people who dressed up in togas (even if they weren't dressed in togas then, it was enough to know that they *would* do so at some point in the summer), but he decided it was something I had to do. This was supposed to be a new life.

I brought Norton along, figuring he'd like to see it. Why not—he already knew most of the people who were there.

I have to say, I didn't quite get it. The whole concept slid right by me. Why would people come from New York City—the stress and dress capital of the world—to the most beautiful, quiet, relaxing beach imaginable and *re-create New York?* Why would anyone wear stockings on an eighty-five-degree Saturday night when they didn't have to? Or silk sport jackets? Why wouldn't people wear shorts and a T-shirt? And what was this fear of spending an evening alone? After five days of pushing and shoving your way through several million people crammed into a few square miles, why would anyone want to cram into a few square feet with several hundred of the same people?

Norton was a big hit at his first sixish—he got many compliments, from old friends as well as new, on his ears as well as his personality. I was less of a hit. No one complimented either my ears or my personality. I think I found it a little too hard to conceal my despair at the amount of exposed cellulite. It was as if I'd been suddenly transported into Jack La Lanne's personal hell. (For those of you who have already been captivated by Norm's charm and think he's a much more sensitive guy than I am, please note that after this first dockside experience of mine and ensuing state of shock, he devised the perfect sixish lure for a member of the opposite sex: First, tie a piece of danish to a string. Any flavor will do, though cherry, prune, or cheese are preferable. Casually drop said danish on the ground. When your unsuspecting prey bends over, thinking he or she can surreptitiously shovel away some free dessert, yank the string, pulling the delectable pastry several feet closer to your house. Your prey will pursue. Repeat as long as necessary, which is until you've got the poor sucker trapped in your living room. This simple trick should be good for up to a solid three blocks. For best results, have lit candles, a batch of frozen daiquiris, and some peanut M&M's all set up, waiting at home.)

Norton, to his credit, seemed to share my lack of interest in the sixish. There were certainly no other cats to befriend. The only other quadruped was a small sheepdog whose idea of fun was barking loudly and chasing Norton into the bushes by the market. We left after I overheard a conversation Norm was having with a woman psychologist. Her specialty was people with ego problems. "Sometimes," she was saying, "I want to shake these people and say, 'Don't you understand? I'm the best damn psychologist in New York! Why don't you just get better?'"

Norton let me carry him after that one. We both wanted to get home as quickly as possible.

~~~

Norm, Norton, and I shared a summer house for three years. Norm set new records for popularity on the island and—I like to think that rooming with me was some help here—wrote some of his best sketches for Oscar the

Grouch. Norton had a very happy transition from kitten-hood to adolescence, acquiring all of the traits that go with the teenage and early twenties years. He became an incredible know-it-all. It was impossible to tell him anything. If it was raining and he wanted to go out, all my explanations of how he was going to be very wet and miserable if I opened the door went for naught. He insisted on learning everything for himself. He also became much more independent, taking to staying out all night when we were at the beach (or *almost* all night—he'd usually meow very loudly for me to let him in at five A.M.). I never questioned his whereabouts; I did give him the benefit of the doubt that he was staying away from the all-night disco. Probably the most traumatic event of this period was the removal of Norton's . . . uh . . . manhood. Although I would have loved to have a kitten fathered by him (I'll try to stay away from any grandparent comparison), everyone and anyone who ever had a cat impressed me with their vehemence about avoiding all the things that went with breeding. It was the thought of a cat (and Norton, during this thought process, became *"a* cat," not *"my* cat" or "that cute little guy" or anything like that) spraying all over my apartment, my clothes, my work, my life that finally swayed me. I couldn't face it. So I made an appointment and took him to the vet.

Norton's vet, who has his practice down in the Village, looks exactly like Santa Claus. He's large, jolly, and has long white hair and a white beard. He's a terrific doctor with a great bedside manner. When I took Norton in for this dreaded operation, I was in desperate need of that manner.

"Really," he told me. "It's painless. He won't feel a thing."

"Maybe I should stay," I said. "I could get a cot, set it up in his room . . ."

"He doesn't have to spend the night," Santa told me. "You can pick him up at five."

"Should I do anything special for him? Buy him a soft bed? Should I get the cable guy to disconnect Channel J?"

"He'll be *fine*," the vet said. "This is not going to be traumatic for him."

The vet was right. Norton handled it like a champ. I, however, was a wreck. I spent most of the day doubled over with cramps in the groin area. I was also sure that Norton would hate me when I came to pick him up. I was positive there'd be lots of resentment. I was already dreading his shrink bills.

At five sharp, I returned to the vet's, and there was Norton, slightly groggy but looking none the worse for wear. Santa showed me the incision, and when the room stopped spinning around, I had to admit that it didn't look bad. He told me to make sure Norton took it easy for one night— and then the whole thing would be forgotten and he'd be completely back to normal.

He was certainly right about that. Norton showed no ill effects from the operation, neither psychological nor physical. It certainly didn't keep him from catting around all night on Fire Island. He didn't even gain weight, which I'm sure was due to his outdoor life climbing trees and prowling the Fair Harbor undergrowth.

As for me, during these house-sharing years, my tennis

game improved tremendously, I progressed from grilled chicken to a superb (if I may say so myself) cold poached salmon with an aioli sauce, and we had an incredible amount of fun. But I never managed to become an habitué of the sixishes. I also never dated any egotistical psychologists; nor did I have to resort to The Mayor of Fair Harbor's Original Danish Lure.

But I did enter the full-fledged world of hemming and hawing, awkward embraces, and tentative intimacy. In fact, I did more than enter. I plunged in headfirst.

My first real post-Cindy involvement was with a woman named Sarah. Sarah and I, it would eventually turn out, had about as much in common as Madonna and the Pope. But for the first three months we went out I thought she was perfect.

To begin with the superficialities, she was absolutely stunning. She had dark hair and skin that tanned a deep, deep brown. She had long, perfectly tapered legs and—remember, I warned you this was during my Shallow Period—she wore the shortest skirts I'd ever seen this side of the Twiggy era. She was sensuous and sensual, and to top it all off, as I got to discover when she decided she could trust me, she didn't mind doing a certain amount of her clothes shopping at Victoria's Secret.

Unfortunately, after beginning with the superficialities, I couldn't come up with anything else. And what kept poking through and causing serious trouble was that there were two areas in which we could never resolve our differences. One was *sense of humor*. Sarah's philosophy—which she happened to mention fairly often—was that "A sense of humor is fine, but there are certain times in life that are inappropriate for humor." She would get rather upset when I would unleash *my* philosophy of life, which was that she was probably right but that "I just haven't ever found any of those times yet."

The other great area for our fights was none other than Norton. Sarah was terribly jealous of him, most specifically because I often used him as an excuse not to spend the night at her apartment. She used to insist that Norton was my means of avoiding commitment. I suppose, if forced to analyze it, she was right, though I prefer to think he was just my means of not having to actually *tell* Sarah I was avoiding commitment. My excuse for not spending the whole night in her apartment was that I didn't like leaving Norton alone.

"He'll survive a night alone," she'd say.

"I know," I'd say back. "But he won't *like* it."

As far as excuses went, this one was mostly true. I *didn't* like leaving him alone. But there were other reasons, too. I also didn't like Sarah's apartment. It was one of those new, white brick buildings that have the same sense of warmth as Stalin's Russia. She had filled the apartment up with little knickknacks and kinetic sculptures and modern art prints. It looked like the kind of place I always figured Andy Warhol would go to die.

We once had a huge fight when, at two in the morning, I slipped out of bed and told her I was going home. She was furious. I told her about my Norton and the Predator Theory. She became even more furious. As I kept trying to explain away my leaving, Sarah finally burst into tears and told me she absolutely couldn't see me anymore. She was ending the relationship. A little surprised at the extent of her reaction, I wanted to know exactly why she felt this way.

"Because Norton is just a cat," she sniffled. "And he only has cat feelings. I'm a person. I have *people* feelings. But you don't care about my feelings. You really don't." By this time she was crying. "I think you like your cat better than you like me," she said through her tears.

"Sarah, that's just not true," I said.

"What isn't?" she asked hopefully.

"I don't think Norton only has cat feelings."

Needless to say, this turned out to be one of those inappropriate times for humor. Sarah wouldn't see me for two months after that.

Sarah was constantly refusing to see me for two months or announcing that our relationship was over. Somehow, though, we'd always get back together. Our reunions usually came about when we'd run into each other at a restaurant and realize we liked each other better than the person we were with, or when she'd be depressed about her job and need someone to talk to, or when I'd get the new Victoria's Secret catalogue in the mail and happen to be browsing through it at bedtime. We couldn't seem to stay together and we couldn't seem to stay apart.

One Valentine's Day, on the spur of the moment, I decided to take her up to Vermont for a weekend of skiing and romance. Sarah was so appreciative of gestures like this it was a little scary. We rarely took vacations or trips together. Again, chalk this up to that lack of a commitment.

Once, we almost went to Arizona for a few days at the Phoenix Biltmore, just about my favorite place in America outside of the Liberace Museum in Vegas. But the Biltmore refused to accept cats so, outraged, I canceled the reservation. As soon as I did that, Sarah canceled me for three weeks. Now, with the promise of a long, snowy weekend ahead of us, I don't think I'd ever seen her so pleased and affectionate. Even I felt a little guilty when I realized that all I had to do was, on two days' notice, find a romantic Vermont inn that took cats.

By my twentieth phone call, Sarah was a lot less pleased and substantially less affectionate. As I made my twenty-first call, I was a desperate man. When the innkeeper answered, I went through my by-now rehearsed Norton pitch. I sensed a hesitation on her part—which was far better than the immediate turndowns I'd received already—so I really poured it on. I was almost ready to go the whole route—and tell her about the time Norton rescued my poor lost grandmother in that horrible snowstorm—when the innkeeper cracked.

Which is how my Scottish Fold came to go cross-country skiing.

The day after we arrived at the inn, Sarah told me she was pretty good at downhill but had never gone cross country. We set out to remedy this. First, however, we thought we'd experiment with Norton and snow. He'd never been outside in snow before; most of his outdoor experience up to this point was in the summertime. But in Vermont, summertime was a distant memory. There was a foot-high blanket of soft powder, so we gently tossed Norton out the front door of the inn and waited with bated breath.

The first thing that happened was that he sank without a trace. He was so light and the snow was so high and so soft, Norton was simply enveloped. In the next moment, however, he went flying up into the air, so caked with white flakes he easily could have fit in with Siegfried and Roy's act.

Much to my surprise, he loved the snow. He ran to the nearest tree, raced up halfway, and dove back to the ground. He burrowed, gopherlike, forging a tunnel with his nose and face. He rolled over on his back, now-white paws clawing at the blue sky. I don't think I'd ever seen an animal having so much fun.

After half an hour of this, I think it got too cold for him. He showed up at the inn, snowflakes and tiny icicles dripping off his coat. I wrapped him up in a towel, dried him off, which he seemed to appreciate, and then he lay down in front of the living room fire for a nap. By this time, of course, the owner of the inn was ready to adopt Norton as one of her own.

After lunch, Sarah and I put on cross-country skis and headed out. Norton, as usual when I went for a walk in the country, followed. I tried to talk him out of this one, but he insisted. Snow or no snow, cold or no cold, he was ready to explore.

When we hit the nearby woods, Norton didn't exactly stay on the trail with us. He zigzagged around like a lunatic, jumping onto trees, bounding into snowbanks, then suddenly stopping and meowing like crazy until I'd come and carry him for a while.

All in all, he was happy. And he was even happier when, two hours later, we repeated the toweling and fireplace routine. Even Sarah was happy and had to admit—over a late-night cognac and backgammon—that Norton was a worthwhile addition to the Valentine's Day weekend. She sighed contentedly and told me she thought she was falling in love.

Two days later, however, when I refused to spend the night at her apartment, she decided she never wanted to see me again.

~~~

In between the various romantic interludes with Sarah, there were other romantic (and not so romantic) interludes. Norton managed to involve himself in almost all of them.

For about six weeks, I fell head over heels for a woman sportswriter who lived in Boston. This meant some serious weekend commuting, either to Boston or to some college basketball game in some southern town where lox and bagels were only a disturbing myth.

The first time I went to Boston to see her, I showed up with two steaks, a bottle of red wine, and a cat.

Norton liked Boston (the Pan Am Shuttle stewardesses, er, flight attendants, are *very* nice to small, friendly animals), but the sportswriter couldn't envision interviewing Dean Smith with a cat on her shoulder, so that cooled off fairly quickly.

I went out with an editor at a rival publishing company who used the word "Dickensian" more than anyone I'd ever met. When she was introduced to Norton, she admired his looks but made the mistake of asking if I'd named him after Norton Simon. The idea that someone thought I could actually name my cat after the world's dullest billionaire was a staggering concept to me. If she'd said Kenny Norton even, she might have stuck around for a reasonable period of time. As it was, we lasted two weeks.

One week was spent in the company of a fashion designer. She probably wouldn't have made it through the whole week except that we met a few days before Halloween and she confessed to me over our first lunch that the previous Halloween she'd gone to a costume party completely naked—except for one coat of body paint. The reason she didn't last longer than a week was that she had a tattoo of a snake on her shoulder, and Norton kept leaping at it in the middle of the night, doing his best to remove it from her skin. For some reason, she felt this a sufficient reason to end our brief fling.

One of the best things about dating was watching Norton's reactions to the women I brought home (or, in the case of the sportswriter, brought him to). Most of them he liked. The normal routine was as follows: I'd come home after dinner, usher the woman into my apartment. Norton would get a late-night Pounce; I'd introduce them. We'd go through the "Oh, what funny ears" exchange, while Norton sized her up. If he liked her, he'd nuzzle up to her with the side of his head, pushing it against her quite seductively. This was a considerable help in encouraging my date to think more seriously about my charms.

As she and I sat on the sofa, listening to music, talking, trying to figure out what the rest of the evening had in store for us, Norton—again, only if he approved—would sit a few feet away, turn over on his back, and peer up at us. This was so startlingly cute that once eye contact was made between date and cat, almost all female reservations could be overcome.

Of course, if Norton *didn't* like someone, forget it. No cute nuzzling or adorable backward glances. Oh no. In these cases we got a lot of running around, scratching at the legs of the couch (and sometimes of the woman), possibly even a little throwing up. We usually had the same taste in women, Norton and I, so when his behavior turned, it was hard for me to get annoyed. In fact, except for the couch scratching, I often felt like joining him.

Cindy and Norton had adjusted expertly to a mutually agreeable sleeping arrangement. None of her successors was ever able to work things out quite as smoothly (particularly one named Michelle, who would wake up every hour on the hour, sputtering, gasping for breath, and waving her arms wildly because Norton kept putting his tail in her mouth). Norton, unlike his dad, was extremely fussy about whom he'd let scritch him under the chin in the morning.

I tended to trust Norton's judgment when it came to women, and for the most part, he gave me the benefit of the doubt. The only time we ever had a serious disagreement was over Karyn.

Karyn was a Danish model whom we met in Paris (on one of Norton's first trips). She was twenty-two years old, six feet tall, and the most gorgeous woman I'd ever talked to without actually drooling. She also spoke and read many languages, was overwhelmingly sophisticated, had a sharp and nasty sense of humor, and . . . I suppose you're getting the picture that I was smitten upon first meeting. Miraculously, she was smitten, too. Life seemed perfect.

Except for one problem.

A certain member of my family decided that he absolutely couldn't stand this tall blond woman who occasionally took up his side of the bed. Norton hated her.

My cat doesn't hiss—but he hissed at Karyn. My cat doesn't bite—but he bit her. He liked to wait until she was sound asleep, and then he'd jump on her pillow and meow as loudly as he could, scaring her to death. He once urinated in her shoe—just as she was rushing off on a modeling assignment.

I tried to convince him he was wrong. I also tried to convince Karyn that I couldn't leave him in New York when I came over for a brief Parisian stint. I had no luck convincing either one of them.

Happily I never had to choose between them. It is probably a sickness, I know, but in a choice between someone who could have won the Miss Universe contest (and probably performed some sort of simple brain surgery as her talent) and a temperamental Scottish Fold, my little cat would have won hands down. I might have killed him—but he would have won. Before it came to that, however, I learned once and for all to abide by Norton's judgment when it comes to women.

On my first date with Karyn—which lasted a week—we had a spectacular time. We ate at little, out-of-the-way Parisian restaurants, we drank great wine, I sampled my first peach champagne, we danced cheek to cheek, we held hands in underground *caveaus des jazz.* Then I came back to New York. We wrote letters, we ran up phone bills that rivaled the national debt, we made plans to meet in all kinds of exotic places.

The second stretch of time we spent together was also fantastic. It lasted only five days, which was how long I was able to get away for. That trip, two friends, Nancy and Ziggy Alderman, happened to be in Paris. Nancy, who is extremely attractive but five-feet-four with dark, curly hair, was a little thrown when she strolled into my room at the Tremoille for a glass of champagne, only to find a blond goddess—wearing something not much bigger than Captain Hook's eye patch for an outfit—busy pouring the bubbly for us all. Zig, in one of his suaver moments, panicked completely at the sight of Karyn and told us he just had to step into the bathroom for a moment. His only error was that he stepped into the closet—and was so embarrassed, he *stayed* there for a good five minutes, hoping somehow that we might not notice.

The next trip to Paris, Karyn and I went out to dinner to celebrate my first night back and our love-starved reunion. I hadn't seen her in several months. She looked as lovely and inviting as ever—and Norton hissed just as loudly as ever when she came to the hotel.

When dinner was over, we strolled back along the streets of Les Halles, holding hands, kissing adoringly every few steps. We arrived back at the Tremoille and went upstairs. I prepared for an evening of extraordinary passion. Then she mentioned, "Oh, by the way, my boyfriend is a little bit upset that I've been seeing you."

It's amazing how that kind of line puts a damper on extraordinary passion.

"Wh-what do you mean, your boyfriend?" I asked. "You

told me you'd broken up with him a long time ago."

She looked at me, confused. "Broken up?"

"Yeah. That first time we went out . . . when we spent a week together . . . you told me you'd just ended your relationship and . . ."

"Oh, *that*," she said. "I just had to wait until he went out of town. He was gone that whole week. I didn't really break it off with him."

"What about the last time I was here?"

"He was gone, too."

"Well, why didn't you *tell* me?!"

"Because I thought you wouldn't see me."

I started pacing around the room. I wouldn't look at Norton because I was sure he'd be smirking.

"What's his name?" I asked. "Your boyfriend."

"Robert."

"What does he do?"

"He's a podiatrist."

If he'd been a race car driver or perhaps an international clothing designer, I probably could have settled for some kind of sophisticated if painful sharing arrangement. At least I could have salvaged some pride. But a podiatrist?!

"How . . . um . . . how does Robert know that we've been seeing each other?" I asked.

"Oh, I had to tell him this time, since he's in town."

"And what did he say?"

"Robert has a very bad temper," Karyn said with a shrug.

"What did he *say*?"

"Something about killing you."

"Does Robert also have a very good sense of humor?" I wanted to know.

"Robert has *no* sense of humor," Karyn told me.

That was the end of Karyn. It turned out that Robert really *didn't* have a sense of humor and really *did* want to kill me. He had some Arab blood in him, and it seemed that killing was an acceptable solution in whatever country that blood came from. Even if he wasn't actually going to murder me, I must say some very unpleasant images—my being strapped in a chair, shoes off, podiatric instruments of torture being put to good use—did flash through my mind. I had no intention of spending my life with no feet, even for a beautiful Danish model.

Norton, to his credit, never gloated. I have deliberately never taken him to Denmark, however, and I doubt I ever will. The last I heard of Karyn, she'd moved to Rome and was living with some count. I can only hope it's Dracula.

One of Norton's regular trips was a yearly jaunt down to baseball's spring training in Florida. I went every year in March with the nine other guys from the Rotisserie League. Originally it was men only and some serious baseball was watched. Gradually, wives and girlfriends were added; then, as we all got a little older, golf somehow became part of the trip. Over the years, as we wrote about our outing in our annual Rotisserie League book, players from other leagues would show up. Now it's turned into something of a big deal—a Rotisserie League convention with a few hundred stat-crazed fans coming from all over the country to watch and talk baseball with us.

The Rotiss weekend isn't for the casual girlfriend. Sarah made it one year (and managed to sell more Rotisserie

League T-shirts than anyone ever imagined possible; she looked a *lot* better in one of them than any of us did), but this weekend usually fell during a period when she wasn't talking to me. So for a couple of years, Norton was my only companion. He loved the hotel we all stayed at, the Belleview Biltmore, an absolutely spectacular turn-of-the-century sprawling monster with all the old Southern charm one could want. Part of that charm was that the people who worked at the hotel loved Norton as well.

The second year that Norton went with me, I also took two married friends, the same ones who met Karyn in Paris, Nancy and Ziggy Alderman. (Ziggy is not his real name. His real name is John, but because he works at a rather straitlaced investment brokerage, he doesn't want them to know that to most people he's something out of a David Bowie album—which makes it somewhat complicated being friends with him. When he's with his officemates, we're supposed to call him John, even though they call him Aldy. As if that's not confusing enough, there's another hotshot named John at the firm, a hotshot with more seniority than Ziggy, so Zig's bosses told him they were going to refer to him as Jack to avoid confusion when people in the office yelled out for John. As a result, some people now know him as Ziggy, some as Aldy, some as John, and some as Jack. It's a lot like being friends with Sybil.)

On the way down to St. Petersburg with the Aldermans (or, if you prefer, Alderpeople), Ziggy/John/Aldy/Jack was giving me a very hard time about my bringing Norton. He couldn't understand how I could lug a cat along to such a macho affair as a spring training trip. I was made an object of ridicule for the entire flight—something my pal Zig is an expert at. Several years ago, the three of us went out to the Arizona Biltmore for five days of tennis and golf (right— Sarah wasn't speaking to me that week). The second day we were there, three friends of mine came down from Tuscon for a meal. We all ate a lot and drank a lot at the fairly expensive hotel dining room. When we were all done, Ziggy insisted on picking up the check. I argued with him— these were my friends after all; he'd never even met them before—but to no avail. He signed the bill with a flourish and basked in our profuse thank-yous the rest of the night. For the next two days, overcome by guilt, I did my best to pay for everything—Nancy and Zig's breakfast before we played golf, the round of golf itself, drinks at the nineteenth hole, you name it. When it came time to check out, as I was handed my bill, Nancy said to her hubby, "Don't you think it's time to tell him?" It was—and Zig broke it to me that he had indeed signed for the big dinner check—only he'd signed *my name.*

Anyway, the expression on his face as we stood in our Florida hotel's lobby didn't make up for the near-millions he'd stuck me with in Arizona, but almost. After hours of tormenting me for bringing my cat, Zig had to stand at the check-in desk and watch every attractive woman who worked in the hotel (no more than ten or fifteen of them) screech, "Norton? Is that *Norton?*" Then he had to watch them come over, play with you-know-who, smile at me, and say, "Remember—if you need anything, just call."

Now that I think about it, it *did* make up for the check.

The annual Rotisserie convention was also the site of perhaps Norton's greatest adventure.

A couple of years ago, I went down as usual to do my

Rotisserie scouting. Also as usual, Norton came along. My plane was quite late, so we didn't arrive at the hotel till after eight P.M. After the celebratory greeting of Norton at the desk, I put him in our room on the second floor, set up his food and litter box, then went downstairs for dinner. After a couple of hours of decent food, good beer, and excellent baseball chatter, I was exhausted, so I went back up to the room. The rest of the gang went to the outdoor patio restaurant for more of the big three.

This year, I had a balcony off the bedroom. When I entered, Norton was standing by the balcony door, anxious to be let out. He was used to having the run of the Belleview Biltmore. They have a huge pool area with lots of grass and many bushes for him to skulk around in. His favorite part of the hotel, for some reason, is the basement. He has spent many a day wandering its nooks and crannies. He particularly likes one dusty, concrete corner; it seems to be the perfect napping spot. But he'd never, at least to my knowledge, played up on the various steeples and levels of the roof.

After a moment's deliberation, I figured I'd give it a try. What could go wrong? So I opened the door. Norton scooted onto the balcony, hopped up on the railing, and then went over, exploring the peaked roofs that seemed to stretch for miles. I waited ten or fifteen minutes, called out for him as a test, and sure enough, he came running. That let me know it was safe, so I told him he was free to roam.

Forty-five minutes later, I was ready for sleep. As I stepped over toward the balcony to call Norton in for the night, my phone rang. I picked it up to hear the voice of

Glen Waggoner, an original Rotisserian and one of my best friends.

"I think you'd better come down here."

"What's going on?"

"Norton just fell through the roof of the dining room."

You know the cartoon of the Road Runner, zipping along the road, covering many miles in mere seconds? That was me racing down the stairs to find my cat.

When I got to the patio, the Rotiss group was hysterical with laughter. Glen led me over to the middle of the dining area and pointed up. Ten feet above my head was a gaping hole in the green-and-white striped awning. Apparently, Norton, bored with the roof, had crawled out onto the awning. Midway, he reached a weak spot and the thing gave out. He plummeted sixteen feet down, landing inches from a table where two seventy-year-old women were finishing their dinner. Needless to say, they screamed—you'd scream, too, if you were calmly eating in a restaurant and a cat came flying through the air, landing three inches from your head—and one of them came very close to needing CPR. They were very nice about it, however, as I began apologizing (over the background din of an entire Rotisserie League crying with laughter), and they suggested I find my cat, as doubtless he was far more terrified than they were.

Glen, whom Norton knew well, had tried to catch him after the great fall, but Norton wouldn't be caught. He'd gone racing around in the dark until Glen lost sight of him.

Having no idea where he'd run off to, I stumbled around the giant lawn, calling out his name. No response. I kept stumbling for fifteen or twenty minutes with no sign of Norton, until I suddenly realized where he had to have disappeared to. I went over to the creaky, wooden basement door, opened it, and stepped inside. My eyes took a few minutes to adjust to the pitch dark; then, when they had, I inched my way toward a familiar, dusty corner. There, sound asleep, was Norton.

"Pssst," I said.

Norton's eyes opened; he *brrrmeowed* and came into my open arms.

For the rest of the weekend, people fussed and clucked over him. But he stayed close to me for the remainder of our stay. He'd had enough adventure. I saw him nuzzling up to only one person who worked at the hotel—a very attractive blond woman who worked at the desk. When I went over to get the little troublemaker, the woman smiled at him, then at me.

"Is he yours?" she asked, practically batting her eyes. "He's so *sweet.*"

If I didn't know better, I'd swear that Norton winked at both of us.

The cat who went to paris

7

Over the course of Norton's first few years on earth and in my care, he had, for the average cat, led quite an exciting existence. He'd been lugged around the streets of Manhattan in a pocket. He'd taken cab rides and boat rides and train rides. He'd explored the beaches of Fire Island, the snowy peaks of Vermont, and the antique stores of Bucks County, Pennsylvania (a trip that was relatively uneventful, except for the fact that I bought a beautiful eighteenth-century maple cradle that became Norton's favorite and nearly unbearably cute place in which to nap). He'd also become a regular at my office—spending the day with me on the average of once a week—and as soon as that was established as normal behavior, he began coming to company sales conferences. As a corporate guest, he'd been to Phoenix, Arizona; Laguna Beach, California; Bermuda; and various places in Florida. Basically, if the trip was no more than an hour or two on the plane, he came with me no matter how long or short my stay was going to be, even if it was an overnight trip. If it was a cross-country expedition or something else that could turn out to be grueling for him (e.g., more than five hours without a litter box), then I wouldn't take Norton unless I was going to be away for at least five or six days.

One of my fantasies in my pre-Norton days was to have a dog that I could one day take to France. The French love animals; they treat them a lot better than they treat tourists. Even the fanciest restaurants allow dogs to come and make themselves at home during mealtime. It is not uncommon to see tuxedoed gentlemen and fur-clad society ladies dining in Jamin or Rovuchon or L'Ambroisie with their poodles or their dachshunds lounging under the table. Several years ago, a French publisher put out a restaurant guide rating every restaurant in Paris by how they treated dogs: what kind of scraps they gave them, whether they were allowed in leashless or not, how friendly the waiters were when petting was called for.

It had never actually occurred to me to take Norton overseas. I'm not sure why there was this mental lapse. Perhaps it was simply that in the first few years I had him, I wasn't making a lot of European trips.

That all certainly changed in a hurry.

The change came when I got a phone call from Roman Polanski.

"Peter," he said in his distinctive accent, which combines a bit of Polish rebel, French intellectual, English dandy,

American rogue, and Jewish uncle, "have you ever seen Paris at Christmastime?"

Roman and I first worked together in 1982, on his autobiography, *Roman by Polanski.* We'd worked extremely well together and, for some unknown reason, immediately became fast friends. I know he's been surrounded by controversy for most of his life, but to tell you the truth, I've never seen a particularly controversial side to him. We thought alike on a lot of issues, shared the same sense of curiosity combined with approximately the same amount of cynicism. From a friend's point of view, he happens to be an extraordinarily generous guy—there's nothing he won't do for you if he likes you—and he has a great sense of humor. He tells wonderful stories and likes nothing better than to sit around La Coupole, sipping champagne, slurping raw oysters, and swapping good jokes.

I have met a lot of very, very smart people, but Polanski is probably the only genius I know. He speaks something like twelve languages, has one of the most interesting interpretive minds I've ever encountered, has made some of the finest, most original films of modern times, and, to top it all off, knows somewhere in the vicinity of a million long-legged models named Suzette. All of this is to say he doesn't ask questions like "Have you ever seen Paris at Christmastime?" without having something in mind.

"Uh . . . no," I said, cleverly. "I don't think I have."

"It's very beautiful. Very beautiful. The snow comes down, the lights go up. Ohhh, the lights in Paris, mmmmm, magnificent. It makes you cry. And the women . . . there is a tremendous influx of attractive women at Christmas, Peter."

"Can I ask you one question, Roman?" I asked from my New York City apartment.

"Anything. Anything."

"Why are you telling me all this?"

"How would you like to come to Paris for Christmas and help me write my new movie for Harrison Ford?"

The man has style, *non?*

Of course, I played hard to get. No pushover am I. I told him that it would take me at least four or five seconds to pack and catch a plane out of New York. It actually took me a little longer than that—but not much. Within a week, Norton and I were on our way to Europe.

Many people think that taking an animal overseas is some kind of major deal. A lot of them think there's a quarantine (only in England) or that the travel arrangements are extraordinarily complicated or that hotel accommodations are impossible for pets. The truth is nothing could be easier than lugging one's cat to foreign shores—if you do it right. Naturally, the first time I took Norton I did it all wrong.

Polanski was going to be in Amsterdam to promote his newest film. As I was making my—excuse me, *our*—arrangements, he said, "Peter, why don't you fly to Amsterdam? We'll have a great dinner, do our best to get in some trouble, and then go to work the next day in Paris. Amsterdam is the perfect place to recuperate from jet lag."

Makes sense, doesn't it? It certainly did to me. So as a result, Norton's first European stop—after a one-hour layover at Charles de Gaulle Airport—was Amsterdam.

Before we left, I had to take my pal to the vet so he could

get his cat passport. This procedure was quite simple: the vet gave Norton a shot, swabbed his ears out with a Q-tip, looked down his throat, then filled out a small green card saying that Norton Gethers, an eight-pound Scottish Fold, born in Los Angeles but living in New York, was healthy and able to change continents at his owner's discretion.

The flight was a breeze—with one tiny exception. Norton had been on a number of flights on various American airlines. As a result of their rigidity, I was a strict rule follower. I usually put Norton in his box, kept him under the seat for the whole flight, and only dared to bring him up and out onto my lap if a—okay, I can say it now—flight attendant asked to see him, which didn't happen all that often. But on Air France, Norton was greeted as warmly as if he'd paid full fare. The attendants *loved* having a pet on board and immediately told me to take him out of the confining box and make him comfortable. We were flying first class, thanks to Warner Brothers, and we were both treated in a first-class manner all the way down the line. When I was served champagne and caviar, Norton got a little dish of smoked salmon with a cup of milk. At dessert time, I mentioned that Norton had a weakness for chocolate, and *voilà,* his own personal *mousse au chocolat* arrived *tout de suite.* They were so incredibly nice to my traveling companion that I relaxed. I relaxed so much that about two hours over the Atlantic, with Norton resting contentedly on my lap, I fell sound asleep. I would have slept all the way to Paris except for the fact that, at some point, one of the male attendants gently poked me in the shoulder, waking me up. When I rubbed my eyes and oriented myself, I realized that there was no cat on my lap. When I looked up,

I saw that that was because the attendant was holding him by the scruff of his little gray neck. Horrified, I grabbed Norton, put him back on my knee, and began apologizing to the steward. I was so intimidated by the strictness of American stewardesses, I apologized profusely for a good five minutes before I realized the kindly French steward was saying to me, "Eet's all right. We don't mind. 'E was 'aving a goot walk." Eventually I came to understand that the steward really *didn't* mind. So I got up the nerve to ask the one question I really wanted an answer to: "Where did he go?"

At that, the steward crinkled up his nose disapprovingly. Clearly Norton had done something that this man found repugnant. In fact, by French standards, my cat had committed the ultimate sin.

" 'E was back in toureest," the steward told me with disdain, "talking to a *dog.* "

I stayed awake the rest of the trip. Norton spent most of his free time staring out the window, down at the Atlantic. He seemed to find it just as fascinating as the Fire Island bay.

When we landed in Amsterdam, we took a cab to what turned out to be a wonderful hotel, the Amstel. I was all prepared to either hide Norton or lie my head off, claiming that he wasn't actually spending the night there; I was merely dropping him off to some Dutch friend. But there was no need for the cloak-and-dagger routine. The woman who checked us in gave the cat a warm smile, told me to take him out of his bag, and then watched with an amused look as Norton plopped himself down on the counter and made himself at home. The manager of the hotel came over immediately to get in a few friendly pats on Norton's head; so did a couple of bellboys. The check-in woman asked if Norton was indeed staying there for the night, and when I nodded hesitantly, she immediately asked if he would like a small plate of fish. I sensed that Norton's ears, what there were of them, pricked up a bit at the word "fish," so I told her that would be very nice.

Up in the room, I set up Norton's first international cat litter box, waited for his fish to arrive, then called Roman. After a quick nap, I was ready to go.

Norton was content to spend his first night in Europe sleeping on our down bed while I was wined and dined at a spectacular Indonesian restaurant by a few Dutch journalists. (Okay, Roman was the one being wined and dined—but they let me come along, didn't they? That counts!) The next day was a little more eventful, at least for my gray companion.

I didn't really know what our Amsterdam plans were before I arrived. But I soon found out. We were to check out of our hotel at noon, go to a screening of Roman's latest movie for all the top Dutch distributors, go to a taping of some Dutch quiz show that Roman had agreed to appear on to promote the movie, have dinner with the TV people and some of the distributors, and then catch a late plane to Paris.

It all sounded great except for one thing. What in the world was I going to do with Norton from noon till ten o'clock at night?

Since I didn't really have a choice, I simply took him with me.

The first highlight of the day was our introduction to the distributors. We were at a large screening room and were

seated at a podium toward the front of the room. The studio
publicity person assigned to Roman gave a little speech,
telling everyone how excited they all should be to be dis-
tributing another Polanski film. He went through the litany
of Roman's successes in Holland—from his *Knife in the
Water* days through *Chinatown* and *Tess*. "And now," he
said to the crowd, "I would like to introduce some very
special guests. To my right is a man who needs no introduction. One of the great directors of our time, Roman Polanski."

There was a great burst of applause.

"To Mr. Polanski's right is the writer of Mr. Polanski's
new film, which they are going to Paris to begin work
on—Peter Gethers."

I got some polite applause, considering no one had ever
heard of me and probably would never hear of me again.
And then came the best announcement, as the publicity
person realized there was one other introduction he had to
make.

"And to Mr. Gethers's right is . . . his *cat???*"

Rarely have I heard anyone sound as confused. And
rarely have I been as proud of my cat. Norton didn't exactly
take a bow at the mention of his name, but he did sit up as
straight as he possibly could when he heard the very puz-
zled-sounding applause.

We spent the rest of the day at the taping of the quiz show.

The name of the show translated into "Wanna Bet?" It
was the most popular TV program in Holland (also in
Germany and Belgium). The only way I can possibly de-

scribe it is as a cross between "Truth or Consequences," "Laugh-In," and the ever-popular Vegas review, *Nudes on Ice.*

"Wanna Bet" is ninety minutes long and takes about three hours to shoot. Of those three hours, Norton spent two-and-a-half sitting next to me in the audience—the producers were nice enough to give him his own seat—mostly staring at the flashing sign, which, I assume, said "Applause" in Dutch.

The other half hour he spent in the dressing room—where I was not allowed—being petted by the thirty gorgeous and statuesque topless dancers who participate in the show's sketches.

Norton doesn't usually allow strangers to pick him up and carry him off, but when one of the nearly naked women rushed over to him during a break and asked permission to bring him backstage, he didn't even wait for my okay. He hopped onto the ground and followed her, without so much as a backward glance at his envious dad. When he was returned to me at the end of the show—by three of the dancers, none of whom could bear to part with him—it was yet another time in our relationship when I was very sorry Norton didn't speak English. From the look on his face, however, even if he did, I wasn't ever going to get the details of this particular adventure.

When the show was over, we went to dinner with the heads of the TV studio and several of the distributors who'd earlier been introduced to Norton.

We were taken to one of the city's top restaurants. Norton came along as if he were accustomed to dining out every evening. He hadn't been near his litter box in hours and hours *and* he'd never been out to eat in public, so I was a tad nervous. However, my boy came through with flying colors. He was the hit of the evening.

The first thing that happened was that our waitress practically fainted when she saw how cute Norton was. When she saw how calmly he sat on my lap, she insisted on bringing him his own chair, which she slipped in next to mine. Next, she brought him his own dinner—a nice little plate of herring and potatoes, which Norton gobbled down appreciatively. He was having such a good time that I was almost insulted when she didn't offer him a glass of wine—although he did seem a lot happier with his dish of milk.

This was supposed to be a business dinner, with Roman talking up his movie, but very little business was discussed. Most of the conversation centered around the newest—and smallest—guest of honor. Every few minutes, someone would insist on switching seats with me or Roman, who was on the other side of Norton, so he or she could be near the cat. By the end of the evening, I was on the complete other end of the table, and Norton was in between the head of the Dutch film distribution industry and the woman producer of "Wanna Bet," doing his best Cary Grant impersonation—politely chewing on his herring, sipping his milk, sitting up in his chair, and basically appreciating the restaurant and the attention.

When it was time to leave, several people offered to let Norton stay in their homes if I ever came through the city again, and several asked if they could visit him on their next trip to New York. By the time we boarded the plane for Paris, he was one exhausted cat. In fact, I had to wake him up as we circled over the city, holding him up to the window so he could get his first glimpse of the brightly lit Eiffel Tower.

〜〜

Norton took to Paris like, well, like a *canard à l'eau*.

We stayed at one of my very favorite hotels in the world, the Tremoille, which is on the corner of Rue de la Tremoille and Rue du Boccador in the eighth arrondissement. It is gorgeous, it is small, it is elegant, friendly, it is *very* Parisian, *and* they *love* my cat.

Last year, when I was writing another movie with Polanski, my agent, Esther—she of Norton's encounter with the stewardess from hell—popped into Paris for a couple of evenings of fun and good food. I was there for three months and, to my regret, wasn't staying at the Tremoille—the studio had decided it was too expensive for such a long stay, so I got an apartment—but I insisted that *she* stay there. After dinner, I walked her back to the hotel and talked about how nice they always were to Norton. As I was elaborating, she stopped me on the street and said, "I don't believe you. You are definitely making this up." Indignant, I insisted I was absolutely telling the 100 percent truth. She refused to accept this. So when we reached the lobby, I went up to the front desk, smirked confidently at Esther, and said to the concierge, "Good evening. Do you remember me?"

"Of course," he responded. "And 'ow is your leetle cat? Is 'e well?"

"Very well," I told him.

"Please send him my best," the man said, to Esther's total

astonishment. "Tell 'im to come visit anytime 'e weeshes."

Esther now believes everything I tell her.

Over the years, Norton has stayed at the Tremoille six or seven times, usually when I'm working with Roman. Our writing routine is as follows: start around ten-thirty or eleven in the morning, break for lunch at one o'clock or so, a nice leisurely lunch, then work from three until seven or eight. After an hour- or two-hour break to relax, to have a glass of icy Polish vodka, or just to get away from each other, we usually have dinner. I'd always go back to the hotel to check on and play with Norton, either during our lunch break or our pre-dinner break. After a while, I realized that playtime was unnecessary. Norton didn't need any more playing with. Almost every time I returned to the room, there was at least one maid, usually two, petting him, scratching him, playing with some new toy they'd just bought for him. Once he became an accepted member of the hotel family, they let him hang out in the lobby during the day (one of the people on the desk or one of the maids would bring him back to the room if they felt things were too hectic) and let me bring him down to the formal dining room for dinner.

One day there was a near catastrophe. I came back at seven P.M. for my daily check-in, strolled jauntily into the hotel, and asked for my room key. One of the managers looked at me very gravely and said, "Oh, Monsieur Gethers, your leetle cat, he is very seek."

Without another word, I grabbed the key and raced up the two flights of stairs to my room. When I ran inside, a maid was sitting on the bed, soothingly petting Norton and cooing at him. He was snuggled up on my pillow, curled into a ball. All in all, he looked pathetic—and was clearly sick.

The maid didn't speak any English, so I didn't catch all of what she said. Basically, I picked up on the fact that she'd come into my room early that morning to clean, began her usual play routine with Norton, only he didn't respond. He wouldn't leave the bed, he wouldn't pick his head up, he wouldn't move at all. She tried to give him some Pounce— I'd brought over a lifetime supply and had shown all the maids where I kept it—and he wouldn't even touch that. This was serious.

Norton had never, ever been sick before. I didn't know what to do. Roman was surprisingly understanding when I told him I was going to skip our usual dinner and carousing because of a sick cat. He was pretty attached to Norton by this time, too.

Norton didn't eat that night. Nor did he move from my pillow (I slept on his side of the bed all night). I did my best to reassure him that everything was going to be all right, but he was not a happy kitten. If you ever hear anyone say that cats don't think or feel, all you have to do is tell them to spend the night in bed with a sick one. If you looked up the word "mournful" in the dictionary, you would have seen a picture of Norton that night. I decided to give him twenty-four hours before calling a French vet.

He seemed to be feeling better the next morning. (I, on the other hand, wasn't doing too well since I'd tossed and turned with worry all night.) He wasn't particularly active—he wouldn't get out of bed to eat his breakfast—but he did munch on a couple of Pounce when I brought them to him, and he did lick my hand appreciatively afterward. When I left to go to work, Norton roused himself slightly, standing up for a moment on the bed. I came back, told him he'd be fine, and then watched him settle back onto my pillow.

At lunchtime, I came back to see how Norton was feeling. The manager gave me the thumbs-up sign when I picked up my key. Sure enough, in the room were two maids, hovering over Norton, who was now resting playfully on his back, enjoying their gentle scratching and friendly babbling. They had bought him a present—a little catnip tree, which they'd placed on the end table by the bed. They told me that he wasn't quite ready for it, but they thought it would be a good incentive for him to get well.

I went back to work knowing my pal was in good hands. At that night's dinner break, he was back to normal. Not only did he gulp down his dinner and leap at the Pounce when I held it out to him, he munched a few leaves off his new catnip tree. When it was time for bed, he was well enough to sleep on his own pillow. I had no idea what had brought on his one-day illness—perhaps it was all that rich French cat food—but with a sigh of relief, I told him I was glad he was feeling better and kissed him on the top of his head. He gave me a quick lick with his sandpaper tongue and made me feel as if, at the very least, I'd been an understanding and supportive nurse.

We fell into a fun Parisian routine, Norton and I. Since I didn't have to be at work until at least ten-thirty, I got into the habit of going to one particular café, across the Seine from the Eiffel Tower, for my morning café au lait. After a few mornings of this, I didn't see any reason not to take

Norton. So every day he'd hop into his shoulder bag, we'd leisurely stroll the few blocks to my regular haunt, and I'd sit in my straw café chair, sipping coffee and reading the *Herald Tribune* while he sat in his chair, sphinxlike, watching the passersby and, once the waiters got used to his presence, lapping at a small bowl of water or milk.

After breakfast, I'd usually take him back to the hotel. Sometimes I'd take him over to Roman's apartment. That first trip, when I was rewriting the script for what became the film *Frantic,* Harrison Ford came over to spend a couple of weeks working with us. He was the star of the film and, as such, quite properly wanted to have input into character motivation, action, and thought. He and Roman were friends but had never worked together. I'd never met Harrison before. So the first few days were spent feeling each other out, seeing how we'd all get along, all of us trying to be firm with our convictions for the movie yet flexible and sensitive to the other two's egos and desires. Harrison has a reputation—which my experience certainly bears out—for being a remarkably intelligent actor. It's remarkable because actors, in general, are not considered much higher on the intelligence scale than your basic, everyday dining room table. They are also known for screwing up scripts in order to make their characters look better. Not only is Harrison smart, he's more concerned with the *movie* than whether or not his character is braver, brighter, and cleverer than all the other characters. I liked him and respected him a lot right from the beginning. However, my guess is that Harrison wasn't overly impressed with me the first day he showed up. We shook hands, started discussing the first draft of the script, which was written by Roman with his longtime collaborator, Gerard Brach—what was wrong with it and what was right with it—and then, just as we were really getting into it, just as some passion was coming out in the conversation, Roman started sniffing the air.

"What smells so terrible?" he asked.

"Wait. Hold it," Harrison said, getting excited. "I think I'm on to something here. I think this guy, this doctor, has to really love his wife, has to be *incredibly* jealous of her—"

"Whoooo, what could smell so bad?" Roman was clearly distracted. His face was scrunched up as if breathing were a painful matter.

"Roman, Roman, listen to me! I think we need a scene between me and my wife, something tender, right at the beginning . . . Jesus, what *is* that smell?"

Eventually, all discussion of the script stopped. The entire apartment was starting to smell as if someone had died— about three weeks ago. Both heads turned to me when I muttered quietly under my breath, "Uh . . . I think I know what it is."

I marched them into Roman's bathroom. There in the tub sat my cat. There next to him sat a very large pile of . . . well . . . what can only be described as cat shit.

"I forgot to bring his litter box today," I explained meekly. "He usually goes in the tub when there's no litter box."

"That's pretty smart," Roman noted.

"This is *your* cat?" Harrison asked.

I nodded.

"You brought him from New York??"

I nodded again.

"I'm working with a writer who brings his cat to Paris so he can shit in the bathtub?"

"I know it looks bad," I said, "but give him a second chance."

"It's not *him* I'm worried about," Harrison said to me.

This was my introduction to a lifetime's fantasy—writing a movie in Paris with a brilliant director and a superstar actor: the brilliant director and the superstar actor on their knees in the bathroom trying to scrub away the smell of cat shit while I held the cat, trying to assure him that he hadn't done anything wrong.

Over the years, I believe Norton has come to prefer Paris to New York, much like his dad. He likes his morning alfresco breakfasts; he enjoys his occasional restaurant dinners. (By coincidence, Norton and I were in Paris when I signed the contract to do this book. He *definitely* enjoyed the celebratory dinner I took him to that night. We went to my very favorite joint, L'Ami Louis, where Norton received his own giant plate of Louis's specialty, the best foie gras one could ever hope to eat.) This cat has even been to a nightclub or two. I will go out on a limb and say, absolutely, that he is the only cat ever to have danced the night away at Bains Douches, one of Paris's very coolest clubs. A lot of people get turned away by the doorman at Bains Douches—but Norton has guaranteed entry when he shows up.

One of my little cat's favorite pastimes was exploring the famous rooftops of Paris. He had access from our room at the Tremoille. The hotel has those old-fashioned, very heavy windows that swing open. (Wait a second—perhaps, at last, I understand why they're called *French* windows!) Norton used to sit with his nose pressed up against the bedroom window, just waiting for me to get the hint that he was desperate to go outside. At first I was hesitant, but once again logic lost out to a cat's desire and the window was thrown open. I held Norton in my arms for a few moments, explaining to him that he was in a strange city and that he shouldn't go too far away—then up over the balcony he went, scrambling out onto the red tile rooftops of the city.

I don't know how far he actually traveled. I once saw him three peaks away—perhaps half a block. He always came back when called, so he couldn't have been out of hearing distance. Eventually, I relaxed with his outdoor prowling, and as soon as I could get the maids to understand that if he wasn't in the room, they shouldn't ever shut the windows, I even began leaving them open during the day so he could strut his stuff when I wasn't there.

The other thing Norton enjoyed for a while was our unusual Paris–New York commute. Although it's usually a safe rule of thumb for a writer to assume that everything he does is either going to fail or never come to fruition, there was a stretch of about a month where everything I was working on happened at the same time—the Polanski movie, a novel I'd written, a TV pilot—and Norton and I spent this particular February practically living on the Concorde. Once a week I'd go to Paris for a few days to work on the screenplay. Then I'd hop back on the speedy plane, zip back to New York, do whatever I was doing there—I could barely tell one activity from the other by this point—and then head to the airport and jump back on the Concorde. I would spend the quick flight either reading, writing, or rewriting. Norton would spend the few hours wandering around the small cabin, making friends with the attendants and fellow passengers.

This was definitely the height of luxury for a cat and the highlight of his European travels. The Concorde attendants got to know him so well they didn't even make me bring his box. After a while, all I needed was his cloth shoulder bag. He was so much at home on the plane that I half expected, on one of the flights, to hear the following message over the loudspeaker: "Ladeez and gentlemen, we have ze guest pilot for zis flight today. Monsieur, please say hello to ze passengers." Then the pilot would come on the loudspeaker and I'd hear: "Meow."

Things never went that far, of course, but it wasn't for lack of trying on Norton's part.

In fact, if you're thinking of flying to Paris anytime in the near future, I wouldn't rule out the possibility. If you want to make sure your plane lands on time, I suggest you bring a good supply of Pounce.

The cat who fell in love

My cat was getting older, and with age was coming a certain complacency, a slightly existential, lackadaisical attitude. Plus, he was starting to get fat.

So I did what any normal person would do for his cat. I bought a house.

During the summers at Fire Island, Norton would run everywhere, all the time, having a ball, and every season he would lose a pound between Memorial Day and Labor Day. By the time the leaves started to change colors, that Scottish Fold was one lean, mean fighting machine. Over the autumn and winter, however, he never left the confines of my apartment (except for the occasional cross-country ski trip), which meant he did a lot of sitting, sleeping, and begging for Pounce. I knew that wasn't good for him. Since I tended to do the same thing—the lazing around part, not the begging—I suspected it probably wasn't good for me either. So I decided to go house hunting.

Well, I didn't actually house *hunt*. As usual, I house *stumbled*.

Nancy and Ziggy had a place in Sag Harbor, and I went out to visit them one weekend. Norton was supposed to be left at home because Zig is highly allergic to cats. At the last second, however, my trusty cat-sitter wimped out. (I haven't really discussed what happens when my traveling cat occasionally has to be left behind. Luckily, a friend named Lynn Waggoner has decided that sitting for Norton is comparable to chauffeuring Tom Cruise around the city. Well, perhaps I'm exaggerating, but Lynn takes awfully good care of Norton—buying him toys, taking him for walks, all those good things he's come to enjoy and expect. Once, when Lynn was unavailable, my assistant took him for a weekend. She brought him to her in-laws' house in Montauk. Norton had been in the house for all of two minutes when someone left the front door open—and Norton took off. Laura, the by-now terrified assistant, and her husband spent the night in the woods searching high and low for him. They gave up somewhere around two A.M. and came home—to find Norton waiting patiently by the front door. Laura later told me the story—*much* later—and also revealed her strategy on how to break it to me that she'd lost my cat. It was going to be in the form of a suicide note.) Anyway . . . since no cat-sitter was available, I surprised my weekend hosts and brought Norton after all.

My surprise was greeted with all the enthusiasm of an earthquake. He'd be no problem, I assured them. He'd stay outside the whole day. He'd come in only at bedtime, and then he'd sleep with me. I wouldn't let him out of my bed. Zig would never know there was a cat in the house.

That was true. He didn't know there was a cat in the house—until the middle of the night, when Norton, slipping away while I was asleep, went upstairs and decided he'd sleep on Ziggy's head.

That night at the Aldermans was not dissimilar from what I imagine Krakatoa must have been like. At three A.M. I went upstairs, grabbed Norton off the sputtering master of the house, and took him back into my bed. At three-thirty A.M. he was back on Ziggy's head. We repeated the procedure. At four A.M. Norton had returned to his new favorite spot, covering most of Zig's face with his entire body. At four-thirty A.M. Zig gave up. At five A.M. he realized he wasn't sneezing anymore. By morning, he'd decided Norton was the first cat he'd ever met that he wasn't allergic to. Fury and despair turned to delight and triumph. I was not a favorite house guest (in fact, I won the poll for Most Annoying Weekender)—but somehow Norton had wormed his way into their hearts.

The next day, we went to check out the real estate. My search was only a halfhearted one. I can't say I *really* wanted a house. For one thing, I'm not the handiest guy in the world. I still wake up screaming in the middle of the night at the thought of my high school wood shop. The idea of using a drill or repairing some electrical wiring can quickly bring on my best Curly Howard impersonation, with all the face smacking, high-pitched blubbering, and floor whirling trimmings. For another, I loathed the idea of any kind of commute, even if it was just on weekends. I had no desire ever to do any gardening or to rake up leaves or to shovel snow off the driveway. In fact, I didn't even want a driveway, since I didn't own a car.

But Norton needed a year-round playpen, so . . .

The first four houses we looked at were all nice, all spacious, and all wrong. They didn't have any personality or charm. The realtor, a woman named Peggy Meves, to whom I am forever indebted, asked me to describe my ideal house—my *affordable* ideal house. I did so: at least a hundred years old, in such good shape it needed no work, original wood floors and beams, a fireplace or two, eccentric rooms, two stories, an office that was so nice I'd *want* to go sit at the typewriter, a manageable size—perhaps two or three bedrooms but not cramped and not so spacious that I couldn't take care of it. In other words, something that was so perfect I'd never find it.

When I finished my description, Peggy said, "You know, I think you should take a look at this one place. But the people have received an offer on it. I think they've accepted, so I don't think you can have it—but it sounds like what you're looking for. At least it'll give me an idea of what your taste is like."

I agreed to go look at the house, knowing that I couldn't buy it. That was all right with me. Again, I didn't really want to buy anything. I mostly just liked looking at nice houses.

I didn't even make it upstairs. One look at the living room—with its original 120-year-old wood floors, its antique potbellied stove, its *personality*—and I heard myself saying, "I'll take it."

Peggy, being that rarest of breeds, a completely honest person, tried to tell me again that I couldn't have this house.

She was just showing it to me for taste purposes.

"This is my dream house," I said. "I think I *have* to have it."

"At least look upstairs before you decide it's your dream house," she advised.

Upstairs made it even worse. There was a tiny, heartbreakingly charming guest bedroom, a large master bedroom (the bathroom had an old claw tub in it!), and to round out my fantasy, there was a small office that hung over the driveway, with French windows that looked out onto the beautifully landscaped garden. I haven't even mentioned the outside of this place, which looked as if Hänsel and Gretel could have comfortably settled in and been right at home.

I ran down the steps, outside to my rented car, and opened the door. Norton came bounding onto the front lawn. He stepped cautiously inside the house, looked around the living room, then plopped himself down in the middle of the floor, directly catching a ray of sunlight streaming in through the window. He looked up at me and meowed happily.

The next day, I bought the house.

All of a sudden I had a country house, I had a cat, I had good friends for neighbors. I was just missing one little thing.

Despite a rather flip exterior (hiding, many people would say, an amazingly shallow interior), I was becoming a bit concerned that Cindy's parting words—"you don't know what love is"—had more than just the hollow ring of truth to them. I was beginning to think that too many years of going for the gag, hanging out with Danish models, and working round the clock had possibly limited my capacity for "something more." Of course, every time I began to think this, I tried to imagine what could be "something more" than laughs, Danish models, and satisfying work. I have quite an active imagination, but in this area, my imagination had run totally dry.

And yet . . .

There was Janis.

This was an unusual affair because Janis was not at all my type. Physically she was quite lovely but not the kind of looks I usually go for. She was short and slightly round rather than long and lean. She was extremely classy looking, elegant, and sophisticated, where my taste usually ran to the slightly trashy. She was Deborah Kerr in *An Affair to Remember* as compared to my usual leaning—the soap-covered girl who washed the car in front of the prisoners in *Cool Hand Luke.* Even her personality was off-kilter alongside any past infatuations. I wasn't wild about confrontations. To say Janis was combative would be like saying Lawrence Taylor has an aggressive streak. She had the independence and confidence of British royalty and was as stubborn and opinionated as anyone this side of Saddam Hussein. Yet, despite all our differences—or perhaps because of them—she was the most intelligent, most stimulating, least boring person I'd met in a long, long time.

There was a slight hitch, however, to my having a long-lasting, perfect, satisfying relationship with Janis. She didn't *want* a long-lasting, perfect, satisfying relationship. At least, she didn't want one with me.

The closer we became, the more she'd pull back. Eventually, she pulled back so far I needed a telescope to find her. Which was a good sign the romance was over.

The relationship didn't end, however. What happened was that Janis and I became best friends. Without the threat of a romance, we became as close as two people could be. We even wound up working together. We saw each other during the day, we had dinner several times a week, we even went away on weekends together a few times—strictly platonically. She saw me through a couple of tough romances, through several professional crises. I did the same for her. Despite the Sarahs and the Karyns and the sportswriters and the Dickensian editors, it was Janis who always seemed to be there, whether the "there" was for fun, for support, or for anything that struck either one of us as interesting. We became so inseparable that most people thought we were still a couple. But she didn't want that. She didn't want a relationship because, in her experience, relationships only pointed toward the *end* of relationships. With ending came pain (and the better the relationship, the more painful the ending). With pain came bitterness. With bitterness came sorrow. You can take it from there.

Over time, I accepted that there was never going to be any kind of real relationship with this woman. It took some doing—a lot of teeth gnashing, a good bit of stomach hurting, and way too much head banging—but I did eventually accept it.

Only one person didn't accept it.

And I suppose I have to use the word "person" loosely.

Norton liked Janis.

It was particularly noticeable because she didn't much

care for him. Animals were something else she didn't want to get attached to. She didn't see the pleasure in such an attachment. She didn't see the point. But Norton didn't let up. Usually, when someone ignored him, my cat was happy to be ignored. Janis was the only person other than my father that I ever saw him pursue. When she came over, she wouldn't pet him—but within moments he'd be by her side, rubbing his body up against her leg or trying to burrow his face into the palm of her hand. Rarely did she so much as respond—but over the course of several years Norton never gave up. Whenever he saw her, he rolled over on his back in his best impersonation of the world's cutest cat. If she refused to look at him, he'd move to her, rubbing, cuddling, purring. Janis was tough—she knew the dangers of getting involved. But Norton was tough, too—he knew the *pleasures* of getting involved.

For a lot of this period—Norton vs. Janis—I was content to remain neutral. Then came Sag Harbor.

When I bought the house out there on Long Island, I had already rented a house on Fire Island with Norm for the summer. The thought of one last season avoiding the six-ishes appealed to me (especially since I'd already paid for it), so I came up with the perfect solution. I arranged for Janis to live in my new house for the summer, rent-free, on the condition that she fix it up—furnish the kitchen with utensils, buy and put up drapes, start to get the garden in shape. All the things that I would never have either the time, taste, or inclination to do. It was a fair deal and she accepted happily. At the end of the summer, Norm and I drove out to Sag Harbor to check up on the house and to have dinner with Janis. She insisted on cooking; dinner was served amidst delicate candlelight on the front porch. When I stepped inside—this was my first time there since I'd signed the papers three months earlier—I was amazed. The place was no longer just charming—it was beautiful. It no longer just had its own personality—it had Janis's. It was clear to me that she loved the house as much as I did. It was clear to anyone who bothered to look inside and see what she'd done with it.

That night we had a wonderful time. The food was delicious, we drank a lot of wine, everyone laughed until we were too tired to laugh anymore, and—for the first time in several years—it didn't feel right leaving Janis. It felt as if there was unfinished business.

Driving back to the city with Norm, we discussed it. He noticed that Janis had seemed softer than usual, that her guard was down, or at least lowered (she usually had barbed wire and German shepherds surrounding and protecting her vulnerability). We discussed the question of the homing instinct—was it actually enough to push two people into a relationship?

Norm thought that it was—if the two people were finally ready for a relationship. He also thought it was interesting that Janis had gone out of her way to do one thing she'd never done before. Right before we got in the car to head back to New York, she'd bent over the couch and petted Norton. Stroked him once, gently.

It had started to rain during our drive, and I remember looking at Norton through the rearview mirror. He was sitting comfortably in the backseat, relaxed, dozing. I wondered if I could really use a cat as a gauge for a relationship.

Norton didn't open his eyes to peer back. He wasn't going to make it easy for me.

Janis's birthday comes in the middle of September. It was on her birthday that we decided to bring our relationship to a new level. Or just bring it back to what it had once been. Or bring it back but make it different. As you may gather, we weren't exactly sure *what* we were doing.

What I *am* sure of is that whatever we were doing or becoming, we wouldn't have done it or become it without Norton.

My house became *our* house—mine, Janis's, and Norton's. Norton was fun to be with on the weekends in Sag Harbor, and he made us both laugh. Janis couldn't get over the fact that he'd walk with me to Sean's Murray Hill Market, three blocks away from the house. Unlike Fire Island, Sag Harbor had traffic, so it was difficult to get him to take mid-afternoon strolls. But early in the morning, before cars started clogging up the streets, Norton would leisurely walk along behind us, meowing forcefully as usual. He'd wait patiently outside the market while we shopped, then hike back with us. Initially, Janis would get impatient if Norton decided to duck into the bushes for a two-minute (or ten-minute, depending on his mood) time-out from the walk. She'd try to convince me to leave him behind when it was time to buy groceries. Soon, however, she was coaxing him into taking the walk with us. And once he was along for the journey, if I started walking too fast for the cat, she'd urge me to slow down. "Don't be so impatient," she'd lecture me.

She stopped complaining when he got sidetracked and welcomed him back happily when he rejoined us.

She also liked to watch Norton prowl the garden. There were no bluejays to torment him in Sag Harbor, but there was a mockingbird, and he quickly became my kitten's new nemesis. Once the mockingbird had sized up the situation—the macho-level of the gray, furry animal in the backyard—he started zooming out of his tree, landing on the ground a few feet from Norton, and then would stand there screaming at the poor cat. Norton was totally intimidated. Janis would urge him on, try to get him to beat up on the puny bird, of course to no avail. She began to take it as a personal insult, and I would often find her explaining to Norton—as I had years before on Fire Island—about the law of the jungle and the concept of the food chain.

She grew catnip in the garden for him. It never got high enough for us to cut it and let it dry. As soon as she'd plant it, Norton would make a beeline for the spot, dig up the ground around it, and spend a happy few hours rolling around in the dirt while Janis would mock-scold him.

It was fun to watch a relationship develop between the two of them, both so independent. I'd gotten used to Norton's near-magical powers over the years, so it was rejuvenating to see his effect on her and to watch her witness his effect on others.

Janis was with us one day as we were driving along the L.I.E. out to Sag Harbor. I was driving, Janis was passengering, and Norton was in his usual position, lying down in the back, staring out the rear windshield. (When just the two of us drive, Norton will sit on the front seat, but Janis doesn't like him up there. For one thing, she thinks it's dangerous. For another—the real reason—Norton's claws will occasionally come out, to help him balance himself if the car lurches, and he will ruin her stockings or rip a small hole in her blouse. So Norton will lie patiently in the back, content to watch the countryside zip by, until Janis falls asleep. Then he'll sneak up cautiously to the front and make himself comfortable.) It was a beautiful day; I was lost in thought and, apparently, also speeding like a lunatic. When the motorcycle cop pulled us over, he already had his ticket pad in hand as he broke it to me that I'd been going seventy-five miles an hour. Before he could write up the ticket, though, he glanced at the backseat.

"Is that a Scottish Fold?" he asked.

I nodded. I'm much better nodding than I am talking to policemen.

"He's beautiful," this leather-jacketed cop said. "I have a Fold, too."

I won't bore you with the sappy details. Suffice it to say that Norton let himself be held and petted by the arresting officer—and the arrest was never made. My record remained unblemished and the ticket was torn up.

Janis was around for another car confrontation with Norton, this one without quite the happy ending of the earlier one.

I had driven to the office that day and had decided to take the cat. He was a perfect corporate companion, spending the whole day either lying on my desk or resting on the couch in the corner. Periodically, he'd wander out of my office and stroll along the hallways, stopping to visit the people he liked. It was no longer a surprise to anyone at the publishing company—even the Chairman of the Board—when a cat would wander in to say hello.

It was a brutally hot summer day, and naturally enough, the air conditioner in my car was broken. Driving home—Janis in front, Norton in the back hoping she'd doze off—all the windows were wide open. Downtown, in the Village, on the way to the garage, we stopped at a red light. On the street corner was a bag lady, filthy, kind of crazy seeming, clearly homeless. It had been a hard day at work, it was too hot, whatever the reason, but when the woman came up to our car and asked for money, both Janis and I looked right through her. It was as if she weren't a real person, as if she didn't exist. Perhaps we'd been in New York too long, where homelessness is a way of life, something too easy to inure yourself against.

As the car idled, the woman asked me a question.

"Is that a special breed of cat?" she said, pointing to Norton, who was looking out at her, his paws up on the back door, his head sticking through the open window.

Without really thinking about it—except snobbily to decide I didn't want to explain Norton's pedigree to a homeless woman—I simply said, "No. He's a regular cat."

"Oh," she said. "He looks like a Scottish Fold."

The light turned green. Before I could drive on, she added with a wistful sigh, "I used to have seven Siamese."

She stuck her hand through the window, gave Norton a pat on the head, and with astonishing dignity, walked on.

Much to Norton's delight, Janis allowed him onto the front seat for the few-block drive to our garage. She even hugged him. I'm sure also to his delight, neither one of us has ever looked at a homeless person in quite the same way. It was a good cure for our haughty superiority.

Janis was also present for Norton's one and only cat fight, a sorry affair by any standards.

I had long suspected that Norton was no Rocky Marciano. In the garden, he liked to hunker down and stalk the occasional and ever-dangerous butterfly, but that was the extent of his aggressive tendencies. Unfortunately, when one rears an outdoor cat, one must face up to the fact that other outdoor cats will come a-calling.

We had noticed a large orange, furry guy who seemed to enjoy strolling around our backyard in Sag Harbor in the late afternoons. If Norton was outside for these appearances, he would either meow immediately to be let in or he'd quickly disappear around the front of the house to one of his secret hiding spots. If this bully was visiting while Norton was safely inside the house, Norton would bravely stand at the back door, protected by a screen, and hiss loudly. He'd arch his back and release his claws, then he'd look over to us for approval. Either Janis or I would tell him what a tough guy he was and how proud we were of him. Perhaps that's what made Norton cocky.

One afternoon, while sitting upstairs in my office working away, I heard the most god-awful noise. It was a wail of pain and fear, and it seemed to stretch on forever. That was followed by Janis's scream. She screamed my name and then yelled for me to come downstairs.

I made it as quickly as I could, but in the few seconds it took me, I heard violent hisses and howls, high-pitched growls and what sounded like two sumo wrestlers thudding into each other. By the time I got outside, the orange monster was walking triumphantly across the lawn. I screamed at him and waved my arms. That didn't seem to scare him—he gave me a look that made it clear he felt he could take me, too—but he did get the message that he wasn't welcome. Once he had hurdled the fence and landed in my neighbor's yard, I went looking for Norton.

Now, my cat *always* comes when I call him. *Always.* But not this time. Janis and I spent twenty minutes searching for him high and low. No Norton. I really began to be afraid when I finally heard a very soft and rather pathetic meow. I stopped and listened, heard it again. So did Janis. It seemed to be coming from under my car, which was parked in the driveway.

I got down on my hands and knees to look, and sure enough, Norton was cowering there. It took several more minutes of coaxing, but I finally got him to come out. When he slunk out between the rear tires, Janis gasped. Norton was bleeding above the nose and on his right shoulder. His fur was matted and sticky, and he was so frightened, he seemed to have curled up to half his normal size, which wasn't very big to begin with. When I picked him up in my arms, I realized he had been so terrified, he had also defecated, somehow all over himself.

I calmed him down as best I could, then carried him upstairs to the bathroom. Putting him down in the bathtub, I turned on the water, just a gentle stream from the tap, and did my best to clean him up. He made no effort to resist. Once he was clean, I could see that his scratches and scrapes were minor. The physical wounds were surface, but the emotional scars seemed to run deep. After I dried him off, talking to him and cooing at him the whole time, he timidly went into my bedroom, hopped onto the bed, and crawled under the covers. He burrowed his way to the foot of the bed and stayed there for the rest of the afternoon. Every so often, I'd try to get him to come out, but, ashamed, he wouldn't even look at me. By dinnertime, he still hadn't poked his head out from under the quilt.

At that point, Janis decided the situation called for a woman's touch. I watched as she sat on the bed and gently pulled the covers back. Norton curled up into a ball, his face hidden. But where he had refused to look at me when I'd tried to cheer him up, he slowly began to uncurl as Janis stroked him and whispered to him. Within a few minutes, his little tongue was out, licking her fingers. When she told him it was now time to come downstairs and eat dinner, he rose, jumped off the bed, and followed her down the steps.

It took Norton a couple of days before he was up to snuff. He didn't look me in the eye for quite a while. It was more humiliating for him to face his dad than his new mom after his run-in with the orange Chuck Norris. I did notice a new bond between Norton and Janis after that. Somehow, he trusted her more than he had before. And somehow, she knew it and responded in kind.

Because Janis was so resistant to a relationship, it was easy to chart her ups and downs by her responses to the cat. When she would be overcome by fear or the claustrophobia of a relationship, she would push Norton away. When she was feeling affectionate toward me, it was easier to show it to the cat. It was safer.

Our biggest arguments at the beginning were over Norton's sleeping arrangements. She *hated* that he slept with us. I had reached the point where I couldn't sleep well if he wasn't in the bed with me. She felt smothered by him—

especially because he insisted on sleeping directly to her left, by her head. Since I was directly to her right, she was caught smack dab in the middle of us—for eight hours a night.

Norton would get in bed before either of us, usually settling down on Janis's pillow (he still slept like a person—head on the pillow, body under the covers). She'd crawl into bed before I would, pick Norton up, and unceremoniously toss him onto the floor. I'd finally come in, ready for lights-out, call for my pal, and he'd come running. He'd start out sleeping by my side, but as soon as it was feasible—which meant as soon as Janis was asleep and couldn't protest—he'd move to her side. She'd start out distant and comfortable, only to wake up in the middle of the night surrounded again.

The First Stage of softening came when she stopped dumping Norton off the bed. She started moving him over to my pillow instead. Then she'd go crazy watching me try to get into bed without disturbing him.

"He's just a cat!" Janis would say. "Throw him off!"

"No, he's too comfortable," I'd say while I was trying to squeeze my tired body into two feet of available space.

"Get rid of him!" she'd say scornfully—but we were both aware that *she* hadn't gotten rid of him.

This stage lasted a long time. Over a year. It was the period in the relationship when neither person knows whether what they have together is permanent, but each is starting to think it *might* be, if such a thing as permanency is humanly possible. She wasn't throwing anything away—not me or my cat—but she wasn't exactly embracing anything either.

During this period, our relationship grew and strengthened—we both relaxed; we both stopped trying so hard and just accepted what was—and so did Janis's relationship with Norton.

Stage Two arrived when I came upstairs one night to find Janis asleep and Norton curled up against her—on *her* side of the bed. He was taking up half her pillow. She hadn't moved to accommodate him, but she hadn't moved him away from her. It was about that time that she first told me she loved me.

Stage Three came months after that, soon after the infamous cat fight. Exhausted, I had fallen asleep early, long before Janis was ready for bed. Norton, overjoyed that he had me all to himself, plopped himself down directly in the middle of her pillow and got into our old sleeping position, me with half the bed, him with half the bed.

I didn't really fall into a deep sleep, so I was half awake when Janis finally crawled under the covers. I was conscious enough to watch her carefully climb over the sleeping Norton—*very* carefully, so as not to disturb him. Exactly as I had done so many times over the years, she scrunched herself into two feet of sleeping space, wedging herself between me and the cat. I fell asleep soon after I felt her gently kiss my forehead—and saw her put her ear against Norton to listen to his purring, then softly kiss him good night.

It was around this time that we began to realize we might be spending a good chunk of our lives together.

Stage Four came about in a complicated and roundabout way. One thing I can say about it is that it was certainly a good test of the relationship. It all happened because I agreed to take my cat *back* to Paris.

It started with another phone call from Roman Polanski, who called to say he thought we should write something together. Not a rewrite—this time he wanted to do it from scratch.

We decided we would adapt a book. Neither one of us was brimming over with wonderful, original story lines, and we thought an adaptation would be fun, easy, and, from a technical standpoint, interesting. Within moments of this decision, I thought of a book I wanted to adapt. It was brilliant, it was dramatic, it was wonderfully funny and tragically sad. I pulled it down from my bookshelf, stared at it for several seconds, and then stuck it right back where it came from. Too weird, I decided. They'll think I'm crazy. The book was *The Master and Margarita* by Mikhail Bulgakov. I never mentioned it to anyone. Not to Roman, not to the studio.

I didn't find another book. Neither did Polanski. The studio kept sending us thrillers. The director kept rejecting them. Then, a full year after we'd decided to work together, Roman called me. "I know what I want to do," he said. "Have you ever heard of a book called *The Master and Margarita?*"

I thought it had to be a joke. He assured me it wasn't. My heart soared, and two weeks later Norton and I were in Paris adapting one of the greatest literary works of the twentieth century. I do not know if our screenplay will ever get made. Probably not is my guess. Too expensive and too weird. No chance for a sequel. Those are the vagaries and frustrations of working in the movie biz. But I do know one thing about that job:

It was not easy.

The work was torturous. (Or at least as torturous as writing can be. I don't ever like to confuse writing clever dialogue with fighting oil fires or harvesting the rice paddies.) Roman is obsessive about research and meticulously faithful to whatever material he's working from. He read the novel in English. Then he read it in American (they are two different translations). Then in Polish, French, and finally Russian. Every time he read a different version, it would spark a different idea or direction. With every new idea, there was a new night I spent working—and working alone; nighttime for Roman was definitely not for working—until two or three A.M.

Thank god for Norton. Never had I appreciated having him around quite so much. Most evenings, I'd come back from a day at Polanski's spent and exhausted, intellectually and emotionally drained. I'd collapse on the bed for an hour or two, Norton cuddled up against my side; then I'd order room service or take Norton out to a café for a quick bite—then back to the apartment for several hours huddled over the typewriter, trying to make sense of the day's notes and decisions. Norton would sit on the desk, directly to my left, watching me struggle trying to whip this book into shape. By ten in the morning I was supposed to have new scenes, new ideas, new dialogue for Roman to see.

As I worked, trying to make sense of this twisting, turning novel, as I talked it over with Roman—and over and over—something started to click. The morass of political and intellectual theories that abound in the book started to come into a very definite focus. As we wrote and discussed and argued and yelled and struggled, this great and dense fantasy of a novel began to make sense to me in a way it never had before. Oddly enough—*very* oddly, since my life could not be farther from the lives depicted in the book—

the sense of the book and the meaning of the screenplay came from the relationship that had developed with Janis. And, yes, with Norton.

The Master and Margarita was written during the 1930s, finished in 1939, and it was considered finished only because the author died, blind and destitute, a victim of Stalin's repression. It is easy to tell what happens in this novel. It is not easy to tell what it's about. The main characters are the Devil, a suicidal writer, a bad poet, a six-foot cat in a top hat and waistcoat, Jesus Christ, Pontius Pilate, and the most beautiful woman in the world. There are brutal murders, public humiliations, crucifixions, and a confrontation with the ultimate evil. There is also sharp satire, laugh-out-loud slapstick, political parody, religious revisionism, and devastating philosophical insight. There are ghosts and people flying through the air and magical transformations. Oh—it also happens to be one of the greatest love stories ever written. All in all, I suppose it's understandable that so far it's been difficult to get a Hollywood studio to give this movie a financial green light: we're not exactly talking sequel to *Home Alone*.

Anyway, after much sifting, sorting, researching, cutting, and stalling, I ultimately made a decision about what *The Master and Margarita* is all about. It all came back to Cindy and her parting words of years before.

You don't know what love is.

Thanks to that trip to Paris, thanks to Janis and our developing relationship, mostly thanks to a little gray cat with a round head and folded ears, I *do* know what love is. I not only know what it is, I've found it. I've seen it work and seen what it can do.

Days before I wrote the ending to the script, I got a call from Janis. She was out in Sag Harbor. It was early in the morning her time, early afternoon for me.

"What are you doing up so early?" I asked.

"I couldn't sleep," she told me. "I haven't been sleeping well lately."

"Why not?" I wanted to know.

"I miss you," she said.

As perhaps you've noticed, I'm a sucker for this kind of stuff. "Awww," I said. "That's so nice."

"But it's not *just* that," she added.

"What else?"

"I don't sleep well anymore unless Norton sleeps by my side."

So it was Janis reaching Stage Four that gave me the nerve to decide that our screenplay for *The Master and Margarita* should be, above all, about love. Love in its most real sense. Love between two people. Two real people. Love surviving politics and oppression and art and history and cruelty and even death. The script for the movie ends the way Bulgakov ends his book. The Master and Margarita ascend, not to heaven but to a world of two, where they can escape the often vicious and always absurd world into which we are born.

My interpretation of this great novel was that the most important thing any of us can do is to live in a world where love is a greater priority than pain. Only in my case, as now in Janis's, it is not just a world of two. As I am reminded by Norton, who this very moment sits on my desk, six inches to my left, watching me write these words, it is very definitely a world of three.

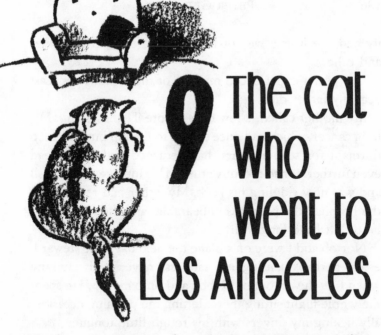

9 The cat who went to Los Angeles

All of our lives, those of us who live in Western civilization, are not really so very different. We all suffer the same constraints—of time, of strength, of laws, of expectations. Within each life there are purely individual peaks and valleys, wild swings of ecstasy and despair, great triumphs, noble failures, yet, taken as a whole, there is a definite commonality of experience. The thrills we experience, which we feel no one can ever appreciate the same way, are thrills experienced by everyone—love, sex, success. The sadness that envelops us, in such a life-changing way that we are sure we are unique in the power of our feeling, envelops us all—illness, separation, poverty, death. There are two ways to go after experiencing one of these highs or lows—one can either withdraw into isolation, or one can accept the commonality and use it as a way of learning more about ourselves and others.

Last year I experienced my first of these sadnesses. Last year my father died.

My mother called, a few days before Thanksgiving. His lung cancer, which had once spread to the hip but had been dormant for several years, had returned and had spread even further. It had recently crushed his hip like an eggshell and was now riddling his back. My father had returned to the hospital, the pain was unbearable, and the feeling was he didn't have long to live.

Norton and I were on a plane the next day. The stewardesses, perhaps sensing my sadness, never said anything when I let the cat out of his box and onto my lap. He spent the whole flight sitting there, letting me pet him, occasionally licking my fingers with his rough little tongue.

I remembered when my dad had had his first operation. He'd had a lung removed. We were all terrified of what would happen, and Norton and I had flown out then, too. When my dad got out of the hospital, he was in tremendous pain. Every breath was agony, and the only way he could get comfortable was to sit back in a giant, ugly, cushiony Barcalounger that my mother bought just for this purpose. He would sit back, practicing breathing with one lung, trying to cope with the agony of broken ribs (that's how the surgeons get to the lung, through the ribs). What I remember most was how afraid my father was. Afraid of death, sure, but even more afraid of the pain.

The Barcalounger was set up in my parents' bedroom, at the foot of their bed. My dad would lie there for most of the day, watching television, the pain spoiling the concentration required even to read.

He'd been set up in the chair like this for two, maybe three days, spending most of those days just being afraid. I was in my room, maybe forty feet away, when I heard my dad call my name. It wasn't a friendly call, or even a weak one, at least not as weak as he'd been sounding. It was a fearful call and I came running.

When I got to his room, I saw what my father was afraid of. Norton was crouched below his chair, ready to leap, eyeing the blanket on my father's lap. It looked like an inviting spot to sit and be petted—especially since these two had long ago befriended each other. But my father's face was not a friendly one. He was afraid that Norton would jump on him, would jostle him, would possibly even land right on the long, jagged scar, and hurt him even more. My father was too afraid even to move.

I didn't get to Norton in time to stop him. When I came into the room, he somehow took my presence as further encouragement. And so he jumped.

I distinctly recall feeling frozen in time, as if everything were moving in slow motion. The cat was floating through the air, aimed at my father's chest. My father was staring aghast, perhaps as afraid as he'd ever been in his whole life.

Of course it was over in a split second. Norton landed on the cushioned arm of the chair, not even touching my father. My dad sagged back, exhausted from the effort of being so afraid, and Norton, ever so gently, as if he weighed not a pound, settled onto my father's lap and began to lick his hand. My dad, trembling, used his other hand to pet my cat. The blood came back into his face and finally he looked at me. He smiled—not much of a smile but a smile—and nodded weakly.

I came back an hour later to check up on him. My father was asleep now, his head back in the chair, his body relaxed. His hand was still resting on Norton's body, and Norton was still curled up on the blanket in his lap. My dad woke up when I came into the room, and he smiled again. This time a real smile. Somehow he didn't look as afraid. I think he felt a little foolish that he'd been so terrified of Norton. At the same time I think he was relieved. The possibility of pain had been very real, yet the pain hadn't materialized. I actually think that moment was the first time my father thought he might get better, the first time he realized he wasn't going to die.

Three years later, as I saw him in the hospital room, he *was* going to die and this time he knew it.

My brother, Eric, and my mother had been under an incredible strain, living with this pressure day to day, so I was, by reason of being the newest and freshest face on the scene, elected designated strong person. The decisions weren't pleasant ones—levels of medication, when to stop the therapy, when to stop fighting and give in to the inevitable. Within a few days there weren't many more decisions to make, however. There was very little to be done. My father was in and out of lucidity, usually out. In a ghoulish way, we actually got some laughs out of the situation—final proof that I was right and Sarah was wrong: there don't seem to be any inappropriate times to find humor.

At one point, my dad, totally under the influence of pain-killing drugs, mostly morphine, was convinced Pete

Maravich was playing basketball in the hall. (My dad had never met Pete Maravich to any of our knowledge; however, as Eric pointed out, since Maravich had died several months before this, it probably wasn't a good omen.) In one coherent moment, my dad was confused by the hallucinations he'd been seeing on the wall—confused because they'd suddenly disappeared. "But they were so beautiful," he said.

"At last," I told him, "you can understand why Eric and I took all those drugs back in the sixties and seventies."

"So *this* is why," he said. And then he said, "Now what I don't understand is why you *stopped.*"

My dad did not want to die in the hospital. So when we knew there was nothing else the doctors could do, we brought him home.

A round-the-clock nurse had set up a hospital bed in his bedroom, and that's where he settled. The bed was near his old Barcalounger. For the several days he stayed alive at home, Norton never left that Barcalounger. He stayed there all day; he slept there at night, keeping my dad company.

One night I wanted him in my bed. It was late, maybe two A.M., and I wanted the company. I slipped into my dad's room. He was asleep—rather, by this time he'd slipped into a semi-coma—and the nurse was reading. Norton sat in the chair, awake, staring at my father as if waiting for word that he was allowed to jump onto his bed and comfort him. The word didn't come, at least not while I stood watching. I didn't bring Norton back into my room. I left him there in the chair and went back to sleep on my own. Just in case the word did come, I figured he might as well be prepared.

The next day my father died. It was in the late afternoon. I wasn't there. I'd gone out shopping for groceries. Somehow, pulling into the driveway, I knew. When I stopped the car, my brother and my mother came out of the house. They were crying. I'd missed it by just a few minutes. Eric had been by his side. One minute he was breathing deeply, asleep, the next minute the breaths stopped. That's all there was to it.

I'd said my good-byes a couple of days before. My dad had been slipping in and out of consciousness. When conscious, sometimes he would call for one of us, or all of us. Sometimes when the nurse told us he was awake, we'd just come in, never knowing if it was our last opportunity to speak or listen.

At some point, the nurse told me that he was awake and I should say whatever it was I wanted to say to him. She said I might not have another chance. So she left the room, and I stood next to my dying father, holding his cold, clammy hand. I knew he knew who I was. He couldn't talk by this point, but he was shaking his head, rolling his eyes as if to say, "What a bitch, huh?"

I didn't have anything to say to him. We'd been very close when he was alive—I mean *really* alive, not barely alive—and I'd said a lot to him when it meant something. I didn't have to tell him I loved him. He knew that. I didn't have to tell him I'd miss him. He knew that too. Anything I could say to him now would somehow seem fake or overly dramatic or ultimately meaningless. So I didn't say anything. I just held his hand and waited until he fell back asleep. My dad was never one to tolerate the bullshit. I think he preferred the silence.

That afternoon, Janis had arrived from New York. My dad had been crazy about her and vice versa. They had a great relationship, a lot of banter back and forth. He gave her a very hard time and she returned it with gusto. He appreciated anyone who could give him a hard time.

When she came up the stairs, the whole family was sitting around my dad's bed. He'd been unconscious, but when she walked in he seemed to stir. He was always a bit of a ladies' man.

"Dad," I said, "it's Janis. Janis came here to see you."

He lifted his head, saw us all, then saw her. She smiled at him. He looked back at my mother, at my brother, at me—and rolled his eyes. A big, exaggerated roll, done for Janis's benefit. The roll said, "Jesus—as if things weren't bad enough, *now* look who shows up!"

We all got hysterical; even my dad did his best to laugh. Then he fell back asleep and never woke up.

There's something comforting in the fact that his last act in life was to make people laugh. He kept his sense of humor right up to the end, and it made everything a lot easier on all of us.

We didn't have a standard funeral. We had a party instead. That's the way he would have wanted it—my dad loved parties. He loved being a host.

My dad was in a wine group, and the members of the group brought exquisite wine to toast him. We had one of the best restaurants in L.A. cater the event. Three of Dad's closest friends gave speeches, talking about him. Their talks were wonderfully funny. I would say that, through the tears, there were as many laughs at the funeral as at any party my dad had ever thrown.

That night, after everyone was gone, after Janis was asleep, I went into my bathroom, the bathroom I'd had as a little kid, and I broke down and cried. I cried for perhaps fifteen minutes, real wracking sobs. I cried until I was exhausted, until I not only didn't have any tears in me, I didn't have any emotions left at all.

When I was done, I looked up to find Norton staring at me. He'd pushed the bathroom door open with his nose and had come in to seek me out.

I picked him up, kissed him on top of the head, and held him while I sat in the bathroom, staring out the window at our backyard. Norton didn't meow; he didn't even lick me. He just let me hold him as long as I wanted. I appreciated the silence, too. I wasn't in the mood for bullshit either.

I don't know how long I was in there. I do know it was almost light when I got back into bed.

I lay down, my head on the pillow, closed my eyes, and went to sleep. Norton put his head on my pillow and snuggled in against my chest.

When I woke up, it was a new day. Many things had changed, but not Norton. He was still asleep, still by my side, still content to let me hold him.

Afterword

Sometimes I worry that perhaps it's just me, that perhaps I make up all this stuff about Norton being so great, being so special. But every so often I'm reminded that that's not the case.

Not long ago, my friends Nancy and Ziggy had a baby, a truly marvelous little boy named Charlie Elroy Alderman. (Yes, if any of you are wondering, it is indeed Elroy as in "The Jetsons.")

Soon after Charlie was born, Nancy walked him down, in his stroller, from their house in Sag Harbor to mine. It was a Sunday morning and it was early. Ziggy was still asleep and so was Janis. This was Charlie's first trip down the block to visit his neighbors.

Nancy wheeled him up to the back door, picked him out of the buggy, and carried him inside.

Norton, who'd been napping on a kitchen chair, raised his head to check out the newcomer in his life. Nancy took her tiny little baby and held him down toward Norton.

"Look, Norton," she said. "This is a baby."

Norton looked up at Charlie, took him in, and sort of nodded as if assimilating the information.

There was a very long pause, and then I heard Nancy gulp.

"You've finally done it," she said to me.

"What?" I wanted to know.

"Most mothers would have said, 'Look, Charlie, this is a cat.'"

I started to laugh.

"Not with Norton," I said.

Nancy started to laugh, too.

"No, not with Norton," she agreed.

a cat abroad

THE FURTHER ADVENTURES OF NORTON, THE CAT WHO WENT TO PARIS, AND HIS HUMAN

peter gethers

To Danie, Anne, Sylvie, Jean-Guy, Anette, Philippe, Elisabeth, Gwen, Ailie, Jenny, Jim, Maureen, Margit, Georges, Mike, and Deborah, who welcomed us, taught us, fed us, and became friends forever.

contents

acknowledgments

Leona Nevler and Betty Prashker believed, encouraged, and fixed.

Esther Newberg did her usual tooth-and-nail job and continues to be the perfect agent.

Janis seems not to care (well, sort of), no matter how grumpy I get or how many weekends I work.

And I especially want to thank Norton for letting me share the chair at my desk with him. For the next book, I hope I get a full half, but I won't count on it.

foreword

Recently, I was in Paris with my rather astonishing and extremely handsome Scottish Fold cat, Norton. We were having dinner with Danielle, an old friend of mine who lives in the 17th arrondissement, and her daughter, Priscilla. I met Priscilla when she was four years old and the only English sentence she knew was, "I like ze Beeg Mac 'amburgair." By the night of our dinner, Priscilla was no longer four. She was twenty-three, spoke fluent English, and wanted to take us to a restaurant where her boyfriend worked. Which means I'm getting longer in the tooth (not to mention thicker around the middle).

I say "we" and "us," by the way, because no one was all that excited just to see *me*. Norton was the star attraction. Danielle had made it quite clear that they would certainly be happy if I came along, but they were *really* interested in my little gray pal as their primary dinner companion. Danielle even let me know that the owner of the restaurant,

1

when told about Norton and his adventures traveling the globe, had insisted that *le chat* come to dinner as her very special guest.

When we arrived at the restaurant, Bistro d'Albert, a charming and perfect place that could exist only in France, Norton was greeted the way I imagine Ike was when he arrived at the Champs-Elysées immediately following D-Day. He was given, as he always is, his own chair, which he settled into quite comfortably. The owner, a typical somewhere-over-forty-year-old blond Frenchwoman for whom you'd happily give up the rest of your life if she'd only so much as smile at you, smiled up a storm. But not at me. Oh, no. At my innocent-looking furry friend, who, just to annoy me, I'm sure, purred like a motorboat, rolled over on his back, and practically begged the owner and all of her gorgeous waitresses to come over and scratch his stomach, which, of course, they did. Meanwhile, I was doing my best to order a *kir*, but I couldn't get anyone to even look at me.

Eventually, the waitresses returned to their regular duties, went about their work, and dinner settled into a normal routine. The three humans had a delicious bottle of red wine with their kidneys—the specialty of the house—and the cat worked away on some broiled chicken and a small bowl of milk.

One of the most satisfying things about being in Europe is that animals are treated with enormous respect. You can go into the very best, most expensive restaurants in Paris and it is almost guaranteed that someone will have brought his or her dog along for the meal. No one bats an eye, no one thinks it odd. The general feeling is that a dog has as much right to eat at Robuchon as any human. This night, at Bistro d'Albert, *five* people brought their dogs along. Which meant that at some point—I think it was during the cheese course—Norton looked up from his *lait froid* to find five curious canines of varying sizes and temperaments sitting in a circle around his chair. One of them growled. Another worked up his courage, stuck his nose right in Norton's face, and took a particularly antagonistic sniff. The dogs seemed to be of the opinion that Parisian restaurants were *their* domain and that cats should stay where they belonged—curled up by the fireplace in a turn-of-the-century apartment or prowling around a garden searching for tasty mice. Certainly they did *not* belong in places where they could actually compete for affection, much less the *boeuf bourguignon.* For just a moment, the room froze. I didn't know if French people had ever heard of the Gunfight at the O.K. Corral—but I had a feeling they were about to. Except that Norton, in the peacekeeping role of Wyatt Earp, simply looked determinedly at his ring of potential tormentors, stared each of them, one by one, straight in the eye, then calmly went back to eating his chicken and sipping his milk. When one dog barked, demanding a little more attention, Norton finished chewing his last piece of chicken, then glanced at the barker with pity, as if to say, "Please. This is France. You're embarrassing me. Haven't you read your Sartre?"

That was the end of the confrontation. Deflated, the dogs went back to their respective masters and sat under their own tables, hoping to receive a morsel of food now that their bluff had been called.

The rest of the dinner went fairly smoothly until it came time for dessert. Danielle, Priscilla, and I ordered our mousse and our pastries, and when we were served, the chef emerged from the kitchen with a big bowl of ice cream. Priscilla had mentioned to him that Norton was an ice cream fiend.

"Zees is for ze incredible cat," he told me. "I made *chocolat*—his favoreet."

Now, Norton likes his chocolate ice cream, no question about it. But he's also quite particular. He loves Ben & Jerry's. Häagen-Dazs gets an A-plus. He will eat frozen yogurt and ice milk but only in an emergency. If offered some chocolate *non*-fat frozen yogurt, he will turn his back disgustedly after one lick, making you feel as if you'd just offered a Sabrettes chili dog to the Queen of England.

The chef dug a spoon into his ice cream and held it up toward Norton. The cat eagerly took a lick, hesitated, gave some thought to what he'd just eaten—and disdainfully turned his back on the chef. I immediately had visions of the chef pulling out a glove, slapping me, and challenging me to a duel—and I was not so far off.

"It's not posseeble," he told me, totally bewildered. "Our ice cream is superb!"

"I'm sure it is," I agreed. "He's probably just full."

"But Priscilla told me he *loves* ze ice cream."

"Why don't you try giving him another taste," I suggested, although I knew my cat well enough to know this would be a useless gesture. By this time, the owner had come to the table to see what the problem was. When I explained, I could see the existential pain in her eyes.

"We have never 'ad a complaint in all our years," she told me. "Zis is outrageous."

"Give him another taste," a waitress urged.

So the chef held out a second spoonful of the stuff. Norton licked cautiously, looked at the brown lump, and, if cats can shake their heads—and I am one hundred percent certain that mine can—he shook his head. *No way,* is basically what he was saying.

Thus ended the meal. The chef stalked back into the kitchen, offended and insulted. The owner made it chillingly clear that the cat was not nearly as special as she had been led to believe. And I was fairly certain that the next time the Larousse French/English Dictionary put in the phrase "ugly American," my photo would be next to the definition.

I gathered Norton in my arms, tried to figure out how I could explain to a cat about the concepts of tact and eating to be polite, gave up, and stuck him back in his cloth shoulder bag, his favorite mode of transportation.

As we were going out the door, one of the waitresses pulled me aside.

"Your leetle cat," she said. " 'E was right."

I looked at her curiously and she explained.

"Ze chef, he made a batch of ice cream and eet was not good," she went on. "He thought he could put one over on ze cat and get rid of it." She put her hand on the top of Norton's head and scratched him, something that ranks in his top three activities. "Zat is a very impressive cat," she said. "And his taste is *soo-pairb.*"

"I never doubted it," I told her and looked at my "leetle cat," just a bit awed. He looked back at me, dubious. "Honest," I said to him, and held my hand over my heart. "I never doubted you for a minute."

PART ONE

a cat at home

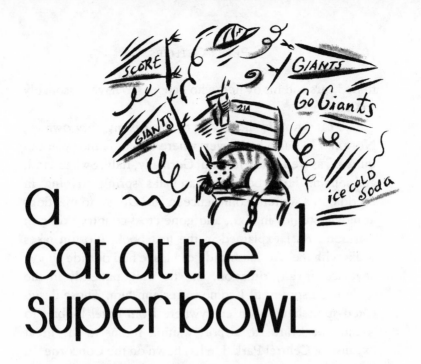

a cat at the super bowl

1

It's been said—by Edmund Wilson among other scholars—that the only great subject for American writers is the rise of America in the first half of the twentieth century.

That may be true, though I would argue that there needs to be a slight revision to such a narrow way of thinking. Without going off the deep end, let's just say: A very *good* subject for American writers is the rise of the American cat in the second half of the twentieth century. Especially if the cat happens to be a brilliant, handsome, good-hearted Scottish Fold with a round head and flat, folded ears who looks more like an owl than a cat and who has traveled all over the world, having more adventures in his travels than Gulliver.

Of course, I may be a little biased here, especially since this book is a sequel to one called *The Cat Who Went to Paris,* which was all about the aforementioned cat with folded ears and his owner, who happens to have reasonably straight ears.

The cat who did indeed go to Paris is my very own cat Norton. He's also been everywhere else in France you can think of, as well as to Holland, Germany, Italy, Switzerland, and Spain. He's been to baseball's spring training in Florida, to a writers' conference in San Diego, to meetings at movie studios in L.A., and gone cross-country skiing in Vermont. As I explained in the first book, Norton takes walks with me *sans* leash and I can leave him outside almost anyplace, in any situation, and he waits patiently in the designated spot until I come to reclaim him. Those designated spots have been everywhere from hotel lobbies to friends' backyards to airport waiting rooms to the great expanse of Central Park. He has flown on the Concorde. In Europe he goes out to restaurants with me and sits in his own chair, where he behaves like someone who has just graduated from a Swiss finishing school. He is, common to the breed, extraordinarily sweet. He is also, not common to any animal I've ever met before, shockingly smart. I really do take him everywhere I go, have ludicrously long conversations with him, and I like him so much I willingly admit it borders on the demented. Very little is done in my life unless Norton approves of the doing.

Since the publication of *The Cat Who Went to Paris,* I've discovered that, as I venture out into the world, I have begun to fade more and more into the background while Norton has slowly poked his way into the limelight. This is fine with me except it means that too often I find myself being compared, one on one, to something—excuse me: some*one*—I used to foolishly regard as my pet.

Believe me, it is not always a comforting exercise to compare cats to people, particularly if the one doing the comparing happens to be a flawed human rather than a member of the near-flawless feline race. For instance: People lie. In fact, people lie all the time. Cats do not *ever* lie. People happily kill other people in the name of everything from a god to a country to an overly developed sense of annoyance when someone cuts across two lanes on a freeway without signaling. Cats will, on occasion, kill other cats but, for the most part, they are content to puff up their fur, yowl like banshees, and rip the occasional ear off—and all this is usually done for the sake of food or protecting their own territory (which may not be condonable, but it is at least rational). People are often cruel and cause great emotional damage to others, sometimes deliberately, sometimes in blissful ignorance. The worst thing a cat will do, when it comes to inflicting emotional pain, is to make it clear he wants to be left alone. This causes nothing more than a sense of relief in other well-adjusted cats and a sense of rejection in not-so-well-adjusted, much more neurotic humans. People tend to lower their standards (and almost anything else that can be lowered) if they have the opportunity to win approval from a friend, spouse, boss, or even nodding acquaintance. Cats, on the other hand, are relatively indifferent to such emotional stroking. As a result, their decisions—on matters of personal attachments, lavishing affection, and certainly on such questions as whether or not to get off the comfortable couch to join, if they'll excuse the expression, the rat race—automatically fall on a substantially higher moral and ethical plane. All in all, it is not particularly difficult to make the case that cats are, in almost any and all ways, superior creatures to the supposedly dominant Homo sapiens.

That is why, when it came to making the single most important decision of my life—which I did last year—it is not so surprising that that decision revolved around the actions of my moral, ethical, truth-telling, affection-lavishing, semi-couch-potatoish best friend.

To begin to explain, we need to take a look at one area where people seem to hold their own, or at least can compete on the same field, with cats: courage.

Norton, not unlike most humans I have encountered, is an interesting combination of brave adventurer and wimpy coward. Plop my cat in a strange garden, yard, or even forest and he will immediately roar into action, fearlessly climbing trees, playfully slithering under bushes, joyously romping and running wherever his little gray legs will carry him. Put him down in a strange house or hotel room, and he will explore any and all nooks and crannies, generally making himself quite at home without any thought of potential danger—i.e., irate cleaning women, dizzying heights, or wobbly furniture that might not take kindly to an extra nine pounds of fur bouncing around on top of it. He is not afraid of Parisian rooftops or dark and mysterious ruins or airplanes or boats or even most dogs.

However. Two years ago, I replaced the pillows on my bed with nice, soft, down-filled ones. The night they arrived, Norton jumped up on the bed, ready for sleep, got set to nestle into his usual spot by my head, placed one tentative paw on the new pillow, and, to put it graciously, was off the bed so fast, running away from the terrifying pillow at such breakneck speed, that he made Lou Costello in *Abbott and Costello Meet Frankenstein*—and I'm talking the scene with the revolving bookshelves—look like Schwarzenegger in *T2*. It took him six months before he'd so much as *touch* a down pillow again! (Don't worry. For those of you who are already doubting my devotion, yes, I did put the old pillows back on the bed. I kept both sets handy at all times and arranged them so I could sleep on the new ones and Norton could sleep on the old ones.)

Janis—of whom much was spoken in the first book and of whom much more will be spoken in this sequel—and I recently bought a new couch for our Sag Harbor house. Only after the old couch was carried out and far removed from sight would Norton so much as step one gray and black ringed foot into the den. He had an absolute horror of that couch. He was too afraid even to *scratch* it. For those of you who are already wondering to what lengths I'll go to keep my cat happy, no, I *didn't* buy a new couch because Norton hated the old one. We got a new one because the old one was ugly, falling apart, and extremely uncomfortable. The fact that I let my cat live with something he didn't like is, however, totally out of character. In retrospect, I'm already feeling guilty and I just hope he settles in happily on the armrest of the new sofa or I'm sure I'll be furniture shopping before very long.

Janis also just bought a new blanket for our bed. A plain, simple, ordinary, purple, inanimate, wool blanket. There is nothing remotely threatening about this blanket—except to a particular Scottish Fold. To Norton, this blanket has much the same personality as Freddy Krueger in *Nightmare on Elm Street*. The first time Janis picked him up, put him on the bed, and, thus, on the dreaded blanket, Norton did a near-perfect Greg Louganis back flip onto the floor—I gave him a 9.7—and disappeared from sight for the rest of the day.

In addition to the odd piece of furniture and accompanying accoutrements, my dear cat also is terrified of bicycles, jackhammers, and birds. The first two I can sympathize with. Bicycles are ridden by careless humans and are more than capable of squashing a feline flat as a stepped-on morsel of Pounce, Norton's personal favorite between-meal snack.

And jackhammers are loud, earth-moving things and *should* be terrifying to anyone with any sense who's not named Rocco or Deke. The last one on the list, however, is a constant source of humiliation to all who know and love cat and cat owner.

This past autumn, while my round-headed pal and I were spending time in the south of France, I decided to show off *l'intelligence incroyable de mon chat.* We were going out to dinner with a friend and our car was parked several streets away from the house. I decided I'd bring Norton along to dinner—and I also decided I'd let him walk to the car with us. Our friend was a little dubious, especially because the town we were in was a French medieval mountain specialty with winding narrow streets and animals roaming freely wherever they chose to roam. But Norton came through with flying colors: striding boldly out the door, disdainfully ignoring all the dogs and cats frolicking around him, as well as all the kids kicking a soccer ball to and fro and all the adults briskly strolling around with their baguettes tucked under their arms. He followed at an acceptable pace along the cobblestones—until we came to a house, a mere ten feet away from our car, that had a bird cage hanging outside the window. Inside the cage were three tiny yellow birds, whistling and singing away. Norton, having braved all the tough obstacles in town, got within a foot of the cage, heard the birds merrily chirping, turned on his heels, and made a beeline for home, in the process breaking A. J. Foyt's land-speed record by a comfortable margin. I found him huddled pathetically by our doorway, trying his best to make himself invisible.

"They were *birds,*" I told him, shaking my head. "*Tiny* birds. *Really* tiny birds. In a *cage.* In a *locked* cage," I added, hoping to shame him.

It's very hard to argue with a cat, however, particularly a nervous cat, and clearly this cat had no intention of getting close to those tiny, caged birds again if he could help it. Which he could. So I picked him up and carried him all the way back to the car. When we passed those tiny little birds, Norton buried his head under my arm, doing his very best ostrich impersonation. Once we reached the safety of our red Citroën, he settled happily onto the backseat, and then, oblivious to the scorn with which he was greeted from his dinner companions, thoroughly enjoyed the rest of his evening on the town. There were no birds in the restaurant to disturb his meal.

While *les oiseaux* seem to be somewhat of an Achilles heel, Norton has a very wide macho streak as far as mice are concerned. This predatory instinct came as something of a shock to me when it finally surfaced. Norton and I had spent many years together without his ever exhibiting one iota of lionlike interest in chasing after big game. Then, one night, while I still had a summer house in the town of Fair Harbor, on Fire Island, the hunter was unleashed.

I was bacheloring it up this particular Saturday night with my friend Norm, the head writer of "Sesame Street" and, as chronicled in *The Cat Who Went to Paris,* legendary lady-killer of the Fair Harbor "sixishes." With us was my cousin Jon, an actor visiting from L.A. The three of us—the *four* of us, counting you-know-who—were having dinner, male-bonding, and basically having a terrific time, all the while wondering how soon we could ditch the other guys and go out and try to find a woman. As we were talking, I noticed that Jon had a big smile on his face and that he was focused on something a few feet from the dinner table.

"What are you looking at?" I wanted to know.

"Nothing," he said. "I'm just enjoying watching Norton play with his mouse toy."

I nodded, smiling at the thought and listening to Norton thrash around on the floor. And then the smile faded. Norm and I looked at each other, confused, and we both said, at the exact same time: "Norton doesn't *have* a mouse toy."

The ensuing action really should have been captured as an Impressionist painting with the title "Three Jews in the Country" because you haven't seen three fairly creaky guys move so quickly in your entire life. Jon, I believe, was standing on his chair. I'm pretty sure that I was all the way up on the table, saying something constructive like "Oh my god, I'm going to be sick!" Norm was the only one with the presence of mind to move for the broom. Using the straw end, he managed to maneuver the thrashing mouse away from Norton, who was playfully batting it around as if the room were one large knock-hockey board game. Clearly my cat did not realize that the small gray thing moving at the speed of light was a disgusting rodent to be feared and avoided at all costs. He didn't even think it was something to kill and eat for dessert. No, judging from this first close encounter of the mouse kind, Norton thought the squeaking, long-tailed prey was something to have fun with, not all that different from a catnip-stuffed beanbag.

Unfortunately for my dignity and sense of self-respect, at some point I had to climb down off the table and hold the door open while Norm swatted the mouse outside, *way* too close to my bare feet, which I pointed out to him later.

Once the creature was out of the house, we settled down and sanity reigned again. We all applauded Norton for his ability to spontaneously tap into his savage jungle instincts, and we all decided that perhaps city life was better for us humans than this dangerous living close to the ocean. More than anything, the three of us were happy we'd all struck out that weekend so that no one of the opposite sex had seen our rather tragic failure when confronted face to face with the wilds of nature. (In later retellings, the mouse became more of a rat—sometimes something closer to a small alligator—and I was the one with the broom, but I'm afraid Norm might read this, so I'd better stick to the sad truth.)

That was only the beginning, however, for Norton, so to speak, had tasted blood.

Fire Island was behind us, the charming country house in Sag Harbor was now before us, and I no longer had to worry about being humiliated in front of strange women because Janis was now a major part of the equation. I could simply worry about being humiliated in front of my very own girlfriend.

Not long after buying our house, I padded downstairs on a perfect autumn morn, went to the market to buy the papers, made a steaming pot of coffee, carried a mug of java into the safe, warm confines of the den, glanced down at the floor . . . and found a half-eaten, dead-as-a-doorknob mouse waiting for me in the middle of the room.

My very own cat had done this. The cat whom I often (probably too often) kissed right smack dab on the lips. The cat who was quite probably the sweetest, gentlest animal in existence. My genius, world-traveling cat had bitten a mouse right in half and left him as a little present for his dad.

I have to admit that, once I got over my immediate sense of revulsion, my chest puffed out a bit with pride. Okay, so birds were scary—but no three-inch-long cheese eater could push *my* cat around.

The only problem left to solve was how to actually dispose of the body. Norton, by this time, was hovering outside the den, waiting for praise for his newfound role as protector of the household. I indulged him in this, picking him up and petting him profusely, marveling at his courage and physical prowess. Unfortunately, Janis was also hovering around, demanding that I get rid of the corpse immediately.

You may have picked up on the fact that I'm a tad squeamish when it comes to things like dead mice (for the record, also when it comes to live snakes and any bugs larger than a quarter). But, since my cat had moved up to a new level of macho-hood, I was determined to do the same. And despite what Janis would tell you now if you could talk to her directly, I did a very solid and impressive job of mouse removal. It just took me a while, that's all. Like about two hours, because every time I worked up the nerve to try to scoop the repulsive little pile onto the dustpan, I'd get dizzy and go into the kitchen (where Janis, I might add, was safely sequestered!) and take half an hour to get myself back together.

After that first kill, however, the routine got a little easier for all of us. I don't want anyone to get the impression that our house is a mini-version of *Willard* and that thousands of mice roam around freely, rearranging the furniture and making crank phone calls in the middle of the night, but once or twice a year we do have a little critter who decides to explore under the sink or behind the refrigerator. And once or twice a year, Norton goes into action. For a cat whose favorite hobby, as he gets a little older, is to sit absolutely motionless for as long as possible, it is a wonder to behold when Norton's mouse antenna goes up. He will sit, poised to strike, staring at a crack under the fridge, as lithe and graceful as any tai chi master. Suddenly, an object will dart out, so fast it's almost impossible to see, except Norton will not only see him, he'll dart even faster. And before you know it, a victorious Norton will be parading into the living room with a conquered mouse firmly clenched between his teeth. One small step for felinehood, one giant step for a mouse-free home.

I can deal with this sort of disruption much better now. Practice does indeed make perfect. No longer do I freeze at the thought of placing another body into the mouse morgue. No longer does some late, lamented Mickey Doe have to sit in the middle of the floor for hours while I stop my stomach from doing flip-flops. Nope. Now I've got things under control. Either I call my friend David Meves, who lives a couple of blocks away and, as near as I can tell, has no fear of man *or* mouse, or I have David's wife, Peggy, do it.

But I don't discuss Norton's heroics just to show off the fact that, when push comes to shove, my little cat can hold his own in time of macho crisis. I don't want him to turn into a feline Mike Tyson or Stormin' Norman Schwarzkopf. I bring it up because Norton's sense of adventure and general fearlessness had a somewhat larger effect on me and my life than simply getting me to toss out my mousetraps. Last year, I was faced with the major, life-changing decision I hinted about earlier and, as with all life-changing decisions I'd made over the past eight years, Norton was a crucial and essential part of the process.

This particular process began when I was invited to go to the Super Bowl.

I'm your basic sports fanatic, although much less so as I've gotten older, as athletes have gotten greedier, and team owners have gotten stupider. I've been to World Series games and NBA All-Star games and French Open tennis

matches, but I'd never been to a Super Bowl, much less a
Super Bowl in which my beloved Giants were playing. The
thought of seeing L.T. leaping tall AFCers in a single bound
was too good an opportunity to pass up, especially since the
people who'd done the inviting were the NFL, which meant
seeing him leap from fifty-yard-line seats.

Even Janis, who would normally prefer something pleasant and relaxing—like 'walking across hot coals or discussing the right-to-life issue with Rush Limbaugh—to attending a sports event, decided she couldn't pass up a Super
Bowl. So we made our arrangements. A flight into Tampa.
A room at the Dolphin Hotel in Orlando. Dinner with
a honcho from NFL Properties. A cat who was a big
Giants fan.

Norton had, by this time in his life, traveled extensively
all over Europe and America. But even for him, Super Bowl
weekend was something extraordinary.

First of all, the Dolphin Hotel is part of Disney World.
As we were checking in, we were greeted by a bevy of very
friendly six-foot-high, three-fingered mice dancing and
prancing around the lobby, waving at anyone who'd look
at them. For a human being, this is a rather disorienting
sight; I can't *imagine* what could have been running through
the brain of a reasonably sophisticated Scottish Fold. The
prospect of biting one of these suckers in half and leaving
him in the den for Dad to clean up must have been incredibly intimidating. Luckily, as I signed us into our room,
Norton restrained himself admirably and settled for sticking his head out of his shoulder bag and swiveling his neck
in every which direction, awestruck as he peered around
the lobby.

When we went out for a stroll to take in the sights—

neither Janis nor Norton had ever been to Orlando before—the atmosphere was no less circuslike. Not only did my cat get a look at thousands of people from all over the country, drinking up a storm and determined to have as wild a weekend as possible, he saw screaming vendors hawking T-shirts and team sweat suits, screaming kids dragging their screaming parents across the street to Disney World, and screaming NFL marketing men trying to stop everybody else from screaming so they could scream louder about their thrice-too-expensive wares. In addition to the giant mice, Norton also got a very good gander at Goofy and Donald, up close and personal, as well as all the real-life (and sculptures of) fish, which were everywhere you looked in the hotel (the designers obviously felt a compunction to create an artistic theme worthy of the hotel's name).

After two days of hectic touristing and socializing, Norton, Janis, and I had a quiet few moments in our room before we were to join all the screaming people on the bus that was to take us to the game.

"Are you glad you came?" I asked Janis, figuring that with only the upcoming game left on our weekend agenda, it would all be downhill from here.

"Sort of," she grudgingly said. "Although I still say it was Goofy who pinched me at that party last night."

"How about you?" I said to my cat. In response, Norton sprawled out on the bed and turned over on his back, his subtle way of telling me he was both tired and wanted his belly scratched.

"What must it be like for him?" I asked Janis. "Giant mice. Lunatic football fans. Kids with buffaloes painted on their chests. For us this is just a weird and fun weekend. For Norton, this must be like going to *Mars.*"

As we talked, I started to obsess more and more about the level of high adventure Norton had reached that weekend. Sure, he'd enjoyed the café life in Paris, liked sunning himself on Florida beaches, even got used to cross-country skiing in Vermont. But this weekend, this was something he'd never come close to seeing or doing before.

"For *real*," I said, half to Janis, half to myself. "I'm kind of jealous. *Nothing* we do could possibly be as strange and exciting and out of the ordinary as what this cat's doing."

Janis knows enough not to encourage me when I start trying to delve into the mind of my cat (or my own mind, for that matter). So she kept quiet and let me go on.

"It's depressing, is what it is," I began to rant. "We're people, he's a cat! We can't let him lead a better life than we're leading!"

"He leads a better life than anyone else in the whole *world* is leading," Janis pointed out.

"That's beside the point," I came back with. "He deserves it. And I'm not talking about Norton in particular. I'm talking philosophically."

Resigned now, Janis sighed and asked me what I was really getting at.

"Norton's life is exciting. He hunts. He prowls. He goes to Mars. Our life is dull. We go to work, we watch TV. We're stuck in a routine. I want my life to be as adventurous as my cat's!"

"Okay," Janis said, doing her best to humor me. "What exactly do you want to do about it?"

To her credit, when I told her, she didn't gasp, shriek, or faint. What she did was ask me if I was serious, and when I said I was, she said, "Okay."

I decided I wanted us to do something as adventurous as Norton coming to the Mars Super Bowl. So we did.

Which is how I came to quit my very good job, leave my very nice apartment, pack up my entire very nice life, and, with my very understanding girlfriend and my role model of a cat, move to the south of France.

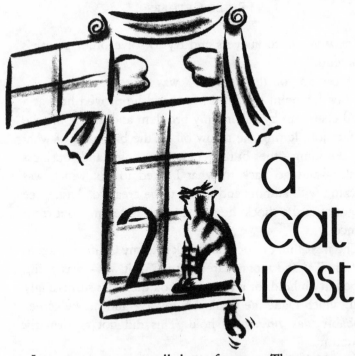

a cat lost

It was not as easy as all that, of course. There were minor odds and ends and major life changes to take care of before the three of us could charge ahead to new glory in the old world.

The first thing we had to consider were our jobs. Janis, who had worked since she was fourteen years old and was something of a workaholic (and a very successful workaholic), arranged for a year's sabbatical from her job in publishing. With that load off her shoulders, she began worrying about a new load: What the hell would she actually *do* for a whole year?

I, as usual, was worried about having *too* much to do. I took care of part of that by resigning as publisher of the company I ran. The chairman of the board I resigned to was quite understanding.

"I no longer get to do what I like," I told him. "All I

do now is talk to lawyers and try to solve other people's problems."

"How do you think *I* feel?" was his response.

I saw his point but I held fast, and he proved he was a good chairman by solving my problem and giving me the perfect job, letting me throw off all the bad parts of what I was doing—the bureaucratic tanglings and business hassles—and go back to what I liked to do, which was working with authors and trying to be creative. And, once he got over the shock, he even agreed to let me do it from France.

The next thing to do was break it to my California agent that my TV and movie career—such as it was—was going to be put on hold for a year. He took the news surprisingly well, which made me think that my TV and movie career probably was *already* on hold. This did not particularly sadden me.

One of the reasons I was able to pack it all in for a while was that my partner, David Handler, and I had been hired to write and produce a TV series that year. It had started out with great promise: a decent premise for the show, a pleasant enough staff of writers, and a terrific cast, TV stars who were actually good actors. The first day the writing staff got together, David and I had visions of a Cosby-like syndication check one day making its way into our dwindling bank accounts.

As is usually the case when one gets one's hopes up in show business, it was not to be.

One of the most amazing things about the television business is the way people delude themselves (which is probably why those delusionless creatures, cats, have never made their mark in TV). People who create shows like "My Mother the Car" and "Pink Lady and Jeff" can't live with themselves if they actually face up to what they're promulgating on society, so they convince themselves that they're really doing Neil Simon. People who do the *good* stuff on TV—shows like "Cheers" and "Taxi" and "Hill Street Blues"—start to think they're Arthur Miller. There's a famous story about a well-known TV producer who had just produced one of the great disasters of a particular season. Not only was the show ridiculed for its shockingly low quality, it was canceled after one episode (which is the only thing people in TV are *really* sensitive to being ridiculed about). After the cancellation notice came, the producer started ranting and raving to his partner. "The problem was, we were ahead of our time," he insisted. "The show was too good! The American public wasn't ready for it!" His partner let him carry on for as long as he could stand it, then finally interrupted with these immortal words of a rare television realist: "You know, you're right," he said. "We *were* ahead of our time. The American public just wasn't ready for total shit."

Needless to say, the partnership broke up.

Unfortunately for us, however, we had one of those I'm-a-Genius mentalities running the show David and I had signed on for. He opened one of our first story conferences by telling us he thought that a good sitcom script was as good as the best poetry. Great. He didn't just think he was Neil Simon or Arthur Miller. We had a producer/director who thought he was W. B. Yeats. Maybe we could do a show called "I Love Leda and the Swan" or a "Gilligan's Island Sails to Byzantium" reunion special.

We knew we were in trouble when, during the course of writing the first thirteen episodes and shaping the show, people all around us started to get fired. The co-executive producer was the first to go. Then a couple of writers fell by the wayside (including one who, after we'd had a discussion about a zany episode that would center around a botched surprise party, said, "This show has the potential to be so Chekhovian"). New writers were hired and then they, too, were fired (one was hired to be a consultant, came in for one meeting, argued with the boss, and was immediately fired. Actually, not so immediately that he wasn't given a large check to keep him happy. This made the other writers, who were working hard but weren't getting large checks, somewhat cranky). Then, as if things weren't bad enough, we got a close-up gander at the female star, who was, according to the premise of the show, supposed to be gorgeous, sexy, and irresistible. Unfortunately, the only person she could have possibly been irresistible to would have been Dumbo because our star had gained a good thirty pounds since her glory days.

Things went downhill from there. But we knew we were in *serious* trouble after we saw what happened to our first script. David and I tend to take the realistic approach. We were aware we weren't on the Preston Sturges level with our contributions to the show, but we were confident that our forty-four-page work was extremely funny. And while it may not have been Yeats (or even Ogden Nash), it was, we knew, coherent. However, when we were given a cassette to watch after the filming and editing, we were a tad surprised to find that not only were all our jokes cut out, the show made no sense. None. I'm talking total gibberish. Our nemesis had managed to rewrite it and then cut it so any stranger watching it would have absolutely no idea what it was about. Plus, what was supposed to be a lighthearted contemporary comedy now had all the wit and style of one of Eva Braun's home movies. To top it all off, *our* names were plastered all over the credits.

Here's how bad it was: Norton, who liked hanging around the set, had, midway through our viewing of the show's first act, gone and hid in the office's heating duct. He decided that crawling around in old, rusty pipes was a lot more fun than watching his dad's career die a slow and painful death.

As soon as the tape finished rolling, the door to our office was thrown open and it was the producer/director, the man responsible for this entire nightmare.

"I think it's the most brilliant thing I've ever done," he announced.

We said nothing.

"I think it may be the greatest show in the history of television," he now proclaimed. I'm not kidding. He really said that.

We still said nothing. If ever the phrase "Silence is golden" had meaning, this was the time, but we knew that at some point we'd have to work up our courage and speak. The psycho in our office decided there was no time like the present.

"Didn't *you* think it was *great?*" he demanded.

"Well," we both hemmed and hawed, "we thought it was very good. But we think there might be room for improvement. Maybe we can give you a few notes."

"I don't *take* notes on something that's *perfect!*" he told us. He didn't actually say the words "you barbarian ignoramuses" out loud, but his tone made it quite clear that the phrase should have been tacked on to the end of his sentence. Then he slammed the door on his way out, leaving us to realize that we were working for a lunatic and we could forget about making enough money from this series to buy a small, private island in the Caribbean.

David and I lasted for three more painful months before

our greed finally gave way to our self-respect and we quit. The only satisfying thing was that the show folded immediately after we did.

I had learned a couple of valuable lessons, though, which I promise never to forget. One is that I will never again work with people who don't believe that something they do can ever be improved upon in some way, shape, or form. That attitude is the antithesis of all creativity. The second thing I learned is that I will never again doubt my cat's taste. The next time he walks out of a show, so do I.

Free at last, I was in relatively good shape for a change of life. Janis was all set, too. Only Norton now had to be dealt with.

Two things were stopping us from leaving immediately. The first was probably the worst and scariest day of my life: the day Norton ran away and got lost in New York City.

The trauma started simply enough. Janis and I made plans to take a short trip—a trip *without* Norton. This is not something I'm usually wont to do, but my back was to the wall. Janis comes from the South, her family's still down there, she still has enough Southern lilt in her voice to sound as if she could have Stanley Kowalski as a brother-in-law, and, to top it all off, her father had a big birthday coming up—so she decided that we had to venture south of New Jersey for a week before we blew off the United States for good. We decided to fly to Memphis, then spend a week driving further down, through Mississippi to New Orleans. This was not a trip Norton could make. He could happily live with the several hours we'd spend every day in the car; I knew he wouldn't mind moving to a new hotel every night; and I was fairly sure he'd like to discover real Southern barbecue. But it simply wasn't practical. When traveling in Europe, he was used to being greeted with open arms by both restaurants and hotels. On the road in America, however, he couldn't eat out with us and we couldn't be sure that any of the hotels we'd find would take him. I had a crucial decision to make. On the one hand I could leave Norton for seven days with his usual cat-sitter, Lynn Waggoner, his favorite nonimmediate family member in the world. On the other hand, I could try being in the car with Janis on a rainy night in the backwoods of Mississippi trying to explain to her that the hotel we'd been lucky enough to find wouldn't let us in because they didn't take cats. I decided I'd rather face Norton's disappointment than Janis's wrath.

Naturally, I made the wrong choice.

We did nothing different to prepare for this excursion, so don't ask me how my cat could possibly know that he wasn't coming along on the trip—but he definitely, unequivocally, one hundred percent, absolutely knew. A couple of days before we were to leave, I noticed that he seemed to be sulking. Whenever I say things like, "I think Norton's upset because he's not coming on our trip" to Janis, she tries to get me to see a good psychiatrist, so I usually keep such thoughts to myself. This time was no different—I kept quiet. But he was definitely out of sorts.

Janis was going to Memphis on a Friday. That was also my final day in the office, the day of the big farewell party, so I was going to stick around and meet up with her on Saturday. I was also having dinner that night with one of the Random House bigwigs, the nephew of the company's owner. All in all, it seemed worth sticking around for.

We—Janis, Norton, and I—spent Thursday night at Janis's apartment. I woke up bright and early Friday morn, fed Norton his breakfast, then went in to take a shower. When I came out, I got dressed, kissed my still-sleeping girlfriend on the top of the head, and went to gather up my cat to take him to the office. When the company told me they were going to throw me a farewell party, they made it fairly clear that they wanted the chance to say farewell to Norton as well.

I called him, waiting for him to come as usual, but there was no response. I waited patiently—still nothing. I began poking around in some of his usual resting places—but no Scottish Fold anywhere. I then spent twenty minutes looking through Janis's apartment and could find no trace of Norton. Annoyed—what a time for him to decide to act like a regular cat—I went in, woke Janis up, and told her I was going to leave Norton behind.

"He's hiding," I said. "I'm sure he'll come out as soon as I leave. Have a good flight and I'll just come back and pick him up after work. See you tomorrow."

And off I went.

At noon Janis called my office.

"I'm leaving for the airport," she told me. "Norton still hasn't come out. I don't know if he's still in the apartment."

"Of *course* he's still in the apartment," I told her, a little annoyed. "Where could he have gone?"

"I don't know," she admitted. "I can't figure out any way he could have gotten out, but I really looked for him. And I don't think he's here."

"He's just being a cat," I said confidently. "Cats hide all the time. We're just not used to *Norton* doing it. He'll be waiting for me when I come to get him."

She acknowledged that I knew my cat better than she did and went off to Memphis. I stuck around, ate some cake and drank some wine at the farewell party, then around four in the afternoon I went back to Janis's to pick up what I was sure would be a repentant Norton.

When I walked in the front door I called his name. Silence. I tried again, gently cooing for him. Zilch. For the first time since cat and I had joined our lives together, I got a nervous flutter in my stomach.

I began to *really* search the apartment.

I looked in the closets. I took things out of the closets. I stood on chairs and peered into corners of the highest bookshelves. I crawled under beds. Gently calling Norton's name every few seconds.

No cat.

Now, I am a reasonably mature person. I have had my share of traumatic experiences and emergencies and have handled them all with, I like to think, a certain amount of grace and strength. I'm not prone to overreaction, panic, or hysteria. But, at the moment I decided that my nine-pound, extremely trusting, wonderfully sweet, and extremely protected cat was outside, loose on the mean streets of New York City, I overreacted, panicked, and became completely hysterical. To make matters worse, the weather immediately turned hurricanelike: Gusts of wind, explosions of thunder, flashes of lightning, and sheets of rain took over the city. As I pictured little Norton outside in all that, I lost whatever inner fortitude I'd ever pretended to have and simply began blubbering pathetically.

The first thing I did was call my friends Kathleen and Dominick. Kathleen is one of my very closest pals and would do anything for me. Dominick speaks with a British accent, so I knew he wouldn't go emotional on me and would keep his head. Through pathetic gasps and strangled sobs, I managed to spell out the problem. Half an hour later, they were down at Janis's apartment, helping me rip the place apart.

"Norton is *definitely* here," Dominick said. "There is no question about it."

His confidence buoyed my spirits a little, but the buoy sank fairly quickly as we kept searching the place to no avail.

We moved couches. We took every single item out of Janis's closets. We lifted radiator covers and floorboards, shifted large, unbelievably heavy kitchen appliances, and called Norton's name as calmly as we could—but there was no sign of him whatsoever. That was when I spied the open window.

You must understand something: We kept the windows closed, except for a crack, whenever Norton was staying in that apartment. But as my eyes were scanning every inch of the place, desperate for any sign of feline life, I spotted a living room window that was open at most three inches— and open from the top, perhaps twelve feet off the ground. It would have been a herculean feat, involving a jump to a chair, another jump to the top of a bookshelf, then an incredibly difficult leap up to and through a three-inch-wide crack—but I was convinced that it was through that crack Norton had disappeared. No matter that the trip down would have been even more difficult—either a tough jump up to the roof and then on to who knows where or a very difficult shinny down the front of the building to the street. I was positive I'd discovered the escape route. So we went in search of the escapee.

We immediately began a tour of the Soho neighborhood, in weather that now seemed to be a full-fledged tornado.

The three of us went to every store within two blocks of the apartment and asked if they'd seen a small, gray, wet cat with folded ears. No one had seen anything except three drenched, crazy-looking people in search of a lost feline.

We then scoured every nook and cranny and back alleyway within the same two-block range, screaming out Norton's name whenever we saw a potential hiding place for a wayward cat. But no wayward cat appeared (and the only positive that came out of this exercise is that I learned Linda Winer's Cat Law #3. Linda Winer is a columnist for *Newsday* and friend of mine who, at various points in her life, has owned several dozen cats, including one named Ishkabibble. Linda's Cat Law #3 is a simple one, written in stone after Ishkabibble disappeared one day and Linda had to search high and low for him all over her neighborhood: Never Name Your Cat Something You Are Ashamed to Yell Out Loud at the Top of Your Lungs).

We split up at this point, having failed to find Norton close to home. Dominick and Kathleen broadened our horizon, moving several blocks farther away, still checking for any buildings and alleys that might look inviting, warm, and dry to a frightened cat. My assignment was to get Janis's landlady to take me into their backyard. They had a decent-sized garden and patio, with a garage/workshop. It was reasonably familiar territory, I realized. Norton might have fled there figuring I'd be able to find him eventually. I was just hoping-beyond-hope that he'd figured right.

Janis's landlady wasn't home yet, but the landlady's mother, who also lives in the building, was. She was kind enough to use her key to let me back. Unfortunately, she also decided to accompany me.

She's a terrific woman, Mrs. Flaymen, but she's also eighty years old and has a slight hearing problem—as in, she can't hear anything anyone says. It's difficult to stress exactly how upset I was; just accept the fact that I was bordering on irrational behavior. So I was not at my best for the conversation that transpired in the pouring rain, in the nooks and crannies of Mrs. Flaymen's backyard.

"Ohhhh, the poor cat," she began.

I didn't want to hear about the poor cat. I wanted to hear

that he was dry and safe. So I acknowledged her despair only with a grim nod.

"How old is he?" she wanted to know.

"Eight years old," I told her.

"Four weeks old!" she screeched. "Oh my God!"

"Eight *years,*" I said again. "He's *eight!*"

"How could you let a four-week-old kitten outside?! And in weather like this!"

Normally, I would find this kind of inane miscommunication fairly funny. Perhaps even hilarious. However, in the midst of my desperate search, I had, possibly for the first time in my life, completely lost my sense of humor. So I did my best to ignore her and started looking through the garden.

"What's his name?" she asked me as I prowled.

"Norton," I muttered.

"Morris?!" she said.

"Norton!" I told her. *"Not Morris! Norton!"*

"Morris!" she began to call. "Come here, Morris!"

"Norton," I growled. "His name's Norton!"

"Morris!" she kept shouting. And then she started muttering about how stupid I was to let a one-week-old kitten outside in a hurricane.

"His name's not Morris!" I finally screamed. "His name's Norton! And he's not one week old! He's not even four weeks old! He's eight!"

"One week, four weeks, eight weeks," she said. "What's the difference?"

"Eight *years!*" I yelled as loud as I could yell. "Eight years!!!!"

"I don't think it makes a difference," she said with a shrug. "I'm sure he's dead."

I'll skip the rest of the conversation, as well as any de-

tailed description of the veins bulging in my neck, and just
say that my scrupulous search of the back of the apartment
house was as fruitful as the searching I'd done up till then.
There was nary a sign of my beloved cat.

I met Kathleen and Dominick back at the apartment at
the appointed time. They were as wet as I was and had also
had the same rotten luck. I called the number where Janis
was staying in Memphis and left the following message on
her friend's phone machine, in a monotone that could,
putting the most positive possible spin on it, only be described as zombielike: "Hi. It's me. Still no sign. He's gone.
I don't know what to do. I'm not coming tomorrow. I have
to wait here until he shows up." I don't think I was even
able to say good-bye. I just choked my message off in mid-
sob and hung up. That was the fourth or fifth such message
I'd left for her.

By this time, the entire block was involved in the search.
Janis's landlady, Sylvia, had come home, heard the frantic
activity, and learned what had happened. She started calling
all her neighbors and pretty soon everybody was calling
everybody else, seeing if anyone had seen a lost cat with
strange ears. One kindly person called Janis's apartment and
told me that she had definitely seen Norton. But, as I
probed a bit, it turned out that she'd spotted a stray cat in
her yard the day before. Sorrowfully, I explained that Norton had only gotten out that very morning, and that it was
some other miserable person who'd be searching for yester-
day's stray.

It was now seven-thirty at night, so in addition to the
storm, it was getting quite dark. It was also time for my
dinner with Mr. Random House. There was nothing I could
do for Norton—not at this point—so I did my best to look
presentable and went off to the restaurant. I decided I'd

return to Janis's after dinner and spend the whole rest of the
night waiting and/or searching.

The dinner was a disaster from start to finish. I'd be asked
a question along the lines of, "Well, what kind of direction
do you foresee for the company over the next few years?"
and I'd come back with a morose reply along the lines of,
"Huh?" Then I'd stare vacantly at the wall for five minutes,
the silence being broken only by my long and loud sighs.
We made it through the salad and main course and on to
the dessert in a leisurely twenty minutes or so. I had no
appetite and my total depression put an obvious pall on the
executive's appetite. I think it also put the same pall on his
opinion of me, but what could I do? As far as I was concerned, life as I knew it was over.

As we were waiting for the check to arrive, the waitress
came over to our table and said to me, "Excuse me, but are
you Mr. Gethers?" When I told her I was, she let me know
that there was a phone call for me.

The call was from Janis and it was the most wonderful call
I'd ever received in my life.

"You're not going to believe it," she began, "but go to
my apartment immediately. Norton's waiting for you in the
living room."

I let out a very loud yelp, tried to calm myself down since
I was in public, then said the hell with it and let out another
yelp, louder than the first. I pleaded with Janis to tell me
how this miracle had occurred.

"I told you you're not going to believe it," she said, and
then proceeded to relate the entire story: After landing at
the airport and going straight out to dinner, she'd finally
gotten to her friends' house in Memphis, where she found
my many suicidal-sounding phone-machine messages wait-

ing for her. Not knowing what else to do, she called her landlady and asked her to send her husband up onto the roof in one last desperate attempt to find the cat. According to the landlady, her husband's not unwarranted response was, "What are you, out of your mind?!" and her response to that was a slow, quiet, and obviously quite effective: "Get . . . out . . . on . . . the . . . fucking . . . roof. *Now.*"

She then went up the two flights to Janis's apartment, figuring that if Norton was indeed up on the roof, he would be so petrified and hard to handle that her husband would need someone to hand him to, through the window. She turned the key to the front door, stepped inside . . . and sitting in the foyer, curled up in a calm, peaceful, untraumatized, toasty-warm ball, was none other than Norton the cat.

Stunned, she ran to the phone and called Janis in Memphis, who immediately called me at the restaurant. I hung up the restaurant phone, told my confused dinner partner—who'd clearly crossed my name off his list marked "People with a Future to Whom I Might Pay Lots of Money Someday"—that life was good again, then I raced back to Janis's in a cab, taking the three flights up to the apartment two stairs at a time. By the time I got there, Sylvia had put Norton in one of the apartment's two bedrooms, closing the door behind him so he couldn't possibly get out and hide again. When I inched the door open—still not believing the little guy was really there—I found Norton sound asleep on the bed in his usual position: head on the pillow, body tucked under the blanket. When I stepped inside, he opened one eye and began purring.

I gently walked over, picked him up, and began a rather lengthy petting, scratching, cooing, and kissing process. When both of us had had enough of that, I called Janis.

"He's actually here," I told her. For the first time in fourteen hours, my voice didn't have that despairing rasp to it.

"And he'd *never* been outside?" she asked, incredulous.

"Nope. He's as dry and happy as could be."

"Then where was he?" she wanted to know—the first of several million times we asked ourselves that question.

We never found out where he was. We did eventually figure out that this day-long hide-and-seek experience was Norton's little way of letting us know he didn't like being left behind for a week while his parents went off on a fun vacation (and, believe me, now Janis accepts it as gospel when I tell her that Norton's looking a little subdued—she instantly goes through her apartment, closing the door to every room). But, more immediately, as we spoke on the phone, as I did everything but collapse in relief and exhaustion, Janis got angry. In her own way, she'd been as unnerved by the experience as I'd been, and she had the same feeling, I imagine, one has when a child falls off a high swing yet doesn't hurt himself. At first you're so relieved he's okay, you'll do anything to make him happy. Then, when the scare's over, you want to kill him for putting himself—and you—through the trauma.

"Don't let him get away with this," Janis told me. "I don't think you should feed him tonight."

"You're right," I agreed, nodding vigorously. "I definitely won't feed him."

"And don't pet him and kiss him and tell him that everything's okay," she ordered.

"Absolutely not," I said. "I'd never do that. I'll be strict and firm."

"Yeah," she said dubiously.

"Yeah!" I said strictly and firmly, if a bit guiltily.

"I'll see you tomorrow," she said, unconvinced. "And I'm glad your stupid cat's okay."

"Thank you. I'll tell him."

"And don't feed him. I *mean* it. It's for his own good."

"As of now," I insisted, "he's on bread and water. Think of me as George Kennedy in *Lonely Are the Brave.*"

When I start making movie references that she doesn't get, Janis usually figures it's time to hang up. I knew, at that very moment, before the phone even clicked down into the cradle in Memphis, she was turning to her friends and telling them there was no way I wasn't going to cave in. I could tell she thought I'd be feeding and petting my cat within seconds. But I was determined to toe the line. Tough love was my new motto for the evening.

Unfortunately for my new motto, it's almost impossible to resist a meowing Scottish Fold. Especially one of his special "I'm hungry" meows.

"No dinner for you," I told him as definitively as I was able. "*You* are being punished. And that is *all* there is to it." I figured he might be intimidated by my refusal to use contractions, but no such luck.

He meowed again. I thought of the anxiety and horror he'd put me through all day long. I remembered how I'd felt trying to imagine him wandering the streets of New York City, wet, lonely, frightened. I remembered my vision of seeing Norton's picture on the side of a milk carton, with the phrase "Have you seen this cat?" All of seven seconds had passed since I'd gotten off the phone with Janis.

"Well, maybe just a snack," I allowed, and instantly opened up a can of his favorite food, scooped it into his bowl, and set it down in front of him. Grateful, Norton munched until satisfied. Then he came over and tried to get back on my good side, once and for all. The first thing he did was look me straight in the eye and start purring.

"No way," I announced. "I was given explicit instructions not to be nice to you. I can't let you starve to death, but I don't have to be friendly."

He jumped up onto the bed, looking shaken and, if truth be told, extremely pathetic. This may have been the first experience of rejection in his life. I reached out and stroked his head in a moment of forgetfulness. Norton immediately took the reassuring gesture as a sign of capitulation and he went in for the kill, rubbing his nose firmly up against my cheek, something I'm usually a sucker for. But not this time.

"Uh-uh," I told him, drawing back. "I am *not* weakening."

He now began rubbing himself against my leg.

"It's for your own good," I tried to explain. It had sounded so convincing when Janis said it.

The purring grew louder, the look in his eye more tender. My resolve, I do have to admit, was weakening rather quickly. After several minutes, when he turned over on his back and wiggled his paws around in the air, my resolve was about as firm as my backbone—which was clearly the consistency of mush.

"All right," I sighed. "C'mere."

That was it. I was a goner. Discipline was thrown out the window and I was on all fours, petting and scratching and telling him that everything was fine, I really didn't mind that he'd put me through the worst day of my life, just as long as he was okay.

This went on for quite a long time—until he was sure I'd forgiven him completely and until I was sure he understood that this hiding business was not something to be repeated in the future.

Peace made at long last, I went into the kitchen and poured myself a well-deserved beer. Then I came back to my cat and spoke two more sentences.

"Don't tell Janis," was the first thing I instructed. After all, there was no real need for her to know the extent of my wimpiness. Luckily, from the look in Norton's eye, I knew my secret soft side was safe with him. I took another long swig of beer. "And where *were* you?" was the second thing I said, very quietly.

But this time Norton only turned his head to avoid my stare. After a few moments, he glanced back at me, quietly closed his eyes, and went straight to sleep.

There are certain secrets a cat just won't share, I suppose, not even with his best friend.

a cat on tour

We made the decision to rent a house in Provence.

There was no particular reason for this, although we did have a certain guiding logic. We wanted to be in the country, not in a city. We didn't want to go *too* exotic since I needed to be somewhere I could get a fax machine repaired at the drop of a hat. Janis wanted warm, or reasonably warm. We wanted good food and we wanted someplace beautiful. This narrowed it down to approximately half the globe, then we got serious and started picking, choosing, and eliminating.

First we ruled out any countries with whom we didn't share an alphabet. Then we crossed off anyplace that might be under attack from Scud missiles. Next we eliminated any country that ate cats. Pretty soon, and without too much difficulty, we boiled things down to Italy and France. We winnowed out a few regions in both of those countries— Sicily was a possibility but I decided I wasn't in the mood to get blown to smithereens in my car; Burgundy was a very real consideration until Janis got it in her head that the weather was exactly like England and thus she'd be cold and damp all the time. Picture the creature in the Schwarzenegger film *Predator* and you've pretty much got Janis's personality if she was cold and damp all the time. Soon we were down to Tuscany and Provence. We compared wines and cheeses, we looked at the dollar against the lira and the franc, we did everything you were supposed to do, and then we made our decision based on one key factor: We didn't speak a word of Italian and we did speak a tiny bit of French. So we settled on Provence.

A couple of years before, while I was working with Roman Polanski on a screenplay, Norton and I'd lived in Paris for three months. Almost every night, Roman and I would go out to dinner, usually with friends of his. Roman had friends who were Italian, Polish, French, Russian, you name it. So during our meals, someone would say something in French, someone would answer in Polish, someone would then respond to that in Italian or Danish or Upper Slobovian. Every fifteen minutes or so, Roman would interrupt protectively and say, "Come on, fellows, speak English for Peter" (translation: "Come on, you guys, we've got a cretinous American here, so say something he can understand"). Rarely had I felt so inept, so when I returned to New York I was determined to learn at least one other language.

I'd had two years of high-school French, but that was so long ago I could really only remember the bare essentials. I could conjugate the verbs *aller, avoir,* and *être;* I could ask for the location of the nearest apothecary; and if someone served me the proper vegetable, I could show my appreciation by saying, *"Bravo! Des asperges!"* Braced by such a substantial background, I began taking French lessons from a rather eccentric woman who lived on the Upper East Side and who had, in a one-room apartment, six birds (including a blind pigeon she'd found in the park), one dog, three cats, and several mice (I *think* the mice were pets, though I wouldn't swear to it). She also liked to keep the room temperature somewhere near a hundred and forty degrees at all times. But I slogged through my lessons and, when the time came to *choisir un pays* (don't applaud, really), I thought my French might come in handy.

Once we'd settled on Provence, the next step was finding a house. This was something I had absolutely no concept of how to do, but I made a decent stab at it. I called the French embassy. They sent me to a French realtor with an American outlet. They in turn sent me to some company that mailed me a videotape showing all sorts of *châteaux* for sale for a mere three million dollars. I even called a realtor in France who told me that what I was looking for didn't exist and that I should stop bothering her.

Eventually, we found a house through friends of friends of friends. It sounds farfetched, but that is the absolute best way to find something. Just start telling everybody you know that you want to rent a place in the south of France. Someone is bound to say, "Oh, Fred did that two years ago. Got a great farmhouse in the country—and boy, was it cheap." It may not be in Provence—but, hey, the Dordogne ain't Pittsburgh—and the odds are that Fred's farmhouse has tripled in price since then, but it's also probable that Fred learned about other places while over there or knows somebody who knows somebody who knows somebody else who has a house for rent.

When word got out that we were looking to shove off, I got a call from a writer friend of mine. His wife was friendly with someone who lived in Paris who had a *deux-ième maison* in Provence that they sometimes rented. I called the people in Paris, who told me that they were no longer renting their place out. But—and this is key; this is why it pays to talk to anyone, anytime—they loved where they lived and were very happy to find someone who also wanted to live there. So, trying to see if they could help me in some way, they asked me what I was looking for. I told them: I wanted a three- or four-bedroom house in the Lub-éron. I wanted old, I wanted charming, and I wanted a garden. I also wanted something that was in a small village rather than in the middle of the countryside (Janis didn't want to feel too isolated). And we wanted something that had a few conveniences—a dishwasher and a washer-dryer would be nice—but that wasn't so modernized and Ameri-canized that we'd feel we were renting a condo in Atlantic City. In other words, I wanted perfect. And not incredibly expensive.

Much to my surprise, they didn't tell me to rent myself a nice little room in an insane asylum, they told me they thought they could help. They had a friend who had exactly what we were looking for. They'd mention our search to her—and if she was interested, she'd get back to me.

The next day, I received an eight-page fax from a woman named Elisabeth, who turned out to not only have the perfect house but who was a classy, honorable, and gener-ally wonderful person. Her fax described the house in great detail—it was three hundred years old, stone, four bed-rooms plus an office, and it had a football-field-sized garden. It also had a dishwasher, a washer-dryer, and a BMW which we were welcome to use. She was French, her husband had been American (he'd died a couple of years earlier), so the house was half-French (the charming part) and half-American (the convenience part). Ooh-la-la! She stressed that it was very countrified, although very comfortably outfitted. "Don't expect a pancake flipper," she warned. "It's still France." Which was okay with me. I wanted a crepe pan, not a damn pancake flipper.

So we were all set. I had an office, Janis had a garden, Norton had three centuries' worth of mice to chase after. There was only one thing still left to do.

Unfortunately, to write about what it was I had to do, I have to break a solemn vow I took with someone very near and dear to me.

Years ago, I made a pact with my writing partner, David, who has as much integrity and taste as it's possible to have considering what we do to make a living. The promise we made to each other was that we would never—artistically speaking—eat our own entrails.

This is not nearly as repugnant as it sounds. Honest. It simply means that when we were younger we decided that if we ever became successful writers we wouldn't join the Philip Roth School of Writing About How Successful We Are. Uppermost in things to avoid: writing about how hard it is to be a writer; writing about how no one ever appreciates how hard it is to be a writer; writing about other writers or editors and critics, because they're all incredibly boring; writing about how all those boring writers, editors, and critics don't like you either; and absolutely first on the list, never, ever, *ever* write about your own publicity tour. It's unseemly, it's uninteresting, and it's just plain obnoxious (as in, "Oh, yeah, sure you've got it rough over in Bosnia, but you should have been in *my* shoes when this little short guy with a bad rug got my *name* wrong on 'Good Morning, Schenectady.' Now, *that* was a nightmare!").

Anyway, Dave, I'm not really writing about *my* publicity

tour. I was all set to go over to the three-hundred-year-old
house in France and keep my last few shreds of artistic
dignity. I swear. Nobody wanted to talk to or see *me,* anyway. But before I could hop on a plane and hightail it out
of here, I had my last little detail to take care of. It turned
out that a lot of people wanted to meet my cat.

The tour officially began in Los Angeles but, in the publishing equivalent of spring training, we got a practice appearance in, on a show on a small cable station in Connecticut.
Everyone thought this was a good idea since no one really
knew how the cat would behave in front of the cameras and,
probably more pressing, everyone wanted to see if I'd turn
into the Chef of the Future once the little red light went on.
   Basically, it went well. Norton was, of course, his usual
perfect self. We arrived early, as instructed, and were led
to the greenroom, which, in case you're interested, was
brown. (Later, in several weeks of touring, I was in many,
many greenrooms. Not *one* of them was ever green. I'm
thinking of calling "Sixty Minutes" to see what they can do
with this.) I paced the room for half an hour, looking in the
mirror constantly, running my hand through my hair,
straightening my tie, doing everything but going "mi mi
mi" and gargling. Norton was already acting as if he'd been
on as many talk shows as Teri Garr. He sat on the couch,
let a few stagehands come over and pet him, and was even
nice to the guest who was to follow me, a woman who'd
written a book about the proper way to pack a suitcase. Ah
yes, there's nothing like doing publicity to make one feel
like an important cultural influence.
   Once we went on the air, the host and hostess of the show
couldn't get over the way Norton just sat on my lap for the

whole interview. He even would sit up and look straight into the camera, thus making sure all thirty-five people watching the show would stop listening to me and pay sole attention to how cute he was. (I think he did this whenever he sensed I was going on too long and was becoming boring.)

For my part, I was fine, except that, being as vain as possible, I'd worn a dark blue suit and blue shirt, figuring that would be my best look for my TV debut. It was, I suppose, at least at the beginning. But as the show went on, Norton began doing what all cats do, especially when they're under hot lights—he began to shed. And he began to shed all over my dark blue suit. By the end of the interview, I had so much gray fur on me that I looked like nothing so much as a large, talking prehistoric bird.

But we'd not only survived the first test, it was clear that Norton was such stuff as stars were made of.

As I said, this was an early interview, a trial run. The book was still a few weeks away from being published. So all we had to do now was wait for the book to exist and then, having passed our test, wait to throw ourselves on the mercy of America.

For a writer as well as a cat, waiting is the hardest part. But, from a literary point of view, the end of the wait is usually worth it.

There is something very special about seeing one's book for the first time as a finished product. No matter the quality—whether you're Daniel Defoe or Danielle Steele—writing a book is damned difficult. Everyone *thinks* he or she can write, but it's fairly daunting to take a look at a blank page and then decide that you have the audacity to fill not only it up but many more like it. So when you finally have finished the first draft, then the second, then the third;

when you've corrected the copy-edited manuscript, then the galleys, then the bound galleys; when you finally get to hold the finished, published product in your very own hands—several hundred pages long, a real jacket, flap copy that hypes till even *your* face turns red, something solid and permanent—it provides a moment pure and satisfying. Bad reviews haven't come in yet, nor have the agent's calls telling you that three days after the pub date the book's already on the remainder tables. All that exists is this physical *thing* that somehow is a mental extension of yourself.

That lasts for all of a minute or two. Then, of course, reality comes a knockin'.

The Cat Who Went to Paris gave me a particularly satisfying couple of minutes because it was so personal and because it had extraordinarily handsome photos of my beloved companion all over the front and back jacket. The day before Norton and I were to leave on our publicity tour was the first time I saw it in a bookstore, B. Dalton's on Eighth Street down in the Village, where Norton and I were making our first public bookstore appearance that evening. I was supposed to sign books and be witty. Norton was supposed to look cute and let people admire him. I can't tell you how often, as the tour progressed, I wanted to switch roles, but everyone from the publicist to the editor to my very own girlfriend told me I'd be making a *big* mistake.

Several hours before the signing, I took Norton and we snuck into the store, incognito. (It wasn't very difficult. No one recognized me since no one had ever heard of me. And Norton's very good—when he wants to be—at slipping down into his shoulder bag and becoming almost invisible. It's why I've always thought he'd make a superb private eye.) As I casually checked the store out, trying not to look too much like an annoying author checking out the store,

I was surprised to see that the book was very well dis-
played—there was even a giant poster of Norton in the
window. Ecstatic, I bought a copy for good luck—figuring
it was probably the first hardcover sale in New York—
rearranged the remaining books on the shelf so they lay face
out (yes, we really do that; any writer who denies it is lying
through his teeth. I didn't want the copy I bought to also
be the *last* hardcover sale in New York), then practically
danced back out to the street. Outside, I showed the book
jacket to Norton, who seemed singularly unimpressed, perhaps wondering why I got my name on the front of the
jacket but he didn't.

Later that night, we went back to the same store, boldly
striding in this time, Norton fearlessly taking in the sights,
both of us hoping the clerk wouldn't recognize me as the
nervous, sweaty guy who'd earlier bought a copy of his own
book. There were perhaps fifty people at this first signing
and three speakers. The first speaker was a woman who'd
written one of the all-time great cat books, *The Natural Cat.*
The second speaker was a man who'd put together a superb
cat encyclopedia called *The Cornell Book of Cats.* (His only
flaw was that he spent *way* too much time lecturing about
the tragedy of cat prostate problems. It was all I could do
to keep myself—and Norton!—from passing out during
that particular section of his speech. At one point, I'm afraid
I did have to cover my ears and quietly hum all the words
to "A Hundred Bottles of Beer on the Wall," but I'm sure
no one noticed.) When it was my turn, I talked about how
I came to write the book (an editor thought it was a good
idea to have a book about a *bon vivant* who traveled around
the world with his cat; I was so thrilled that somebody
thought I was a *bon vivant,* I immediately agreed to do it),
and then told several of the most amusing and amazing

Norton stories in it. Nothing was as amusing or amazing, however, as my cat's behavior during the speeches. When the first two speakers were on, Norton lounged politely, barely paying attention. When I stood up to begin, my little gray partner sat straight up on top of his table, staring right at me in rapt attention, occasionally glancing out at the audience as if to encourage them to laugh. The only problem came at the end of my talk when the cat fans in the store decided to applaud. At the first sound of enthusiastic clapping, Norton spun around so his back was to the crowd and he snuggled down out of view inside his bag. I immediately figured he didn't like my speech and was trying to discourage the positive reaction. It took me a little while to realize that, while he was otherwise totally unintimidated, the loud applause frightened him. For the rest of our tour, I would always begin my talk—even on a TV show if there was a live audience—by explaining that I had the greatest, most courageous cat in the world but that applause scared him, so could they please refrain from clapping when we were done, even on the slim chance that they felt like doing so. That made Norton much happier all along the way. And, of course, made me a bit neurotic. There's nothing like giving what you think is a slam-dunk winner of a talk, then walking off the stage to total silence. But, you know me—anything for El Foldo.

After the seminar/signing at B. Dalton, Norton and I headed back to my apartment. Still basking in the glow of our literary triumph and certain we had a big hit on our hands, I went to my phone machine to check my messages before I began packing for our next day's journey. I had only one message; it was from a middle-aged-sounding man and here it is in its extremely polite entirety:

*Uh, hello, uh, I'm looking for Peter Gethers, if this is
the same Peter Gethers who wrote a book called* The
Cat Who Went to Paris. *I'm calling all the way from
California and I bought this book for fifteen dollars. I'd
just like to say that my wife and I both read it and we'd
like our money back. This is the worst piece of shit we've
ever read. I mean it. What garbage. Total, absolute
shit. You should be ashamed. Thank you.*

In a mild state of shock, my first reaction was to wonder
which one—the man or his wife—had read it first. And
whoever did, did they then turn to their partner and say,
"Honey, I just read the biggest piece of shit I've ever read.
You've *got* to read it, too"? And then, did the other person
read it, curled up in front of a fire, turn to the first reader
and say, "Sugar pie, you're sure right with this one. Hooo-
eeee, this stinks to high heaven! Let's call the author long
distance and tell him"?

Once I decided this probably wasn't a healthy road to
pursue, I called my partner, David, to play him the message.
He didn't seem too surprised. Not because he agreed with
their assessment but because he's written several mystery
novels, one of which won an Edgar Award, and thus he's
come across his fair share of wackos. (It's a publishing rule
of thumb: Science fiction fans are absolutely the weirdest.
No question. Many of them think they're from another
planet—and, in fact, a good many of them probably are. If
you ever want to convince yourself that the nihilists are
right and that life has no meaning, go to a science fiction
convention. After the sci-fiers, though, come the mystery
fanatics. They all dress in black and have memorized everything Arthur Conan Doyle ever wrote. They also meet at

conventions two or three times a year, where they attend panel discussions on things like "What's the Best Murder Weapon?" and "Who's Zanier: Cornell Woolrich or James Cain?") David topped my anti-groupie without hesitation. He told me about one particular fan of his who called him on a regular basis, usually early in the morning before he had the wits about him to screen his calls. David described the fan as sounding a little bit too much like Hal the computer in *2001*.

"Daaave," the guy would say. "I just read your first novel again. Sixth time. And I'm gonna read it *again*. *Tomorrow*." Then he'd usually say something like, "I'm in Chicago today, Dave"—a mere thousand miles from David's house. "How about I drive up and we meet for lunch?"

I felt a lot better after talking to David—demanding fifteen dollars back seemed a lot saner than a twenty-two-hour drive for lunch—and started packing for the tour. I knew enough to pack mostly gray clothes, thanks to my Connecticut experience. I also had the presence of mind to give Norton many extra Pounce that night and to pet him for a particularly long time before working up the nerve to ask him, "Do you have any idea what we're really in for?"

I don't know if he did or not, but he was certainly a good sport about it, and purred contentedly on my pillow until I fell asleep.

~~~

The first stop was Los Angeles and the Four Seasons Hotel, home to several impressive Nortonian moments in times past.

The Four Seasons is where I always stay in L.A. It's convenient, classy, and perfect for conducting business. The staff is also extraordinarily nice to Norton. In fact, every Four

Seasons is particularly gracious toward pets. In the Boston
Four Seasons, they even have a pet room-service menu. I
know this because when we stayed there, I was happy to
find a large bowl filled with nuts when I walked into the
room. Only I soon realized they weren't nuts but dog biscuits—and fairly tasty dog biscuits, I might add. Under the
bowl was a small, printed sheet which was titled "Doggie
Delights." The rest of the menu read as follows:

BARK, BARK!

(Main Courses)

#1   Ruff, Ruff, rrr . . .
(Quickly Broiled Beef Filet with natural broth $6.00)

#2   Aowh, Aohw, Aohwooooooo!
(Boneless "Safe to Eat" Lamb Chops $7.00)

#3   Woof! Woof! Grrr!
(Roasted Chicken Breast with natural gravy $5.50)

BARK!!!

(Side dishes)

#1   Awwrr, Yip, Yip!
(Brown Rice $1.75)

#2   Grrrrrr . . .
(White Rice $1.75)

ARP! ARP!

(Assorted Ice Creams $2.00)

Needless to say, I called down to check this out. At first I
thought it was a joke, but when the room-service person

indignantly assured me it wasn't, I wanted to know why the menu was geared only for canine guests. The voice at the other end of the phone hemmed and hawed over that one but finally said he was sure that cats would also find the food quite delicious; the hotel was happy to admit that dogs were not the only four-legged connoisseurs.

It turned out the room-service maven was correct. Twenty minutes after I hung up, a waiter arrived. On the cart he wheeled in was an array of fine china. And on the china was a delicious—judging from Norton's considered reaction—chicken breast.

But even with the usual fine Four Seasons treatment, I still wasn't prepared for the greeting we got upon our arrival in L.A.

First of all, as the cab from the airport dropped me off in front of the hotel, I heard two men in black suits say, in muffled tones, "He's here." Surprised, I put the cat in his shoulder bag and we headed into the lobby. As we stepped inside, two more men in black suits said, "He's here. Get ready."

I knew Norton was popular, I thought to myself, but I felt a surprise party was just a tad excessive.

The entire lobby seemed abuzz as we walked toward the desk. There was a flurry of activity, people rushed toward me—reporters, hotel staff, more guys in black suits. I smiled broadly and Norton stuck his head out of the bag, craning his neck in his best E.T. impersonation—who are we to reject V.I.P. treatment?—and then we watched as everyone rushed toward us . . . and right past us. As even more guys in black suits stampeded by, saying things under their breath like, "Moving toward the elevator. Cover the doors," Norton and I casually glanced behind us—where

the President of the United States was standing. Yup.
George Bush was there for some kind of money-raising,
glad-handing function. I suppose, if I'd really thought it
through, I would have realized that Norton didn't need *all*
of those Secret Service guys. Nonetheless, I confess to
being just a tad disappointed.

Not for long, however.

With Bush out of the way, I found that cat and I were the
only guests remaining in the lobby. So when I heard a
woman's voice say, "Wait a second, I think he's here," I
again turned behind me to see which top-notch celebrity
had breezed in. Mel Gibson? Liz Taylor? The cast from
"Beverly Hills 90210"? I was determined not to be sucker-
punched again.

So I was even more confused when I realized there was
nobody behind us, not even Herve Villachaize. Norton and
I were *it* as far as lobby loiterers.

Another woman, this time from behind the check-in
desk, said, quite clearly, "It *is* him. He's here!"

This led to a couple of exclamatory bursts from other
women, all exceedingly attractive—one at the cashier's
desk, one from behind the concierge's counter—along
the lines of, "We've been waiting for you! We're *so* glad
you're here!"

I decided that this was definitely more like it. Until,
naturally, I was forced to accept the fact that once again I
was not their obscure object of desire. The real target was
not nearly so obscure.

"Norton," the woman at the front desk cooed with her
arms held out in welcome, "we are *so* glad to see you!"

Now, I've stayed at the Four Seasons ten or fifteen times.
When I'm there by myself, they're certainly friendly—but

no one ever holds her arms out to me and scratches me under the chin while shrieking how cute I look. Norton had stayed there four or five times—and no one had really even done that to *him* before. At least, not quite in this fashion. Because that night, as we checked in, just about every person who worked on the ground floor came out to fuss over their smallest, grayest guest. It turned out that the publicist for the book had sent a few copies over to the hotel several days before. They'd been passed around and read and Norton was now clearly on the Four Seasons' "A" list of desirable celebrities.

"We've upgraded you to a Four Seasons suite," the desk clerk said, smiling at the cat.

"We think you'll like it," another said, petting him.

"And we've got a few surprises for you up there," another one told him, scratching his stomach (by this time, he was lying on his back on top of the check-in counter; I was a little startled at how easily he'd succumbed to life in the L.A. fast lane).

I was starting to wonder if they were going to take Norton's credit card, since it was pretty obvious I was an afterthought, but no such luck. For that part they deigned to talk to me.

When we were finally shown to our room, we had indeed been upgraded to a suite. Norton also had a litter box already set up in the bathroom. On the floor by the TV were two elegant dishes, one for water—with a bottle of Evian next to it!—and one to fill with the cans of food that were stacked on top of the end table. And on the desk in the living room was a gift-wrapped box with a note taped to it.

Flattered and pleased, I tore open the package—only to find that it was a can of shrimp-flavored Pounce. Deflated—I don't know what I'd expected; I think I had my heart set on a lovely crystal goblet—I also opened the note, which was from the manager of the hotel. It read (handwritten):

> *Dear Norton,*
>   *Welcome back to the Four Seasons! My cats, Nicholas and Alexandra, would love to meet you someday . . . you sound like a really neat guy.*
>   *Enjoy your stay.*
>
>   *Kathleen Horrigan*
>   *Hotel Manager*

I prowled around the room (both rooms!), hoping that perhaps Kathy Horrigan had also left a small basket of fruit lying around for me, but not a chance. It was clear from the very beginning that Norton was the star of this little sojourn. And from his contented meowing—over by his bottle of Evian water—I could tell he was not unhappy about it.

~~~

The highlight of our travels around the country came at the very beginning of the trip in L.A. when the publisher threw a party to celebrate publication of the book. It wasn't just a regular humdrum party with potato chips and clam dip. For Norton, they threw a bash at Spago, the most famous restaurant in the country, run by Wolfgang Puck, arguably the most celebrated chef in the world.

Not that I'm jaded or anything, but I'd been to Spago plenty of times. In fact, my mother works with Wolf (she helped him write his last cookbook) and she's part of the unofficial Spago family.

Norton had never dined there, however. In fact, no cat

had ever dined at Spago before—until Norton broke the barrier that night. Broke it in style, I might add.

They closed the restaurant for a few hours for our private party. The guest of honor—a hint: not me—was given his own table, upon which he sat in a princelike fashion and let all the guests come over and pay homage. Wolf, whose renowned specialties are pizzas covered with such delicacies as smoked salmon, wild mushrooms, or caviar, made Norton a pizza covered with Norton's favorite delicacy— Pounce. The pastry chef, an amazing woman named Mary (who, in honor of an annual trip I make to Las Vegas with a bunch of friends, once made a cake in the shape of Sammy Davis, Jr.), baked small cakes and cookies with cat paws and cat whiskers all over them. I was congratulated once or twice by the fifty or so guests, but mostly they fussed over Norton. Many of them had never been out in public with him and they couldn't believe how human he acted (they thought that was a compliment; we know better). During the several hours we were there, Norton perched himself on his table/throne, ate when he felt like it, drank a little milk when he was in the mood, allowed journalists to take his picture, let children talk to him as if he were a grown-up (and I mean a grown-up person, not a grown-up cat), and permitted all his admirers to pet him, stroke him, and compliment him. He even let the manager of the restaurant repeatedly refer to him as "Norman" without swatting at his ankle.

The highlight of the evening, however, was Wolf's wife, Barbara Lazaroff, the designer of and guiding force behind Spago and all of Wolf's other restaurants. Barbara, who's extremely attractive and even more flamboyant, strode into the party wearing a cat outfit. We're talking cat slippers—

with whiskers and everything—cat pants, a cat sweater, and a cat hat. Norton, for one brief, shining moment, thought he'd met the ultimate member of the opposite sex, but eventually, to his disappointment, I'm sure, he realized that Barbara was just another admiring, if stunning, human.

After the Spago party, the rest of our tour was fairly typical—considering that one of the authors on tour was a four-legged feline. Following L.A., for the hardcover and the paperback versions of the first book about our adventures together, Norton and I went to San Diego, San Francisco, Portland, Seattle, Miami, Dayton, Rochester, Detroit, Dallas, and Philadelphia. (After the West Coast tour, I told the publisher that a city a day was just too tough on my little pal. He was an extraordinary trouper and shockingly well behaved—just ask any of the couple of thousand people who came by to meet him—but, still, I felt it wasn't fair to cart him around all day, then put him on an airplane. So, for the other cities, we were put on what I heard referred to as the "old author's tour." That meant we got an extra day or two in each city to ease the travel burden. Me, Norton, and James Michener.)

The routine was pretty much the same in each city. An escort would pick us up at the airport. I carried the portable litter boxes—I had about twenty of them in my suitcase when I started, just in case—but each escort was instructed to show up with a bag of cat litter in tow. As soon as I picked up my bags and got into the car, out would come a collapsible litter box, then I'd rip open a new sack of litter, and the whole thing would go on the floor behind the passenger seat. Then we'd get taken to our hotel. As soon as we were checked into the room, it was time for another fold-up box and more litter. This way, not only was Norton assured of never having to go too long *sans toilette,* I was assured that none of the escorts would sue me for ruining the upholstery in their Buicks.

In each new hotel room, Norton would stake out his territory. He'd prowl around, sniffing along each of the four walls. If there was a desk or chest of drawers, he'd hop up on that and check out the comfort level. If there were thick curtains, he'd disappear behind them, checking, I imagine, for scratching texture as well as hideability level (thick curtains are very nice to hide in when a noisy room-service cart careens into the room).

I had many, many cans of Norton's favorite foods and a reasonable supply of Pounce. (Although once the book came out and people read that Pounce was his favorite treat, a can of the stuff became the gift offering of choice at all autographings. On the paperback tour, Norton received, in two weeks, sixty-four cans of Pounce.) Norton's food and water were usually set down in the bathroom. I don't actually know how a cat can tell which room is a bathroom, but I do know that if he was hungry and I hadn't set down any food yet, he'd go right into the correct room and start meowing his starving head off.

San Diego was Norton's first official TV show after the Connecticut dry run. We went on "Inside San Diego," which proved once and for all that Norton had the potential to be another Lassie if he so chose.

For the entire interview he sat on my lap, not thrilled with the lights and the background noise but certainly not uncomfortable or nervous. Subdued and alert would be my description. The hostess of the show—a cat lover—couldn't get over how adorable and intelligent he seemed throughout our chat. But even she wasn't prepared for Norton's finale. As the show was ending, the director decided to put the camera on Norton as the final credits rolled. They wanted to use Camera 3 (it was a three-camera show, as are most TV interview shows) instead of Camera 1, which was the one focused on Norton during the rest of the program. Just as the countdown began to signal that the credit roll was about to start and that we'd be back on the air, the director's voice boomed from above, over the microphone linking him from the control booth to the set: "Do you think you could try to get the cat to face Camera Three?" Without missing a beat—and with no prodding or prompting from me—the newest TV heartthrob sat up on my lap, turned a hundred and eighty degrees, and made sure he was directly facing Camera 3. Just a split second before the countdown ended and the sound and cameras went on, the director summed up what he saw quite magnificently, also over the mike. "Holy shit," he said. "That cat's a fucking genius."

As we did more TV and radio, Norton became even more at ease in front of the cameras and the mikes. On various radio shows, I'd try to be my usual witty self, while Norton would sit next to me, probably wondering why he was there, since no one could see him and no one was asking him to talk. The deejay would usually exclaim, several times for his listening audience, "I know you can't see this cat, ladies and gentlemen, but he really is unbelievable!"

In San Diego, we did Michael Reagan's radio show. Much to my surprise, he turned out to be Ronald Reagan's son. I wasn't looking forward to the interview, since Reagan ranked up with Iago and Roy Cohn in my top five list of villains, but the son wound up being perfectly pleasant and funny. He also turned out to be highly allergic to cats.

The entire week before we arrived to do the show, he'd been going on the air talking about how he was dreading meeting this genius cat. He was afraid he'd be sneezing during the entire interview. Naturally, as in all cases, Norton managed to accomplish the unexpected. Not only was Reagan *not* allergic, he wound up petting him and declaring over the air that he was now going to get a Scottish Fold.

We went back to L.A. to do a Book and Author Luncheon. What happens at these lunches is that a group of book lovers, usually women, decide it would be fun and interesting to bring in two or three authors to lecture and discuss their latest works over a lunch of overcooked vegetables and undercooked chicken. I was chosen for this particular lunch and thus was up on the podium, speaking to a lot of fur-clad women, along with a woman who wrote about the emotional problems children were having in high school, a man who had an easy, step-by-step formula for everyone to reach inner satisfaction, and a woman who wrote best-selling true-crime books and lectured about the mind of the psychopathic killer. It didn't really matter what I said to this group because Norton decided to steal the show. I stood up in my nice new suit (the gray one, where all the cat hairs weren't nearly so visible), glasses perched, looking as professorial as I can, and began to talk. In the meantime, Norton decided to plop himself down right next to the podium, looking for all the world as if not only did he belong up there as one of the speakers, but as if he were, in fact, my translator. The whole time I spoke, he kept glancing back and forth between me and the audience, as if to say, "Come on, folks, he's really trying hard." Whatever I was doing, it worked. In order of popularity, I think I came in a solid third. The psychopathic killer came in second, and Norton, of course, finished first.

Seattle, Portland (it was Norton's first trip to the Pacific Northwest), and San Francisco all went as smoothly as possible. Outside of San Francisco, in Larkspur, we made an appearance at a wonderful bookstore called A Clean Well-Lighted Place for Books. The evening was sponsored by the local SPCA. I spoke, Norton sat by my side, translating as usual, and several cats found new homes. So the entire evening was a terrific success. (Not to pat myself on the back, but I do find it admirable that throughout this entire book as well as the first one, never once have I succumbed to the temptation to say things like "a purrfect success." I just wanted to point that out to anyone who felt that, in general, cat books are too cute to bear. Although I don't have any compunction about relating stories of *other* people who show overly cute tendencies in front of Norton. Once, when we were in Philadelphia, I ordered up my dinner from room service after another grueling day of being witty and charming for TV, radio, and print. When the woman from room service brought me my dinner, she couldn't help but notice Norton and give him a few friendly strokes. She left, then fifteen minutes later reappeared. This time with a bowl of cat treats and a small catnip ball. These gifts arrived with a note. The envelope was addressed to "Kitty Cat Gethers" and the note read, "Hope your stay with us is pu-u-urfect!" It was signed: "The cat lovers in Room Service." You didn't *really* think I could write an entire book like this without having one of those "pu-u-urfect" anecdotes, did you? Grow up!)

In Seattle, I did have the stupidest experience of the entire tour. What people have to understand is that while writers are thrilled to have the opportunity to promote their books, since that's the only way they can possibly hope to collect any royalties, it really ain't a lot of fun. The reason it's not is because most of the talk-show hosts and interviewers who you're talking to haven't read the book and have no idea what you're doing there with them in the first place. At one newspaper interview in San Francisco, I went into the reporter's office, sat down, and after he introduced himself, I told him who I was, then pointed to the sack on my shoulder and said, "And this is Norton." His eyes widened and he said, "You brought your *cat* to the interview????" Slightly taken aback, I shrugged and said, "Well, yeah. He goes everywhere I go." "He *does????*" the guy responded. "That's unbelievable." About this time, I began to suspect that the reporter hadn't actually read the book, so I said, "Well, see, the book's called *The Cat Who Went to Paris* because I travel all over the world with the cat." "And he's actually been to Paris?" the guy now asked. "Uh-huh," I cleverly responded. "That's where we got the title from." "Wow," the guy said, stunned at this heavy new info. "This is unbelievable. Well . . . what do you want to talk about?"

Some of them are bad but not quite as bad as that. One otherwise well-done newspaper story that came out in Boston repeatedly referred to me as *Sam* Gethers (I'd spent two hours with the reporter, but I guess I didn't really make a big impression). I did one radio interview outside of Detroit and moments before it was was supposed to begin, the hostess of the show rushed in, introduced herself, and said, "We only have a minute. What's the title of the book, what's your name, what's the book about, and what the hell are we going to talk about?!" Refusing to panic, I calmly gave her the title, my name, the subject of the book, and fed her several reasonable questions to ask. We were then given the signal that we were on the air and she began the interview by announcing to all those listening, "I have here today an author, Peter Gethers, who wrote a book called *The Cat Who Went to Paris*. Now, I have to be totally up front about this: I hate cats and I hate cat books."

One good thing about that opening: The interview had nowhere to go but up.

Throughout the entire tour, Norton behaved impeccably. Rarely did he stumble and start to act like a . . . well . . . like a cat. I think he was fairly exhausted by the end, as was his dad, but generally he got to eat a lot, sleep a lot, and have tons of people tell him he was the greatest thing that ever walked the earth. So, while I was glad to get him back home, where he could curl up in his favorite and familiar spots, I think he had a fine time overall on the road.

In San Francisco, I realized he'd just about had it, though, when, one day at a radio interview, he decided to hide.

When I was being interviewed, he'd usually sit right by my side, but this afternoon he was restless. The interviewer, a woman named Ginnie Waters, who hosted a show on KKSF Radio called "Something Different," loved cats and encouraged Norton to stroll around the little broadcast booth as much as he wanted. Since he'd been absolutely purrfect . . . uh, perfect (sorry) . . . for the entire tour, and this was the very last stop for a while, I relaxed and didn't bother to keep my eye on him. The interview took half an hour, went quite well, and when it was over, I called for Norton to come and hop into his shoulder bag. Only there was no Norton. I knew I was in trouble because he'd been a little cranky all day. I should have seen it coming—he'd had a tough trip and was just plain tuckered out—but his timing was not great. For one thing, we had a plane to catch. For another, I'd just spent half an hour telling a good chunk of San Francisco about what an extraordinary cat he was and now I had to spend another half an hour crawling around on my stomach, peering under desks, climbing up on shelves, and searching through strange electronic equipment, while a bemused member of the media watched me try to find my cat. Finally, I heard a meow—he'd decided to let me know he was okay—but there was still no cat in the booth. He meowed again—and kept meowing for another fifteen minutes—but I absolutely could not find him. It wasn't until one of the engineers came in and suggested I look inside one of the speakers that the hiding place was discovered. How he managed to get in there, none of us could figure out. But, cat extraordinaire that he was, he'd managed to slip into the one place in a ten-by-ten room where he couldn't possibly be spotted. He didn't resist when I picked him up, and I sure didn't scold him. He wasn't angry; he wasn't even really hiding. He was just letting me know, in his own inimitable way, that he'd had enough. And I sure couldn't blame him.

But none of this holds a candle to the moment in Seattle. It came at exactly 6:05 A.M. Now, I'm not really the greatest morning person. I can survive it, but I'd gotten into Seattle about 10 P.M. the night before and, between one thing and another, hadn't gotten to sleep until well after midnight. So I wasn't thrilled about getting up at five, slurping down a cup of coffee, and then waiting for the radio station to call me in my room for their morning phoner. Reliable author that I am, however, I did it with as big a grin on my mug as I could muster. And, sure enough, just as I was stifling a major yawn, the phone rang and it was the drive-time radio show. They told me to hold on a couple of minutes while they did the traffic report and then they'd get back to me. So I yawned and held on and eventually heard a typical frenzied deejay's voice saying, "And in just a moment, we'll be talking to Peter Gethers, author of *The*

Cat Who Went to Paris, and his amazing cat, Norton. Hello, Peter . . . are you there?" I told him I was here—and he then asked, in his best slick radio cadence, "Tell me, Peter, what does Norton think of relationships in the nineties?"

I should say right now that I'm usually a fairly glib person. It takes a lot for me to be stumped. Maybe it was the fact that it was the middle of the night, as far as I was concerned. Maybe it was that we'd been touring for too many days in a row. But all I could think of to say was a not-very-glib, *"What?"* And when he repeated the question, I came back with, "Uh . . . well . . . he approves of them."

"Thank you very much," I heard. "That was Peter Gethers, author of *The Cat Who Went to Paris,* and his amazing cat, Norton, on relationships in the nineties." And then he hung up.

I decided I had nobody to blame but myself, wondered how Tolstoy would have responded if he'd been out promoting *Anna Karenina*—"Tell me, Leo, what does Count Vronsky think about relationships in the 1800s?"— then got dressed, kissed the cat, and went on to our next interview.

The best part of being on tour was going to bookstores. Not only was it exciting to see truly great stores—and once again be reminded why I do what I do to earn my keep— it was extraordinarily fun to see how people reacted to Norton.

One woman at the Boston University bookstore showed up at a signing with photos of her family—which consisted of *six* Scottish Folds.

Two women who came to meet Norton at the Village

Green in Rochester were Scottish Fold breeders who appeared with their impressive brochures filled with cute photos of Fold kittens. These two charming women, Barbara Meyers and Grace Sutton, are responsible for the fact that Esther, my agent and lifelong die-hard resister of cats, finally gave in and now has a folded-eared pal of her own named Tate.

When I would sign books, people lined up for books while I sat behind a table and Norton sat on the table. Someone would hand me a book, ask me to sign it (scarily enough, often to someone named Fluffy, Spitball, Pooh, or Peanut Butter), and while I was doing so, he or she would pet Norton, coo over him, and, as often as not, hand him a can of Pounce as a present (one woman tentatively presented me with some M&Ms because she felt guilty that I wasn't getting enough attention; other than that, I was strictly in the background).

If someone had never heard of the book but just happened to be wandering by, they'd usually give me a perfunctory glance, spot Norton doing his shtick, widen their eyes, then sidle over to me to ask a few questions. The questions would usually range from "Is he a trained cat?" (Answer: No) to "Why does he look so funny?" (Answer: It's the breed) to "He's so calm. Did you drug him?" (Answer: No!) to "Did you clip his ears?" (Answer: NO!!!!).

At Gene's Books in King of Prussia, Pa., they had a photo contest. People brought in a picture of their own cute feline and I was supposed to pick winners in the following categories: Fattest Cat, Most Amazing Cat, and Cutest Cat. This was not unlike being put in the delicate situation of having to choose which person's baby is better looking. I did my best, being careful not to always choose photos of Folds, since I didn't want to appear to be too biased. Overall, the winners were gracious and the losers didn't either hit me or tear up my book, so I suppose it could be considered a successful contest.

At Liberties Books and Fine Music in Boca Raton, Florida, people were encouraged to bring their own cats to meet Norton. One guy brought a large St. Bernard dog, for some strange reason, and one couple brought a large black cat who was the calmest cat I've ever seen. Norton, when he's in public, is not particularly nervous or hyper, but he does stay extremely alert. If I lecture for more than half an hour, he may doze off, or may turn over on his back, purr, and demand to be scratched, but usually he sits calmly, checking out the situation, making sure that there aren't going to be any unpleasant surprises. But this black cat didn't care about surprises or anything else that I could see. He simply sat in the audience and was about as tense as a bowl of jello. One of his owners brought the cat over to meet me—and the cat was hanging upside down from the guy's hands like a side of beef in a meat locker. I couldn't tell if Norton was a little jealous or if he was merely scornful of the black cat's eagerness to please. I like to think it was the latter, as I presume he's above any feeling of petty jealousy, but he was definitely standoffish toward this feline competitor.

At Books & Co. in Dayton, Ohio (the country's second largest independent bookstore and a book lover's fantasy), I was the second speaker of the evening. The only problem with that was, while the first speaker was going on—her book and talk were both quite charming, all about various American family traditions—Norton and I stood off to the side, preparing for our own little seminar. So while this other poor author was speaking, people started spotting the cat and coming over to pet him and say hello. Pretty soon, there were fifty people surrounding Norton, praising him to the skies, while three people were left sitting in front of the family traditions woman. I got the distinct impression, when we were both dropped off at our hotel later that night, that her family's newest tradition was going to be hating authors who write books about their cats.

In Dallas, not only did Norton finally get his first taste of real barbecue, he was now so relaxed about appearing on television that he actually fell asleep on a local talk show. The setup was vaguely "Tonight Show"-ish—the host sat in a chair while the guests lined up along a couch. Norton and I were the only guests. He sat closest to the interviewer and I sat next to him. The woman who was the star of the show was a fanatical cat lover and I think she was never really sure to whom she should address her questions, me or Norton. Every so often, I could see a look of surprise on her face after she'd ask something and I was the one who responded. The whole time I was talking, I was rubbing Norton, until somewhere in the middle of the interview, the host said, "Well, I can see the problem with Norton is that he's just too tense under the scrutiny of public life." I looked down and, sure enough, the Perry Como of the feline world had his head tucked into his body, all curled up in a ball, and he was sound asleep, purring away. By the time we got to Taylor's Bookstore the next day, I could tell that Norton was beginning to take seriously to the celebrity life. As the hundred or so people lined up to meet him, I had the distinct impression that he was disappointed there were no cameras around to record his every movement (which, I must admit, weren't many; mostly he would stick his head up to be scratched or stick his head down to be hand-fed a couple of treats. He's kind of a minimalist when it comes to actual public activity).

When the tour for the hardcover book was over, I believe that Norton felt much as I did. There was a sense of relief—it was nice to be home rather than in a new hotel room every day, and it was even nicer to be alone, without having to constantly be performing, something neither writers nor cats take to naturally or are great at. At the same time, there was a little bit of a letdown. For a short burst of time, we were center stage. Don't panic, neither one of us ever fully turned into Sally Field at the Academy Awards, but I do think there was a slight addiction to the public acclaim. Cats and writers are both loners for the most part and there was something gratifying, however uncomfortable it sometimes felt, about people personally acknowledging that we had given their lives some pleasure.

I believe, after the tour ended, that Norton had a slightly different relationship with the human race. Prior to this experience, I was basically the one who'd provided him with the most protracted and strongest feelings of affection and love. Several girlfriends over the years adored him and let him know it, and he'd met all of my friends, who fussed over him more than enough to keep him happy. In our various travels, he'd also encountered plenty of strangers who certainly pumped up his ego. But on this trip it was the first time he was able to sense that *many* people, *thousands* of people, wanted to love him. If not him specifically, then something—or someone—very much like him.

It was an interesting switch. Cats often affect people in strange and mysterious ways and, for the most part, change our lives for the better. It's what they do. It's one of the things that makes them cats. But this was a rare occasion when people were able to substantially change a cat.

Since Norton can't really talk—even though I'm able to interpret many of his meows, it's fairly difficult to have a philosophical conversation with him—I can't be absolutely certain that this change was as strong as I suspect. But I can turn the tables on my cat and observe him, sit back and watch him in action, and I *am* certain, from my observations after the tour, that he was different after coming in contact with so many people who so clearly adored him, and who just as clearly yearned for him to adore them.

He certainly didn't turn into a lap dog. God forbid. Nor did he lose any of his independence or his individualistic spirit. But I noticed that when a stranger came in the room and reached out a hand, Norton's neck would move just an inch in the proper direction, an admission, however grudgingly, that love was not a one-way street.

For a cat, that ain't bad.

And for a cat, an author, and an author's girlfriend, it also meant it was time to put our past lives behind us and head off across the Atlantic.

PART TWO

a
cat
abroad

4
a cat in france

Then there was the bad weather.

Just kidding—that's the opening line to *A Moveable Feast*. I always like to see who's on their toes.

Unlike Papa, as I call him, when we arrived in Paris the autumn weather was absolutely spectacular. Getting there was not quite as pleasant, however.

One of the drawbacks of giving up the life of semi-high-powered publishing executive was that I also gave up the semi-high salary that went along with that life. Saving money just happens not to be my strong point (I'm much, much better at spending it), so, trying to show me that a careful, considered, budget-conscious life could also be fun and rewarding, Janis convinced me to get tickets using our American Advantage Miles. In other words, we could fly to France for free.

I don't know how many of you have ever tried to actually order whatever Advantage Miles are due you. But let me

assure you, if you don't have a Ph.D in Reading Instructions, give it up. Don't bother. As a publisher, I had to wade
my way through many a complicated contract. I know all
about options and step deals and various parties of the first
part and even something about a few parties of the second
part, but trying to order Advantage Miles was something
substantially beyond my intellectual capabilities. I couldn't
figure out how many miles it took to get an international
'flight. Then I couldn't figure out how many more it took to·
get a seat in business class. Then, to make matters worse,
I absolutely couldn't figure out what dates were restricted
or what dates were okay to fly. The nearest I could come
was that, with the mileage I'd accumulated, I could either
fly nonstop to Asia or I could get an upgrade on a flight to
Seattle, but I couldn't fly anywhere else unless I wanted to
go after two A.M. on the eighteenth day of every other
month. After several hours of trying to make sense of the
back of my Advantage Miles statement, and finally realizing
that whatever I did was going to be one hundred percent
incorrect, I called American Airlines and threw myself on
the mercy of whoever answered the phone. I promised
them that I was a reasonably intelligent person who normally could function in the real world, and then I confessed
that trying to figure out their simple system for free flights
was the equivalent, for me, of those spatial-relations tests
they used to give in junior high school. Sometimes I still
wake up screaming as I remember sitting at my desk, looking at a drawing of two gears, and staring at the caption
which read: *If the gear on the right spins counterclockwise and
strikes the gear on the left, which way will the gear on the left turn?*
Not since those mind-numbing sessions—where I would
spend the entire hour twisting myself into a pretzel trying
desperately to figure out the proper movement, then trying

even more desperately to even figure out what a gear *was*, after which my friendly counselor suggested that I try to stay away from all activity that ever involved any form of mechanical skill or abstraction—had I felt the way I felt reading those Advantage Mile forms.

My only consolation was that the woman at the airline was very understanding, leading me to believe that at least some other customers had run into the same roadblock I had. Not many, but some.

We finally figured out what I needed to know and our tickets were ordered. But after this was all done, Janis asked if I'd made a reservation for Norton. I hadn't yet—that had to be done separately; I was afraid of overloading my sympathetic airline friend—but I assured her it would be no problem.

As usual, I was completely wrong. It was a huge problem. American Airlines no longer allowed pets to fly in the cabin on international flights.

This was absurd, and I said as much to whoever I talked to at the American reservation desk. That may be, she said, but it was also company policy. So I asked to speak to the manager. He was quite nice and friendly, but he also told me it was company policy. But, I argued, I fly American everywhere in the States just because they let me take my cat in the cabin with me. Yes, he assured me, that was correct. But not for international flights. When I asked why that was, he told me it was the law.

Granted, I'm not a lawyer, but I seriously doubted there was a law on the books that forbade cats to fly with their owners from New York to Paris. I was also fairly sure it was nowhere to be found in the Constitution of the United States. And while I knew that such a right wouldn't be covered in the Bill of Rights (I can see it now—Thomas

Jefferson stroking his chin, deep in thought . . . "Hmmm.
Let's see . . . let's give everyone the right to freedom of
speech . . . the right to privacy . . . I know! And the right
to bear cats on airplanes!"), I had a distinct feeling that this
guy from American was not telling me the truth. So I did
what any normal, cat-loving person would do. I called the
president.

Give me a break—not the President of the United States.
I'm not a total lunatic. But I did call the prez of American
Airlines. I explained to him that I had just written a best-
selling book about traveling around the world with my cat,
that I was going to be writing another, and that, for some
weird reason, his airline, which was always so nice to my
little furry friend, would not allow him to fly with me to
Charles de Gaulle Airport. I'm a little ashamed to mention
it, but sometimes this mention of the book works when all
else fails. Once, when Norton and I went down for our
annual spring training trip to Florida, the Rotisserie Baseball guys who organized the trip decided to change from
our usual hotel. No more Belleview Biltmore, where they
loved the cat—despite the time he fell fifteen feet through
the dining-room awning and almost gave two seventy-five-
year-old women heart attacks when he landed on their
table. We were now staying at a large, pink monstrosity
called the Don Cesar. Because Norton had been going on
this baseball trip for so many years, it never occurred to me
to make a reservation for him, which turned out to be
unfortunate because the Don Cesar didn't take cats. I won't
give all the gory details, but there was no chance of getting
into another hotel within a hundred miles, so I wound up
sneaking Norton into my room. The next morning, the
manager of the hotel accosted me, drawing himself up to his
full height of five feet six inches, and telling me that he

heard I had a cat in my room. I stared him straight in the eye—I had to stoop a bit—and, looking as indignant as possible, lied my head off. Later that morning, when I returned to my room after breakfast, who was there but the manager, snooping around. Not only did he find the litter box, the cat food, and the bowl of water, he found the cat. I tried being outraged that he'd broken into my room, but it's hard to sustain outrage when you're caught in a total lie. So I did the next best thing: I offered to bribe him. When that didn't work, I became desperate and told him that I had a book coming out in several months, that the book was expected to be a best-seller, and that if he didn't let my cat stay there, I'd make sure I wrote terrible things about him and the hotel in the book. Even Norton was embarrassed by this feeble attempt to keep him sheltered, but much to our shock, it worked. The manager suddenly looked at Norton, smiled somewhat sycophantically (a trait I personally like in hotel personnel), and said that Norton certainly looked like an extraordinary cat and he didn't see what harm a feline could do for just a few days. Now I know how it feels to abuse the power of the media. It feels just *great!*

However, such a ploy didn't work with American Airlines. The president (to be honest, he was sort of vague about his title; he never actually *told* me he was the president even though that's who I asked to be connected to. My own opinion is that he was a fake president, someone they use when dealing with crackpots on the telephone) told me that the several people I'd already talked to were absolutely correct. It was against company policy to fly a cat in the cabin internationally. "Why is that?" I asked as politely as possible. "I think it's against the law," he told me.

At this point, I had visions of a major Supreme Court case. *Norton* v. *the United States of America.* It had a nice ring to it. I was already beginning to fantasize about Clarence Thomas catching Norton alone in a hallway and making a pass, but, as always, Janis pulled in the reigns on my sanity and convinced me that it would be a lot easier to simply get a ticket on another airline.

So on the day of our departure, Janis flew for free on American Airlines. Norton and I flew—not even remotely for free—on Air France. I was not unhappy paying for the flight, since there was no way Norton was ever flying in the baggage compartment. And for some reason—and this will definitely be brought up when I appear before the Supreme Court—it is not illegal for Air France to fly their cats in comfort and plush surroundings up with their two-legged customers, only for American-based airlines.

Norton and I had a delightful flight. I'd found a brand-new traveling kennel for him. Instead of those hard, heavy cases that fit under the seat but force him to assume a pancakelike position for much of his air time, I'd discovered these wonderful shoulder bags made out of a very tough cloth and which are airline approved. There's mesh in the back, so Norton can look out, and it unzips, so he can even stick his head out, which is his favorite way to travel. For takeoffs and landings, the thing zips up and fits under the seat, but it's extremely comfortable and makes Norton's trips a lot more luxurious.

Of course, on Air France, they are incredibly nice to a certain Scottish Fold, and this trip was no exception. The business-class cabin was nearly empty, so Norton got his own seat, as well as his own meal of smoked salmon and baked *lotte*. All in all, he was quite a hit on the flight. A very attractive and very French woman sat next to me, curled up in a little ball under a blanket. When she saw Norton up on my lap, she squealed and said, "Oh, ees he an American

Curl? I joost saw one of zose." I did my best to explain the concept of Scottish Fold—which, in French, translates vaguely into *Écosse Plier*—but I don't think it really came across. Norton's personality did come across to the two stewardesses, who spent an inordinate amount of time making sure that he was comfortable and well-fed. As we taxied into Charles de Gaulle, one of the attendants made the following announcement over the loudspeaker: "Please remember to take all packages weeth you. Except for ze passengaire in fourteen A. Eef he would like to leave his leetle cat, Norton, we would be very glad to take care of heem. Sank yoo."

Janis and I decided, due to several factors—the number of suitcases we had (whenever we moved, I felt exactly like the elder Charles Foster Kane: baggage stretched out for miles before us); our impatience to get started with our new lives in the house we'd rented down in Provence; the fact that Paris costs several million dollars per minute—not to dawdle in the city for too long. We were headed to the countryside, so to the countryside we decided to head.

We stayed at a friend's apartment for the night, determined to get an early start in the morning. Once we were over our jet lag and had our espresso and croissant the next morning, the first thing that had to be done was to pick up the car we'd rented. One nice thing about moving abroad for a year is you learn all about these strange businesses and services that, ordinarily, you'd never discover. One such business was something called Europe by Car. Instead of renting a European Ford from Avis at a cost of thousands of francs a week, Europe by Car leases Citroëns and Peugeots for up to six months at a time at a very reasonable rate.

We'd ordered a brand-new, shiny red Citroën for ourselves, and all I had to do was go pick it up.

Easier said than done in Paris.

Janis stayed at the apartment; Norton and I headed for some strange part of south Paris that we'd never been to before. I don't think too many other people had been there, either. And those who were wandering the streets all looked like they were trying to collect the reward for killing Salman Rushdie. I did manage to find the garage eventually, and once that was done also managed to polish off all the paperwork and other rigamarole one has to do. Then I was pointed toward another room, followed instructions, and went to get my car.

A very Parisian auto mechanic—overalls, a beret, a thick black mustache; he looked like he'd fix your transmission with a loaf of bread rather than a wrench—insisted on showing me all the fine points of my new vehicle before letting me drive off. I tried to tell him that I had a hard time understanding car talk in English, let alone French, but he paid me no mind. I vaguely followed his explanations of the clutch and the trunk and the hand break, and Norton seemed satisfied with the seating room in the back, which of course was of primary importance, but my interest really perked up when he pointed to some little lever to the right of the driver's seat.

"Ne touchez pas, monsieur," he told me. *"Ne touchez jamais."*

"Why shouldn't I ever touch it?" I asked back.

He gave me one of those French looks. The look that says, "Why do Americans insist on asking questions when all that is called for is simple truth?" And he wagged his finger at me, looked down at the lever, and repeated his words of warning. *"Ne touchez pas,"* he said and shook his head solemnly.

"But what does it do?" I asked.

He looked at me incredulously. *"C'est très important,"* he whispered. The whispering meant it was even more important than I'd already suspected. *"Ne . . . touchez . . . pas."* There was a good ten-second pause before he added the word I knew was coming. *"Jamais."*

I decided to give it one more shot.

"I promise I won't touch it," I said. "I swear. But just give me a hint. What does it do?"

My French mechanic zipped up the front of his overalls, wiped his hands on his pant leg, and walked over to me. He put his hands on my shoulder and stared me straight in the eye.

"Monsieur," he said, in a tone worthy of a head of state announcing the commencement of war. "I would like to say just one thing to you."

"I think I know what it is," I told him.

He spun around, took two steps toward the exit, then spun back around to me. He held out his arm, extended a finger of his hand, and pointed toward the lever in the car.

"Ne touchez pas," he ordered.

"Jamais?" I asked.

Pleased—but still grave and unsmiling—he nodded. *"Jamais,"* he agreed, and left for lunch.

I never did *touche* that lever. I also never found out what the hell it was for. All I know is, for the rest of the year, I lived in mortal fear that a stranger would get behind the wheel of that red Citroën, spot an interesting lever to his right, and either some poor passenger would be catapulted through the roof or some city in China would actually be wiped off the face of the earth.

Of much more immediate concern, however, was getting back to Janis and the apartment where we'd left her.

Aside from my lack of mechanical ability, I have possibly the world's worst sense of direction. I can get lost in New York City—where the streets are arranged numerically!—so driving in Paris turned out to be somewhat of an adventure. All streets in Paris are one way, usually going exactly the opposite direction from the one I wanted to go, and very few streets go for more than a block or two without turning into another name. Which makes it very difficult to get around if you don't know where you're going. It's hard enough driving and simultaneously reading a map, but it's especially hard in Paris, where every two seconds someone either's honking at you or screaming at you or trying to get you to buy some pastry.

I did learn one very important lesson, however: Cats may be wonderful at many, many things, but reading maps is not one of them.

It took me two and a half hours to make the twenty-minute drive to the apartment. But once there, we were all packed and, once Janis was placated, we were also ready to move out.

And so, only a few hours behind schedule, we began our drive down south.

~~~

Norton had never been through the Loire Valley—the Valley of Kings—and for that matter neither had Janis, so we decided to spend a few days meandering through that region's *châteaux* and drinking its superb wine.

Once we finally figured out how to get out of Paris (I don't think I can stand to recount how many times I actually had to drive around the roundabout at the Arc de Triomphe; let's just say it was not a pretty sight), we decided to drive the ninety kilometers to the town of Chartres and begin there.

Perhaps you have picked up on the fact that I am not, in any way, shape, or form, a religious man. I relate to my own culture as I relate to most every other culture—through its food and its women. Thus, except when I once dated a dental hygienist named Rachel, a satisfying Sunday brunch of lox and bagels is about as close as I get to any sort of mystical experience involving my own heritage. Other religions and religious rites leave me cold, too. I'm not much of a believer in spectacle (I can pass just as easily on the Rose Bowl Parade as on midnight mass at St. Patrick's). Neither fear nor guilt work well for me as motivating forces, and I've never thought much of dressing up in long, flowing robes, heavy crowns, and millions of dollars' worth of jewelry except to think that the Pope and Allan Carr would probably have a lot to talk about. I don't believe in heaven or hell (unless you count Anaheim) and I don't think praying for one's soul does any good other than to absolve one from an awful lot of responsibility. I sort of understand the fatalism of various Eastern religions, but I can't say I see much sense in climbing incredibly steep mountains just to find inner peace. I can do that watching Dwight Gooden throw a perfect Lord Charles. As far as walking over hot coals and doing the thing where you sleep on a bed of sharp nails, ix-nay on that. Redemption in the form of pain *really* doesn't cut it with me. All in all, I can't say I believe in god. If, in fact, I ever find out that he does indeed exist, I think I'll stay away from him, because if he's responsible for half the things he gets credit for, he's got to be one mean son of a bitch.

To walk into the cathedral at Chartres, however, makes one understand religion and everything that created it. It's not as if I feel that god was behind this remarkable structure, but it's impossible not to feel the power that *was* behind it—that power being the *belief* in god.

There has been a church at the site of the current cathedral since the fourth century, though the cathedral that stands now wasn't built until 1194. Well, at least it was begun in 1194, and was finished, remarkably, in only thirty years. I am not a student of architecture and this book is not meant to be used as a travel guide, but to stand before the church's facades, the flying buttresses, the *Clocher Neuf,* the overwhelmingly beautiful thirteenth-century stained glass and the fourteenth-century stone choir screen is really to stand before the beauty and power of history. It is as overwhelming a visual experience as I can imagine.

Norton seemed quite floored as well. The three of us toured the inside of the cathedral—Norton on my shoulder, as usual—then sat in a pew to rest and try to absorb what we were looking at. Usually, in such situations, Norton will either be oblivious to his surroundings—i.e., sleeping the sleep of all cats—or he'll be looking every which way, trying to see everything that can be seen, as well as keeping an eye out for any potential dog alerts. At Chartres, however, Norton sat on the pew, head up, and very slowly swiveled his neck, looking first at the huge organ, then studying the pulpit, then taking in the sculptures and paintings and thousands of candles. At one point, a representative of the church ambled over to us and started to say something—I'm fairly sure what he was trying to articulate was that cats weren't allowed in places of worship—but then he saw Norton respectfully eyeing the carved wooden archway to our right, so he ambled back from whence he came. It looked to me as if he realized the cat was appreciating what he was seeing just as much as any other tourist, and he decided the no-cat rule probably wasn't apt in this instance. If only he'd worked for American Airlines instead of god, my life—and probably the lives of countless others—would have been a lot easier.

Going from the splendor of the cathedral to the backseat of the red Citroën, Norton was clearly psyched for his first car trip through the French countryside.

Our next stop was the splendid town of Amboise. Amboise is known for several things: It's where Leonardo da Vinci was buried in 1519; it's where the Mona Lisa was first brought to France; it's where Charles VIII died after hitting his head on a very low doorway. (I'm not making that up! And that would definitely rank near the bottom of ways I personally want to leave this earth.) It's also where Norton jumped out of his shoulder bag and ran away for the only time in his life.

Amboise is down by the river and its amazing *château* is terraced high above it. Before touring the castle, we decided to explore the town, since my favorite thing in France is simply to walk around, watch the people, and stop into as many *pâtisseries* as possible. Janis likes to see how many museums and ruins she can visit in one day; my idea of being a tourist is to find an atmospheric café and spend the day sipping espresso and pretending to be French. For this, our first day in the Loire, we decided to compromise. We'd take the *château* tour, but first I got to walk, drink, eat, and pretend. Norton, of course, accompanied us everywhere. Strolling, sightseeing, caféing. He was right at home.

At one point, we decided to stop at the post office to send back a few postcards. The Amboise *bureau de poste* was in the busiest part of town. After we'd bought our stamps and done our mailings, we headed back to the old town, but before we got there, a large truck decided to barrel past us, its horn blaring, at the exact same time that a bicycle decided to nearly sideswipe me and knock me into the bushes. I was a little unnerved—mostly by the jarring honk from the truck, which wasn't all that close, just loud—but nothing seemed out of place until I heard Janis scream. I turned back to see what she was screaming at, reached into the shoulder bag to make sure Norton was okay, and then realized why she was shrieking—because Norton had jumped out of the bag and was streaking off down the street. He was already a good twenty feet away from us and running as fast as he could. Before Janis could even get out the words "Go get him!" Norton had rounded a corner and disappeared into the heart of a medieval hill town.

I will say one thing for my relationship with my cat—at no time have I ever condescended to him. I refuse to believe he would ever do anything completely untoward. I don't mean something annoying like hiding for the day, I mean something permanently improper—like running away.

Janis, on the other hand, panicked. She kept yelling for me to chase after him, even after I pointed out that even in my best years, I could not run fast enough to catch a cat who didn't want to be caught. Instead, I took a deep breath and told Janis that he would be waiting calmly for me to come get him around the next corner.

Still calm, I led her to the street down which Norton had disappeared. Together we walked—not ran but walked, albeit with a fairly quick stride—the two hundred feet or so

to the next corner . . . and there, sitting in the middle of
the street, waiting for us, was Norton. He had quietly
planted himself in front of a dry cleaner's and had an expression on his face that, without a doubt, was meant to convey,
"So where were you? I've been waiting."

He sat there until I went right over to him, picked him
up, and set him back in his bag.

Janis merely scowled and shook her head.

"He won't run away," I told her.

"Yeah, well *I* might," she said.

I stroked my cat, gave him a quick look, which I'm sure
he knew meant I'd been a lot more worried than I'd let on,
and then we went up to see the Amboise *château*.

It was spectacular. Even Norton thought so (although
every time he shifted in his bag to get a better look at his
surroundings, Janis practically jumped out of her skin). We
saw Leonardo's tomb and the plans and models of his early
inventions (how is it that someone was able to sketch plans
for an airplane and automobile in the early 1500s and I
can't touch my fax machine without getting a paper cut that
slices my finger practically to the bone? It doesn't seem
fair). We also got our first inkling of how far we had to go
with our grasp of the French language.

We'd decided to take a tour of the place, led by a woman
who explained—in French—what we were seeing. She was
obviously well schooled when it came to tourists because,
realizing that very few of us were linguists, she spoke ve
. . ee . . rr . . yy . . . sllooowwwllyy. I thought I was doing
rather well, following almost everything, until afterward I
asked Janis what in the world the guide was talking about
when she told us the story about the shoemakers.

"*What* shoemakers?!" Janis demanded.

"You know," I said. "The shoemakers in the forest who

ran around and—here's where I'm a little fuzzy—found shoes and brought them back for the king?"

I'll actually never forget the expression on my darling's face (or, as they say in France, on the face of my *petit chou-chou*—my little brussels sprout) when she realized to what I was referring. It was a look that combined astonishment, awe, and not a little bit of terror.

The guide had told this long, I thought convoluted story, about the *chasseurs* going out to do their thing for King François Premier (or, François the First to you). I couldn't begin to fathom why *chasseurs*—which I thought were shoemakers—would go searching for pumps and loafers in the woods. It turns out that cha*u*sseurs are shoemakers. And they weren't foraging for leather goods in the king's backyard. Ch*a*sseurs are *hunters*. And they weren't bringing back boots for Frankie either, they were bringing him wild game that they'd shot. To say I missed the point would be a slight understatement, especially since my slant on the entire rest of the guide's story revolved around this whole shoe issue. I was particularly bewildered about the annual "Feast of the Open-Toed Sandals."

Oh, well. So I wasn't ready to resume my dinners with Polanski et al. and seize control of the conversation. Soon, I assured my two traveling companions. But neither Janis nor Norton looked convinced.

I *was* ready—and so was at least one of them—to drink some wine. So we began the *dégustation* part of our Loire trip.

The first place we stopped was Azay-le-Rideau, which in addition to delicious white wine, had a world-class castle. We hit a few *caves,* sampled the local *vin,* then took Norton to see his second *château.* I remembered going to Azay-le-Rideau nearly twenty years before, and I was positive that the word then was that this was the place where the Sleeping Beauty legend grew up.

"Just think," I kept saying to Janis, "this is where Sleeping Beauty was supposed to have slept."

"Prove it," Janis kept saying back to me, because, sure enough, nowhere—in any guide book or anywhere at the castle—was this rather wonderful fact mentioned.

"That's the problem with the modern world," I muttered, when I realized it was my word against Michelin's. "No romance."

"Maybe some shoemakers used to come here," Janis told me, but I made sure she knew that that tack was not going to make me feel any better.

We wound up spending three more days touring *châteaux* and beautiful Loire towns. We never planned ahead, just took our chances on finding a hotel. Twice we went for local dives, which were just fine; once we stayed in a converted castle. Norton liked that room best of all, because it had a beautiful large red satin chair that he used to much the same effect as a throne.

The first couple of hotels we stayed in, I followed the same routine. I'd pull up in front, have Janis wait in the car with you-know-who, then I'd timidly ask the desk clerk or innkeeper if they would let a cat spend the night. Each time, I got exactly the same response.

"Why not?" was the standard reply. "We'd let *you* stay here. Why wouldn't we let a cat stay here?"

I must say, I thought this attitude remarkably healthy, and so, obviously, did Norton. Not only did he make himself comfortable in each room we spent the night, he came down to dinner with us also, and generally had the run of each establishment.

We took Norton to some of the most beautiful places in

France over these few days. We went to the *château* in Blois. (Two interesting facts about Blois: The first is that the name of the town is Celtic and it means "wolf"—and, by the way, so does almost everything else in French; anywhere we'd go for dinner, we'd ask what the name of the restaurant meant and at least fifty percent of the time it was some ancient language for "wolf." The second is that the entire town smells like chocolate. Don't ask me why. I will just assume there's either a large chocolate factory nearby or a really, really fat person with no willpower lives there.)

Norton toured the *château* in Chambord, which looks English to me, perhaps because it was a famous hunting lodge in the 1500s, as well as Cheverny, which still has much of its original furnishings, and he was definitely the first cat since the time of Henry II to tour the two most amazing *châteaux* in the Loire, Chinon and Chenonceau.

Chinon, for those of you who know their history from movies rather than reality, is where Peter O'Toole imprisoned Katharine Hepburn in *The Lion in Winter*. It is mostly in ruins but, perhaps more than any other structure in all of France, strikes me absolutely dumb. It sends shivers up and down my spine. Part of it, I'm sure, is my overactive imagination. Nonetheless, the ruins and history of Chinon inspire dreams and fantasies unlike anyplace I've ever seen.

Chinon is where Joan of Arc stopped to meet the Dauphin—and miraculously recognized the heir to the throne, even though he was dressed a lot like Red Skelton in the guise of Freddie the Freeloader. When Janis, Norton, and I stood above the Chinon moat, having seen Joan's bedroom, and the prison that held Eleanor of Aquitaine, it was a wintry, blustery day. There were few tourists around, fewer cars, and it was remarkably easy to imagine life five hundred years ago. It was not hard to picture oneself in armor, another Richard the Lion-Heart, fighting against Moslem infidels (something I've always wanted to do) and for the survival of civilization. Except in my case, of course, it would be Pete the Cat-Heart.

I let Norton out of his sack for a while and, after he sniffed through the ruins to his satisfaction, the three of us sat in the mostly crumbled courtyard, shivering slightly while we all pictured the past.

The present wasn't too terrible, either. We had a wonderful dinner that night at the Château de Marcay, near Chinon. The hotel is actually a fifteenth-century fortress, surrounded by its own vineyards, with forty rooms which are filled with antiques as well as whirlpools. There, they looked askance when I asked for a bowl of water for Norton—and insisted on bringing him milk instead—and looked absolutely horrified when I ordered the wine I wanted. The *sommelier,* a woman, which is rare over there, quietly and tactfully shook her head and offered to suggest something we might prefer. Although neither Janis nor I are ignoramuses about wine, we put ourselves in her superior hands and we were not disappointed. She brought us perhaps the most delicious white wine I've ever sipped, an Anjou, a Château d'Epire, produced by a M. et Mme. Bizard. I've never seen it before or since, but the taste will stay with me for the rest of my life. Of course, it didn't hurt that we were sipping it on giant oak chairs in front of a roaring, twenty-foot-wide hearth. My guess is that the atmosphere will help Norton remember the taste of that milk, too, a Château Borden, produced by Mme. Elsie.

The local Chinon wine was quite delectable as well, as we discovered the next day (and, if you go there, try the red, which is rarely imported to America—it's superb). We also discovered that small towns in America are not the only places that tend to be rather . . . uh . . . shall we say, rinky-dink.

Picture going to San Antonio to see the Alamo. As soon as you get within thirty miles, you start seeing The Alamo Motel, The Alamo Diner, The Alamo Bar & Grill, and The Alamo Fertilizer & Seed Shop. Everywhere you look, you see nothing but people using the name Alamo to promote something that has about as much to do with Davy Crockett and Jim Bowie as it does with life on Neptune. It's the same thing in the Loire Valley, although most of the touristy come-ons are somewhat more attractive than anything found in San Antonio. When you spend the night in the lovely villages of Loches or Ambois or Blois, every sign in town says something along the lines of CAFÉ LOUIS XIV or BOULANGERIE HENRI VIII or BLANCHERIE HENRI II (Henry the Second's Cleaners—it doesn't have quite the same ring in English, does it?).

One thing in the Loire that absolutely cannot be ruined by commercial greed is the wondrous *château* at Chenonceaux, built on top of a five-arched bridge over the river Cher.

I was first at Chenonceau (And so you don't think I'm a careless speller, please note that the French, typically, spell the town Chenonceaux, but the actual *château* is spelled Chenonceau. What can I say? That's why they're French.) in the summer of 1976, when I was young and hippieish. The place was crawling with tourists and it was brutally hot, but it was so wonderful it didn't matter. I was with David, my partner (yes, we go back that far together, although we didn't know what we were doing back then when it came to writing scripts), and our respective girlfriends (we didn't know what we were doing with them, either, but they're long gone from our lives), and we took rowboats on the river, rowing right under the castle as the sun was setting, then we sat in the middle of the Chenonceau grounds, amidst the alley of plane trees, drank wine and watched the incredible *son et lumière* show explaining the history of the castle.

Years later, when Janis, Norton, and I made our pilgrimage, there were no rowboats and no sound and light show and practically no tourists. It was cold and windy and, if possible, even more perfect than that summer day of long ago. As we toured the castle, nearly by ourselves, all the fireplaces had crackling fires in them. Looking through the windows, it was as if we were looking back into a glorious yet sobering past. We could palpably feel the plagues, the beheadings, the treachery, the splendor, the royalty that had all passed through the stone walls. None of the guards questioned that we were bringing a cat to study the Flemish tapestries, the four-poster beds, the Renaissance furniture, and the mind-boggling underground kitchen. I suppose with all that treachery and all those plagues, a Scottish Fold was no big deal.

Our last stop in the Loire—we were now getting eager to reach Provence—was in the lovely wine village of Sancerre.

This town has always had a fascination for me. When I was twenty-five, I had a novel published, called *The Dandy*, in which the lead character moves to France and chooses the town of Sancerre as his home because it produces his favorite white wine. Years later, the town—and the wine—didn't let me down. We wandered through the old part of the city, parts of which go back to the eleventh century, then we went a tastin'.

Sancerre happens to be Janis's favorite white wine, too, so we didn't hesitate to do as much sampling as we possibly could. And in this town, it's possible to do a *lot* of sampling. There must be over a hundred vineyards in a two- or three-mile area, each producing a wine more delicious than the last one. My favorite, and Janis's, was a small local *cave* right in town run by a father-and-son team. They were shut tight the day we were there, but a sign was posted saying that anyone who really wanted some wine should go three blocks further, make a right, then knock loudly at the door of the second house on the left. We followed the directions—a miracle in itself, nearly on a par with Jeanne d'Arc and the Dauphin—and found ourselves in someone's kitchen. The mother of the whole family, a rather chubby lady in her seventies, was making a huge vat of soup. We talked about their various wines while she stirred; then we sipped some different vintages while she stirred. We kept talking and sipping, she kept stirring, and finally we bought several cases to stick in the trunk of our car. I don't think she ever let go of her spoon the entire time.

Norton's favorite vineyard, however, was called the Cave Fouassier, right outside of town on the Route de Bourges. Norton didn't actually taste the wine, but he was very impressed with the vintner's dog, who, when he wanted to go out, would stand up on his two hind legs, put his two front paws on the doorknob, turn the knob, open the door, and scamper outside. It took us so long to taste and decide what to buy that by the time we were ready to leave, the dog wanted to come back in. So he went back on his hind legs, grabbed the doorknob with his front paws, and in he came.

It takes a lot to make Norton feel insecure. But I could tell from his expression that he was a bit awed by this feat.

"Hey," I told him, "practice makes perfect. It'll give you something to work on while we're here."

"You're talking to your cat again," Janis told me.

Norton didn't tell either one of us anything. He just stuck his head down inside his shoulder bag and thought about what he'd seen and what he was going to do about it.

We loaded our wine into the back of the car—there was now barely room to even put gas in—found the big highway, the *péage,* on our map, and, satiated with history, beauty, spirits, and genius dogs, sped on down to our new home.

5

a cat in provence

The house was perfect. And so was our new hometown.

The photographs we'd seen, convincing as they'd been, hadn't done either of them justice. The house was indeed three hundred years old. It was tucked away in a tiny side street (since the whole town was basically one street long, it wasn't difficult for the side streets to be tiny), the facade for the front was a pinkish, rough stucco, and the back was all the original stone. Downstairs was a small living room (very comfortably furnished), an eat-in kitchen with a fireplace (and no pancake flipper), a small *toilette,* and a separate bathroom with a tub and shower. On the second floor (which, mysteriously, the French call the first floor) were three bedrooms—one quite large, two smaller ones which formed a kind of mini-suite—another *toilette,* and another bathroom with tub. On the third floor (which the French call the second floor—if you think *you're* confused, try having a conversation with a French person about finding something on one of these floors!) was a large, sprawling office, sparsely furnished with a few chairs and a long, glass desk, and then another bedroom, large with its own sink tucked off to the side. There were also closets and cupboards everywhere you looked, all of which were filled with Provençalian napkins and tablecloths and linens and towels, as well as china and such essentials as an iron, a vacuum cleaner, and lightbulbs. The furniture was old and comfortable and inviting; the kitchen was splendidly equipped. Best of all, for my taste, was the sprawling *cave* underneath the house. Using an old turnkey to open the thick wooden door from the street, you then stepped into a stone dungeon. In addition to such modern essentials as a washer/dryer and a boiler, the *cave* was the place to stack the winter's supply of wood and preserved jellies and jams. It also had a wine cellar, protected by an iron gate, which needed another old turnkey in order to pass through. Every time I went into the wine cellar, I was positive some forty-pound guy with long white hair was going to spring out at me and beg me to put in a kind word with the captain of the king's guard.

All in all, this house was made for me.

More important, Norton took to it immediately.

Before we did anything else, I showed him the plump couch and two easy chairs in the living room, explaining to him that this was not our furniture and that he was not allowed to scratch it. Ever. Janis, as usual, thought that I'd lost my mind and that these complicated instructions probably would not penetrate the mind of a cat, but I do have to say—and feel free to call our landlady anytime to verify this—at the end of our year there, not a chair or a couch in that house had so much as one scratch on it.

As soon as the rules were laid down, Norton went exploring. He sniffed around the living room and immediately discovered his favorite exit from the house. The old-fashioned windows that swung open, looked over the backyard—and the entire Lubéron valley as well. A roof extended from right below the window, which functioned as an overhang for a patio. Norton immediately hopped up onto the window ledge, looked plaintively back in my direction until I figured out how to swing the window open (something I learned to do smoothly just about the time our year was up), then he hopped out onto the roof, stretched leisurely, lay down directly in the middle of a ray of sun, and began his life as a Provençal cat. All he needed was a beret and a baguette and I guarantee people would have come up to him and started to ask him what life was like in the *résistance*.

Another window swung open over the kitchen table, and Norton liked hopping out that one, too. He was also happy with the placement of his litter box, on the stone floor right by the back door. It became fairly standard procedure, during our time there, for Norton to pay a visit to his litter box, then immediately stand by the back door, waiting to be let out. Once out, he'd jump up onto the stone wall that ran up alongside the back steps to the house, assume a sphinxlike position, and spend as much time there as direct sunlight allowed.

The garden was a cat's delight (as well as Janis's greatest pleasure, since there is nothing that gives her as much pure joy as sticking her hands in dirt and either planting a beloved perennial or ripping out some dreaded weed). Our Provençal garden was roughly the size of a football field, divided up into four distinct square levels and sections, each square separated by an ancient stone wall. Directly out the back door, the first square had an enormous spruce tree in the middle of it, and next to that, a small fig tree. Around

the perimiters were roses, pansies, tulips, wisteria, and lots
and lots of herbs—including huge hedges of rosemary. Up
against the house, an extension, really, of this part of the
garden, was a stone patio, set up with several chairs and a
small dining table. The weather was so beautiful that we ate
outside almost every day until mid-December.

If you made a right turn out the back door, took ten
paces, and then went down a couple of stone steps, you'd
reach the second square of the garden. This one was dominated by a large lavender garden; the well-defined rectan-
gle of lavender was probably twelve feet wide and fifteen
feet long. Past the lavender, and running along the boundary of the property, was another patio, also set up with a
small table and chairs. Built into the wall there was a stone
barbecue, complete with grill.

Facing straight ahead, still standing on the right side of
the yard, you could go down a couple of stone steps to the
third quarter of the garden. This one was dominated by a
luscious cherry tree and a round stone table, the perfect
place to sit and sip a late-afternoon *kir.*

To the left, and down six or seven more steps, was the
last part of the garden, this one fairly sparse. An olive tree
sat toward the right of the space, as did a bay laurel tree,
and the left boundary was lined with raspberry bushes (we
were eating ripe, delicious raspberries for breakfast until
the first week in December).

Norton spent hours and hours exploring every nook and
cranny of this garden. He loved it out there. For one thing,
there were no mean mockingbirds to torment him, as there
were in Sag Harbor, only a bunch of fairly pleasant black
and white magpies. Plus, I'm sure the mice were particularly delicious, since they had been fattened up on camem-
bert and roquefort since birth.

As much as we adored the house—and we gradually added our personal touches to it: the occasional quilt here, a piece of rough hewn pottery there—the town in which we now resided was even more special.

Goult truly is a village touched by magic. It is as lovely as any of the small towns in the entire region yet has escaped any trappings of tourism, managing to remain completely unspoiled. It's small, approximately eleven hundred people, has a thousand-year-old castle, and is nicknamed "Le Village Caché" ("the hidden village") according to local legend because it's tucked away on top of a hill and seems to disappear, à la Brigadoon, when one is trying to spot it from the road down below. Up until the spring of '92, there was only one restaurant in town; now there are two. Up until that same time, there was one *épicerie* in town; now there are two. There have always been two butchers, though I can't fathom how a town of a eleven hundred people supports two butchers, especially since—and this could only be in France—they are right next door to each other, keep the exact same hours, and are closed the exact same day of the week.

We—the three of us, with Norton lagging behind and periodically disappearing into strange alleys and *caves,* including someone's garage, which turned out to have once been the town's ancient olive oil mill—toured the town and oriented ourselves, once we explored the various rooms and gardens of the house. Satisfied that we'd done well—having no idea yet quite *how* well we'd done—we returned to the house to begin the process of making it our home. The first step was to unpack the various boxes we'd sent on ahead (yes, yes, we had even *more* stuff than the millions of pounds we lugged in our suitcases). There was only one problem: There *were* no boxes.

This brings us to an important rule of thumb that one must understand before ever moving to France: When it comes to anything involving rules, regulations, and laws, absolutely nothing in the country makes any sense whatsoever.

A case in point:

Since I was neither retired nor wealthy, and since my cat was expecting to be kept in the style to which he'd become accustomed, I had to do some work while we were in France. As this is the twentieth century, I needed a computer, a fax machine, and a telephone answering machine to do that work. And thus the nightmare began.

My first mistake was shipping those key items over instead of packing them away and carrying them (this was important because in all the trips we made in and out of the Marseille airport, we never even *saw* a customs official, much less one who would rummage through a suitcase). My second mistake was being honest. On the UPS form, right below the line where they promise you'll receive your goods in two days, is a blank space where you're supposed to list exactly what it is you're shipping. On my form, kook that I was, I put exactly that: a fax machine, a laptop computer, a telephone answering machine, three electrical transformers (which weigh twenty pounds apiece, cost eighty dollars apiece, and are an absolute necessity for any American spending time in France), and some sweaters (which, along with bubble wrap, were used to cushion all the machinery so they wouldn't be smashed into little bits). UPS couldn't have been nicer or more efficient and they weren't even that expensive. All my stuff even arrived in Paris exactly on time. And when it arrived, I got a call from someone named Monsieur Kebé at French Customs. We had a very pleasant chat—although Monsieur Kebé spoke no English and, at this point, my French sounded a lot like Inspector Clouseau; I was basically speaking English with a French accent and hoping that would pass—until I was told that it was impossible to allow my cartons into the country. It seems that the French phone company, which is government-owned, has a monopoly on phone machines *(répondeurs)* and fax machines. So no such machines are allowed to be brought in. Ever. Never.

I was told that no amount of money, no amount of pleading, no amount of *anything* would ever convince them to let me bring these machines into France. It was impossible. Out of the question. End of story. *Tout est dit!*

I did some checking. There really did seem to be a law against bringing in phone machines. The government made everyone buy only French phone equipment. As near as I could tell, however, there were no exact laws against bringing in computers—they're not owned by the phone company, thank god!—but it seems the French just don't really *like* it when one is brought in. They prefer you buy one of their own *ordinateurs.* As far as the sweaters were concerned, they were a little concerned that I'd be opening a sweater store, which would be illegal for an American, so they thought they'd keep those, too.

I'll skip most of the unpleasantries. Like anything else in France, what was needed most here was neither money to bribe nor logic to convince. What was needed was patience. And a French friend named Nicholas who lived in Paris and went to see Monsieur Kebé in person. After three days of conversation, Nicholas called me to say that he explained to Monsieur Kebé that I was a writer and a publisher and that these machines were not to be sold in France but were the tools of my trade. Ah! Although it was still out of the question—absolutely and finally—Monsieur K wanted me to fax him my passport, a letter from my French publisher, and a copy of the jacket of my latest book. I was happy to do that, I explained—except that Monsieur Kebé had my fax machine. That was why we were having this conversation in the first place!

They acknowledged a certain logic on my part, but nonetheless they wanted what they wanted. I found a public fax in the nearby town of Murs and was able to send them what they'd asked for. It only took me six hours, which means I could have taken the TGV up to Paris, dropped the material off, and trained it on back home in the same amount of time it took me to fax something. The reason it took so much time was also fairly typical Provence (and fairly typical me). Janis decided to stay home to begin work in the garden. So Norton and I got in our car and went exploring. First we went to the town of Apt, the largest nearby town. After asking in the bookstore, a café, and a pottery store, I found out that there was no public fax in Apt. The nearest one was in Murs, a town of perhaps seven hundred people. No problem. We headed off to Murs and got to the *mairie,* the town hall, just a few minutes after noon. Which was a few minutes too late because the *mairie* was closed until three. No problem. I was in France; I could adapt to a different speed and lifestyle. I'd simply go to a café in Murs, have a little wine, read a little bit, pet my cat, and wait for three o'clock to arrive. Except that Murs didn't *have* a café. It was too small. So Norton and I drove back to Apt, where we found a café and a carafe of chilled rosé wine. Two hours later, it was back to Murs. But there was some sort of emergency and the *mairie* still wasn't open. (Later, I think I pieced together the emergency: The woman who worked at the *mairie* had a daughter who'd had a fight with her husband. I couldn't understand what they fought over, though I think it had something to do with a beef stew the daughter either had or hadn't made for that night's dinner.) At 3:45 the woman arrived and, apologetically, opened up the town hall. She reminded me of Jo Van Fleet in *Cool Hand Luke,* wheezing and creaking and coughing while she talked. We climbed the two flights of stairs together, then, exhausted, she had to rest for a few minutes before we could get on to business. I showed her my passport and the other things I'd brought and asked her if I could use the town's fax machine. *Of course,* she told me. *Absolutely no problem. Fine,* I told her. *Well, maybe there's* one *little problem,* she said. Then she told me she didn't know how to work the fax machine. No one had ever asked to use it before. So we had to wait for her coworker, a man of sixty years or so, to come huffing and puffing up the stairs, too, to try to send the material. He was the French William Demarest, grumpy, mumbling constantly, very concerned about everything, and extremely tan and leathery.

An hour later, we'd all basically figured the sucker out. Sure enough, when I tried faxing everything through, it worked. (Although when the first sheet of paper passed through, both William Demarest and Jo Van Fleet did double takes. "What eez zat noise?" she asked. "I think it's the fax being transmitted," I told her. She looked at him for confirmation and he just shrugged; now that it was working, he'd washed his hands of the whole matter.)

I then asked how much I owed—and this was a major stumper. She had no idea, so she paced for a while, pursed her lips in that French way, shook her head, and muttered to herself. She tried asking Bill Demarest, but he could only make puffing noises with his mouth and slowly shake his head back and forth. I just let them talk and pace and puff, and at some point they settled on twenty francs, about four dollars.

On Day 5 of the Fax/Computer Hostage Situation, customs told me I should forget about what they'd said earlier: I could have all my things after all—for a mere fifteen hundred dollars in import tax. Outraged, I told them to ship it all back to America. I'd rather buy new equipment, I said. (A mistake: A French phone machine, even a crummy one, costs four hundred dollars. A fax machine goes for about fifteen hundred. Don't even *think* about buying a computer there. Anything electric costs two to three times as much as it costs in the USA.) Luckily, however, they paid no attention to me. French people hardly ever pay attention to anything stupid we foreigners say.

Day 10: They asked me to send them a copy of *The Cat Who Went to Paris.*

Day 14: Monsieur Kebé liked the book. I decided he's more suited to be a literary critic for *The New York Times* than a French Customs official. He also says I can have my equipment for a mere thousand dollars. I get angry but, keeping his superb literary taste in mind, I don't go berserk.

Day 17: My friend Nicholas calls me to say I'm getting everything—for free. No problem whatsoever; it'll all arrive within two days. He said the final conversation in the customs room between Monsieur Kebé and his superior went as follows:

"Hmmm, he really seems to be a writer."

"What should we do?"

"Hmmmm. More wine?"

"Thank you. Do you think he's importing these things to sell them here?"

"No, do you?"

"I don't know. I don't think he could get very much for those sweaters."

"Oh, let's send the stuff to him. It takes up a lot of room here."

"It certainly does. Okay, let's send it. Could I have a drop more of the white?"

Once my home office was set up, I could relax, rather than spend most of the day pacing around the town of Goult muttering about the end of my career. This final settling in also meant that our family of three could develop a routine. (Although here are two hints to help you relax a bit more if you're American and you ever set up a home office in France. Hint #1: Bring a spare phone machine because you will definitely blow up the first one trying to figure out how to hook it up to the transformer without blowing it up on the different current. Hint #2: After you finish ripping your hair out of your head because you can't figure out how to plug an American phone into a French phone jack, go to a French hardware or electrical appliance store. They have special plugs that fit American phones—even though they're not supposed to, because, as we all remember, it's illegal to have an American phone. Don't ask questions, just get one.)

Our routine was a fairly relaxed one, since the purpose of this whole trip was to exchange our insanely hectic New York lifestyle for one that made some philosophical, psychological, and emotional sense (and, since we were in France, we figured we also had to eat and drink as much as we possibly could). I would get up, have my early-morning two-mile run through the vast expanse of vineyards, then, huffing and puffing on my way back up the hill to Goult, I'd stop off at the patisserie in Lumiere, the town closest to us, for a baguette or a couple of croissants. By the time I'd get to the house, Janis would have made coffee. We'd have our breakfast—bread, honey, jam, and coffee—together, on Elisabeth's china and in her giant, soup-sized bowls; sometimes Norton would join us, sometimes he'd already be perched on the roof or the wall outside. Then I'd go upstairs to work for the morning while Janis would garden or go off to a museum or just study her French. Come lunchtime, we'd rendezvous, deciding, depending on our mood, whether to have a luxurious and extravagant lunch, or a quick peasant lunch at a *routier* (truckstop) followed by a two- or three-hour session exploring the region. If I didn't have to work in the afternoon (I was busy working for Random House as well as writing a screenplay and a book; I know that doesn't sound like much of a vacation, but believe me, after running a company and producing a TV series and writing a book all at the same time, working two jobs on my own time was the equivalent of lying on the beach in the Caribbean), we could explore further. For dinner, we'd either hit a local restaurant or expand our culinary abilities (not to brag, but we both became fairly proficient in the kitchen while we were there) or, as our circle of friends expanded, hope that one of our new pals would invite us over for an *aïoli* or a *maigret de canard.*

Norton's routine became fairly standardized also, once we worked out his sleeping arrangements. For the first couple of weeks we were there, we had a tiny bed and he was too outraged at the lack of space to sleep with us. There was barely room for the two humans to get through the night without tumbling onto the floor, though of course this didn't stop me from trying to squeeze Norton in. But he would have none of it. Needless to say, this didn't sit well with me; I do not sleep well unless my cat is within hugging distance at almost all times. So I was delighted when our landlady agreed to buy the house a new and much larger bed, although, like everything else, having a bed delivered in France is not like having a bed delivered anywhere else. More than anything in the world, French people love to talk. It doesn't matter if the tone is argumentative, questioning, sympathetic, informational, or philosophical, as long as talk is involved. So the first thing was that the guys from the furniture store came over to take a look at the house—and talk about it. They examined the front door to make sure the bed would fit. That was good for a five-minute chat. Then they examined the hallway. That seemed worth talking about for ten minutes or so. They examined the curved stone stairway that led up to our bedroom. That was a particularly interesting topic of conversation. How old was the stairway? Was it original? How many steps were there? How steep was it? Did I ever slip and fall down it in the middle of the night?

They managed to examine the bedroom—as well as the three other bedrooms in the house, just in case the bed wouldn't fit in the room for which it was intended. Then they discussed the door and the hallway and the various bedrooms some more. After forty-five minutes of this, I suggested that perhaps it might work best if they actually measured the doorways and the width of the stairs. Yes, they agreed. That was a very good idea. Did I happen to have a tape measure? I did happen to have one, and after another forty-five minutes during which we discussed the furniture in the house, the weather, the advantages and disadvantages of Goult, a date on which they could deliver the bed, and, finally, drank a couple of cups of coffee, they left. A week later, when the bed came, the problem with

Norton was solved. He had enough room to be comfortable and went right back to his usual spot of sleeping near my neck and chest.

The first night of the new bed, we went to the local restaurant in Goult, Le Tunneau, owned by a charming guy and good chef, Patrick, to celebrate. It was Norton's first time at Le Tunneau and he was served a little duck by way of introduction. He was accepted as just another customer. There was no fuss whatsoever, even from the dog dining there that night. During the course of the meal, Norton wandered a little bit (the restaurant is a converted *cave,* so there were plenty of interesting sniffing and scratching places). Every so often, he would hop back up on his seat and help himself to a taste of my rabbit or Janis's chicken. After dinner, stuffed and quite content, the three of us headed home and went to sleep. Janis woke up in the middle of the night to the following picture: I was sound asleep on the left side of the bed; she was lying on the right side. Stretched out exactly in the middle, head on both of our pillows, body under the blanket, was our Scottish Fold, sound asleep yet purring so loudly he'd woken her up.

Once the sleep routine was settled, Norton's day was not so different from our own. After a fine French breakfast (canned rabbit was the clear winner as far as he was concerned), he would sun himself outside in one of his three or four favorite spots. He would, as often as not, come out to lunch with us and explore whenever it was appropriate. Depending on how hard we'd judged his day, he'd either dine out with us or stay home like a normal cat, content to eat more canned rabbit and then fall asleep.

Norton had never been a particularly social animal, not when it came to other four-legged creatures. He was not around a lot of cats in New York (he'd been in one fight—

recounted in extraordinary dramatic detail in the *very* underrated yet moving and puckish *The Cat Who Went to Paris*—which did not end happily or with much of Norton's dignity remaining) and his exposure to dogs, while harmless and uneventful, had also been infrequent. That all changed in Provence.

At my last count, there were forty-two million cats in Goult, give or take a million. They were all over the place, everywhere and anywhere you turned. None of them, it seemed, had a home, although every person in town knew every one of the cats, usually by name. Our landlady, Elisabeth, was a longtime cat lover and, even though she didn't have any of her own, she used to leave food out for *tous les chats Goultois.* Which meant that we usually had several cats strolling the property in search of nourishment.

I don't know whether it was the fact that Norton felt, as an expatriot cat, that he was intruding on the Goult cats' turf, but he was far friendlier and more relaxed around these fellows than he ever was with the felines in Sag Harbor or Fire Island. There was the occasional hiss and unmistakable cat-fight screech, and every so often he'd try to act like a tough guy (usually when he was safely inside and knew all doors and windows to the garden were closed), but on the whole, Norton seemed to accept the French *que será, será* way of life and actually made a few pals.

One of his closer friends was a solid black cat, whose name we learned was Othello. We never learned who Othello's owner was, but Othello's demeanor was befitting of his regal name; he used to preen all around the town, though his special spot was a bench that was placed in a small grass triangle—a *very* tiny public park—from which he liked to survey the townspeople's comings and goings.

I don't think Norton and Othello used to go to soccer

matches together or exchange Christmas presents, but there was a certain amount of male bonding that went on. I do know that one day, as I was strolling to one of the village butchers, I did see Norton and Othello together sitting outside the café. Don't worry: They weren't being served. At least, not when I passed by.

Probably the funniest animal in town was a bulldog named Archie (pronounced Ar-*shee*). Archie was as solid as bulldogs usually are and he was a dead ringer for the older J. Edgar Hoover, except I never saw Archie wearing a dress. Archie's owner was a young woman who would often walk him through town on a leash, but just as often, we'd find Archie hanging out around our front door, leashless and ownerless. Everyone in town knew Archie (I think he must have, at one point or another, drooled several kilos of saliva on every person in Goult), but he handled his celebrity status quite well. He was always friendly, to humans and to Scottish Fold cats. After several weeks of eyeing each other warily, Norton and Archie achieved a certain comfort level. When in each other's presence, Archie would do his best not to snort and breathe so heavily that he scared Norton, and Norton eventually got to the point where he would stroll within inches of the bulldog without having to sprint, hiss, or make all his fur stand up on end.

I know everyone likes a happy ending, but I'm sorry to say that Norton never did come to grips with those little, friendly birds who were in the outdoor cage a couple of blocks from our house. After his wimpy run-in with them, which I mentioned earlier, he stayed as far away from that part of town as he possibly could.

Norton got to be pals—or at least nodding acquaintances—with several animals outside of Goult, too.

One of our favorite restaurants, a breathtakingly charming place up in the mountains, the Auberge de la Loube, in the town of Buoux, was wonderful not only because of the owners/chefs but because of the cats and dogs who populated the place.

The restaurant is a four-hundred-year-old stone farmhouse, quite small, maybe twelve tables, dominated by an enormous fireplace and decorated with all sorts of horse accoutrements—everything from photos to bridles to reins to saddles. The owner, Maurice, is a terrific guy, quite friendly and elegant, a little bemused at how successful his country inn has become since Peter Mayle rhapsodized about him in *A Year in Provence*. (The reason there's so much horse memorabilia around is that Maurice restores antique carriages—as in horse and carriages. Some of them are nineteenth-century American carriages, most are French, all are exquisite. When the weather's nice, it's possible to arrange for a carriage ride in the mountains and a picnic lunch or dinner. One other thing about the Auberge de la Loube: For months, we assumed "Loube" was some variation on the Lubéron valley and mountain range, of which Buoux is a part. However, we asked Maurice one night and he explained to us that—and remember, I warned you about this earlier—*loube* is, in fact, Provençal for "wolf.") His wife, whom we knew only as Madame Maurice, is equally terrific, and she took particular pleasure in Norton's visits to the Auberge.

Maurice and his wife have three dogs, a gorgeous Irish setter, a black lab, and some kind of very friendly mutt, as well as a big, fat, easygoing orange cat. The dogs roam the two rooms of the restaurant, camping under the table of whoever looks most likely to drop food on the floor, either unintentionally or out of pity for the tortured, starving look the dogs can assume at a moment's notice. All three of the

canines also spend a lot of time burrowed in the two hol-
lows that are dug into the stone underneath the huge
hearth. The cat, naturally, is much more dignified. He
strolls around the restaurant, quite haughtily, until he finds
a willing sucker, then he jumps up into his or her lap and
settles in for the night (or until Madame Maurice spots him
and swats him away, yelling at him to leave the customers
alone). The dogs and cat get along famously, and they all
switch back and forth effortlessly from being outdoor to
indoor animals. There is a famous local story about the Irish
setter, who tends to roam more than the others. He was
spotted one day in the town of Apt, which is a good seven
or eight miles away from the Auberge. When he was recognized, as he was walking confidently through the town,
some concerned friend convinced him to hop into his truck
and brought him back to the Auberge, where they suspect
he makes such lengthy sojourns on a regular basis.

The first time we brought Norton up to meet the gang
at the Auberge, he was greeted warmly by all concerned
and fit in as if he'd been born to the French mountain life.
He had quite a few dinners up there, and humans, dogs, and
cat were always glad to see him. When the restaurant wasn't
crowded, he'd be allowed his own chair. When it was
crowded—which was more often than not—he'd either sit
on my lap or find a nice spot on the table in which to settle
in. If we got a window seat, he was also more than happy
to dine in comfort on the stone window ledge.

The food at Auberge de la Loube is a cat's delight, as well
as the delight of any sane person, because it's delicious and
completely satisfying. They also do something that's common in France, which is take the pressure off the diner as
far as having to choose is concerned; basically, they order
for you. When you sit down at Auberge de la Loube, an

enormous tray of Provençal appetizers is placed before you.
On the tray are small dishes, filled with local delicacies. A
typical sampling will include onion marmalade, tiny quail's
eggs, the best *tapenade* ever made, candied carrots, rabbit
pâté, a very garlicy yogurt, *anchois* and pickled cucumbers.
All to be eaten with a basketful of French bread, which is
sliced before your eyes with an antique bread cutter which
resembles nothing so much as the guillotine that sliced off
the head of Marie Antoinette and probably a whole bunch
of other cake-eaters.

Once sated, you're left only with having to make choices
from the good, inexpensive, and mostly local wine list and
four or five options for a main course. In the fall and winter,
the possibilities range from *sanglier,* which is wild boar
(often served in a stew, with a thick, very dark sauce, called
a *civet*), rabbit (sometimes served in the same kind of stew,
sometimes served roasted), stuffed or roast veal, and occasionally a fish, usually salmon or *lotte.* In the spring and
summer, the choices are usually the same base foods, although prepared in a somewhat lighter fashion. Oddly
enough, restaurants in Provence rarely serve chicken, as
that's perceived, historically, as poor people's food.

Perhaps it has occurred to you already, but when one
lives in the south of France, one becomes totally obsessed
with food. We would get calls from friends back in America
wondering whether we'd lost our minds because they'd just
received a three-page letter from one of us which was about
nothing but one luscious and delicious tomato we'd bought
at the market. It reached the point where people were
expecting daily faxes from us to find out what we'd eaten
for dinner the night before.

It didn't take long for each of us—me, Janis, and Norton—to grab hold of this obsession and refuse to let go.

After we'd been there several months, we had the ultimate compliment paid to us by an elderly French woman, who prepared us dinner one night. As we were eating her succulent lamb, we were discussing other great meals we'd had since we'd been in Europe. We're munching on her roast potatoes talking about a pasta dish we'd eaten in Tuscany; we're scarfing down her white beans in *vinaigre* while extolling the virtues of a bouillabaise we'd had in Marseille; we're moaning over her *tarte aux pommes* but manage to get in a few highly charged words about a raspberry beignet we'd stumbled upon at an open-air market. Finally she says, in a throaty voice with just a touch of a French accent, "Congratulations. You are now truly French. To eat a fine meal and do nothing but talk about other foods means you're now one of us."

Hey, when in Rome (or Provence), you know what I mean?

Our days began to revolve around food.

One of the great thrills of living there is to shop at the open-air markets, which move from town to town, depending on the day of the week. When we finally figured out the schedule, we began to move along with them. Tuesday was a small market in the village of Gordes. Saturday was Apt. Both towns were convenient to Goult, so we became Tuesday and Saturday regulars. The biggest and most spectacular market was on Sunday, in the town of L'isle-sur-la-Sorgue. There the appeal was not just food but miles of stalls filled with splendid antiques. Going to market on Sunday became, to me, the equivalent of a five-year-old kid going to Disneyland.

L'isle-sur-la-Sorgue is not a large town—perhaps three thousand people—but on Sunday mornings it quadruples in size. The village itself is quite beautiful. It's flat, unlike most of the towns around it, which are perched on hilltops, and has winding cobblestone streets lurching in every direction. It's also built on a series of canals, which surround the town and, thanks to the clear, rushing water and the waterwheels and the wooden bridges, give it much of its atmosphere. During the week (except Thursday, when there's a mini-version of the big market), the place is subdued, quiet, and charming. But on Sundays, from seven in the morning until one o'clock in the afternoon, it's a madhouse. Every inch of the cobblestone streets is packed with vendors and shoppers. The vendors have staked out their particular territories over a period of years (in some cases, I'm fairly sure that certain families have been selling their wine or their potatoes in the same spot for about three *hundred* years or so); the shoppers mill aimlessly until they see what they want or, especially as the seasons get warmer and more tourists show up, shove their way through the crowds to try to get the best of everything. It's so European it can make you cry with pleasure, especially when the local organ grinder, who happens to look like a young Maurice Chevalier, strolls through the crowded market in feathered cap and glowing cape belting out his romantic ballads.

Norton quite liked being lugged through the L'isle market in his shoulder bag. If he played his cards right, which he usually did, he could come away with little bits of everything from homemade sausage to strong, smelly goat cheese to chocolate tarts. Janis and I also usually played our cards right. It didn't take us long to find our favorite vendors and become regular buyers (many of the same vendors also went to the Gordes and the Apt markets, so we'd see them two or three times a week). One of our favorites was a small, wonderfully nice and cheery man who made mouthwatering tarts and sold them from his truck, with the aid of

his eight-year-old daughter. He baked in the town of Ve-
nasque, about forty-five minutes away, via a curving, mountain road, and then carried his scrumptious works of art to
the marketplaces. His artichoke tart was like nectar of the
gods, as was his *poireaux* (leeks) creation, but his shallot tart
was his masterpiece, as delicious as anything I've ever tasted
that wasn't covered with chocolate. And while we're on the
subject, he happened to make a chocolate and caramel tart
that, in my humble opinion, belongs in the Louvre. Luckily
for everyone's cholesterol count, we figured there couldn't
possibly be more than seven or eight pounds of butter in it.

In addition to our tart guy (that's the way we started
thinking of him: Our Tart Guy), there was a Cambodian
man who made the most delicious *poulet rôti* that was ever
*rôti*ed. He was a lawyer in Cambodia but wasn't allowed to
take the French bar (or whatever the equivalent of the bar
is in France) and so made perfect roast chickens instead.
There was a young Algerian who aggressively sold vats of
incredible *tapenade* and *anchois* (crushed olive paste and
crushed anchovies). There was also an old, cronelike
woman who was missing at least two-thirds of her teeth and
who sold goat cheese so strong you could barely stand up
after a small taste. She sold them in little heart-shaped
cheeses, each one flavored with rosemary or garlic or shal-
lots or—and this one I'm guessing on but I think I'm
close—really old socks. We bought cheese from her every
week and her products became a benchmark for any and all
of our visitors. It was simple: Someone would arrive from
New York, exhausted from the long flight and drive from
Marseille. We'd sit him, her, or them down, set up a glass
of wine from a nearby *cave,* and place a plate of the crone's
goat cheese before them. If they tasted it, and then hungrily
dug in for more, appreciating the earthiness and power, we

knew we were in for a good visit. If, on the other hand, the guest or guests got a slice of the garlic cheese halfway down their throat, then started gasping and calling either for water or a gun with which to shoot themselves, we knew that we'd have trouble sharing our Provençal tastes and pleasures.

Norton, in the meantime, was developing his own very particular tastes and pleasures when it came to French food.

With all our travels, prior to and including this year abroad, Norton seemed to prefer French cat food to any other. His favorites were Whiskas, Gourmet, and the French Friskies. Gourmet was the cheaper brand, more of a peasant cat food, but at times clearly satisfying to the cat palate. The nice thing about Gourmet was that they sold it in a handy three-pack *(le menu 3 étoiles; 3 boîtes de 195 grams)*. They had many different flavors, most of which pleased my cat. In the category of *Les Pavés Mignons,* they had your basic *Délice de Viandes,* your fresh *Au Saumon,* and the ever-popular *Au Foie et Volaille.* In the category of Best Supporting *Terrine,* they had an overload of delicacies: *Au Lapin et Foie* (definitely in Norton's top three); *L'Agneau et Volaille* (yummmmm), *Au Foie et Veau, Délice de Colin, Aux Trois Volailles, Au Foie et Volaille* (a certain pattern does seem to be emerging, though I'm not sure if Norton ever noticed that there were the same basic ingredients, cleverly mixed together in as many different combinations as those Gourmet folks could think up), *Au Boeuf et Rognons* (also quite a favorite), *Panache de Poissons* (not a chance; Norton never succumbed to this one), *Au Gibier* (Norton was quite fond of this can; Janis would leave the room as soon as it was opened—a *boîte* filled with all sort of giblets is not her idea of culinary heaven), *Au Poulet et Rognons* (boring but a solid choice), *Au Lapin et Foie* (now you're talking!), and just before we left, Gourmet introduced the *nouveau* flavor of the year, *Au Rognons et Volaille* (bravo!). As if this weren't enough, they also had a category called *La Mousse*, which only had one flavor, but was nothing to sneer at, *Au Rognons et Volaille.*

Although Gourmet was not, in fact, the crème de la crème of French cat foods, I had a soft spot for them because of the Club Gourmet one could join. On specially marked cans of their food was an announcement: *Vous qui êtes passionnés de chats, rejoignez vite le CLUB GOURMET, un club spécialement crée pour vous: vous bénéficierez des privilèges d'un club prestigieux et des conseils châteaux de CATY.* Translated as best as I can manage, this means: You who are passionate about cats, quickly sign up for the Gourmet Club, a special club created for you: you benefit from the privileges of a prestigious club and the counsel of the cat castle.

Friskies wasn't bad, if you go by Norton's appetite, and they had the advantage of being slightly healthier. Well, okay, I wouldn't call it health food, but at least with their *Au Foie et Volaille,* they added *petits légumes.* After Norton munched on these, I didn't feel so bad about giving him a lick of my dessert.

Whoever was the creative force in the Whiskas kitchen was a fine *chef de cuisine,* also. Norton's favorite *boîte* on their list was the clever combo of *Au Lapin et à la Dinde* (rabbit and turkey; you've got to admit it sounds good). Whiskas also was thoughtful enough to tell you a little bit about their food on the back of each box top:

- *WHISKAS a préparé pour votre chat les "Petits Régals":*
- *des recettes richement elaborées avec de delicieux petits morceaux et une odeur appétissante*

- *une présentation soignée, en portion repas, facile à utiliser, avec un couvercle refermable*
- *Pour varier les plaisirs de votre chat, les "Petits Régals" vous proposent trois variétés raffinées: Au Bouef et aux Rognons, A la Volaille et au Foie, Au Lapin et à la Dinde.*

Words to bring comfort to any cat and cat owner:

- *WHISKAS has prepared for your cat the Little Meals:*
- *recipes richly elaborated with delicious little morsels and an appetizing odor*
- *a careful presentation, in meal-sized portions, easy to use with a recloseable top*
- *To vary the pleasures of your cat, the "Petits Régals" proposes to you three refined varieties: Beef and Kidney, Fowl and Liver, Rabbit and Turkey.*

Bon appétit.

At the beginning, it all seemed exotic and quaint and a little eccentric. The more time we spent there, however, the saner life in Provence became. What was happening, without our realizing it, was that we were becoming part of the community.

Though we'd only been gone a few months, America was receding into the distance. We didn't have a television in Goult—a deliberate choice, mostly Janis's I have to say, but a very wise one—which cut us off from a lot of our own culture. Our French, at this stage, was barely serviceable, but almost no one we were spending time with spoke any English, so we quickly got out of the habit of speaking the only language we could communicate with.

That left us in a strange though not unpleasant kind of limbo.

There were all sorts of things we had not anticipated before we moved from one country to another. Or if we had anticipated them, they didn't turn out quite the way we'd expected.

We knew we'd have to do something about money, which meant we'd have to figure out what to do about using a French bank. Cleverly (I thought), before we left New York, I'd spoken to someone at Crédit Lyonnais, the second largest bank in France. The person in their New York office told me that they did indeed have a branch fairly near Goult, in the town of Cavaillon.

Perfect.

After our arrival and two or three days of doing nothing but soaking in atmosphere, appreciating the local beauty, and screaming at the customs officials, we decided we had to do something practical, so we drove into Cavaillon and found Crédit Lyonnais.

It was easy. The very first street we turned down, once we hit town, had a bank on it with a big LYONNAISE sign. We parked in front of the bank and went inside. (Which was not very easy; the French have a strange system where you have to punch a buzzer to get in one door, then you're trapped in a tiny room before you can open the other door. The problem is in trying to open the second door, which can't be done until the first door is completely shut. Janis, Norton, and I spent a good ten minutes trapped in between doors, until some kindly soul in the bank finally started waving his hands and pointing and shouting and showed us how to get through.) Once inside, we were golden. The bank was very small, almost sleepy compared to most banks. In very simple French, I asked if anyone spoke English.

They told me that the manager, Monsieur Gilbert Rebattu, spoke a little English, and moments later we were ushered into Monsieur Rebattu's office.

When they say "a little English" in Provence, they mean a *little* English. Monsieur Rebattu, a slight man with a dark mustache and a somewhat nervous but absolutely charming manner, knew how to say "hello" and "good-bye" and practically nothing else in between. He was, however, extraordinarily nice and helpful, and spent almost an hour with us, helping us fill out the forms. (Normally, this would have been a five-minute meeting. But between my French and Monsieur Rebattu's English, we needed the hour.) He told us what type of banking would be best for us, he explained how we should write checks, he even explained the French banking system, which makes a lot more sense than the American system. In France, no one asks for I.D. when you write out a check. You don't have to show a driver's license or a credit card; it's exactly the same as handing over cash. Monsieur Rebattu explained that that was because people in France don't bounce checks. There is no system of credit there (one of the reasons that the country's not in debt for hundreds of billions of dollars, unlike other countries we might name). When a French person pays with a Visa card, that money is taken right out of his or her bank account. If a French person ever bounces a check, he loses all banking privileges for a year—which basically means he can't live. I think Monsieur Rebattu also said something about never again being able to drink wine or watch Jerry Lewis movies or eat *tarte tatin,* too, but, again, my French was still pretty rusty.

Once this was all explained to us, we put in enough money to ensure we'd never lose our banking privileges. We received our temporary checks right away—Monsieur

Rebattu had the good sense to ask if Norton would require his own checkbook; the answer was a definite no—and then we were all set. But as we thanked our new bank manager and stood up to leave, Monsieur Rebattu put his hand on my arm and said, in a very soft voice, "Excuse me, *monsieur*. But what is it that made you choose our bank?"

I explained that it was quite simple. We'd been told that Crédit Lyonnais was the most convenient place to bank because there were branches all over the country. We'd also been told that the Crédit Lyonnais in Cavaillon was the closest to our town. There was nothing more to it: the biggest, the best, the closest. *Voilà*.

Monsieur Rebattu nodded unhappily. The smile that had been on his face disappeared. He was not a physically imposing man to begin with and he seemed to shrink before our very eyes.

"Yes, I thought it was something like that," he sighed.

"Is there a problem?" I wanted to know. I didn't really want to know, but I sensed it was a question that had to be asked. I was right.

"This is *not* Crédit Lyonnais, *monsieur*."

"It's not? But the sign out front . . ."

"This is Lyonnaise de Banque."

I looked at Janis. She looked at me. Norton refused to look at either one of us. "That's not the same thing?" I asked, trying my best not to look as miserable as I felt.

Monsieur Rebattu nodded knowingly and wistfully, then, looking much unhappier than I could possibly be, he shrugged and gently said, "It's not too late to change. I will understand."

By this time, Janis was practically in tears and half in love with Monsieur Rebattu for being so kind and thoughtful, so

we both shook our heads—after a moment's hesitation—
and boldly declared, "Absolutely not. Lyonnaise de Banque
is the bank for us!"

They didn't bring out a band or have a parade but it was
close. I don't know when they last had a new customer, but
clearly this was an event of the first order for the gang at
Lyonnaise de Banque. Monsieur Rebattu shook our hands
(and petted Norton) and thanked us profusely. Then he
proudly took us through the rest of the bank, which took
all of fourteen seconds, introducing us to all the other em-
ployees, who looked at us as if they couldn't comprehend
that we were actually putting money in their, shall we say,
"modest" place of business.

It turned out to be a great move. (Except for the time our
friend Norm came over from New York and wanted to
change American dollars into francs. That really threw the
entire bank for a loop. They didn't know the rate of exchange—I swear! I asked three times to make sure I could
believe my ears—so they had to look it up in the paper.
Then Norm watched in astonishment as they scurried
around trying to find five hundred dollars. They looked in
drawers, in cabinets, under stacks of paperwork. Finally,
they scraped up enough francs and proudly turned them
over.) For the entire time we were in France, whenever we
went into our bank, Monsieur Rebattu would stride out of
his office, smile broadly, pump our hands, ask about our
health, and usually give us a calendar or a pen (if anyone
needs six or seven Lyonnaise de Banque wall calendars, just
give a holler). We got a lot of funny looks when we told
people where we were banking, but other than that we
never had a problem. In fact, I've never had better banking
or more personalized service anywhere, proving Red Auer-

bach or Leo Durocher or Vince Lombardi or someone like that to be a genius when he said, "I'd rather be lucky than good."

One of our next points of business was to become fairly familiar with the local wine growers. After a few weeks, we stumbled into a vineyard, only fifteen minutes or so from our house, that sold a local Côte Ventoux. Monsieur Bonnelly et Fils. Monsieur Bonnelly was a man of eighty years or so. As we were tasting his delicious '86 red wine, we struck up a conversation.

"What do you do?" he wanted to know as he was petting Norton. When I told him I was a writer and had, in fact, written about the very cat he was stroking, he asked if I'd ever heard of a Monsieur Beckay. I shook my head and his eyes widened in shock. "Beckay?!" he bellowed. "You've never heard of Samuel Beckay?!!" I finally realized we were having a pronunciation problem. Samuel Beckett is who he was talking about, and when he calmed down I told him yes, indeed, I'd heard of Monsieur Beckett.

"He used to buy his wine here," Bonnelly told me. "Before the war. While he was working on *Waiting for Godot.* He lived in Roussillon and used to come in every Wednesday. He'd buy three bottles of red and flirt with my wife. She was much better looking back then."

Monsieur Bonnelly pulled out a tattered copy of *Attendent Godot.* Not only did Beckett buy his wine there, he wrote about it. In the middle of the French edition of the play, one of the tramps actually says, "Let's go to Bonnelly's for some wine."

Since Beckett is a god to me, in my opinion the greatest writer of the century and the author of the great English novel (a trilogy of novels, actually: *Malloy, Malone Dies,* and *The Unnameable*), this was fairly impressive. Not to mention inspiring. Sparked by the ghost of Godot, we bought several more bottles of wine from Monsieur Bonnelly than we'd originally intended. And as we were leaving, Monsieur Bonnelly called after us. "Perhaps in twenty years, I'll tell people that Monsieur Norton also bought wine from me."

Which is how this book almost came to be called *Meowing for Godot.*

Two of the more interesting local characters whom Norton won over were Gianni Ladu and his wife, Chantal, Sardinian goatherders who ran a rustic *auberge* up in the mountains above Sivergues. Gianni was very much a Sarde, which meant he always had a three-day growth of beard and liked doing nothing so much as slicing open and skinning a goat right in front of you. That could be a little intimidating while trying to have a conversation, I have to admit, but Norton seemed to soften Gianni up a bit. He liked to roam about Gianni's property—not exactly mingling with the goats, but not really avoiding them either. Norton seemed fascinated by those animals' bleats and bla-aaa-aaas, and I got the distinct feeling he wouldn't have minded taking a day-long trek in the mountains with them. Gianni had seen many things in his day, but he'd never seen a cat in his restaurant, especially one who'd hang out with his herd. The restaurant was usually fully booked—they served their meals to a select few at long tables in an ancient room of stone and wood beams—but when I'd call to say we wanted to reserve a table, he'd say, "Is the cat coming?" If I said no, it was fifty-fifty at best that we'd get in. If I agreed to bring Norton, Gianni would usually say something along the lines of, "Okay. We're full—but for you and the cat we have room." We'd then get to sit up in the mountains and eat a whole roasted goat (Norton, for some reason, didn't

mind that one of his pals was being consumed right before
his very eyes), some of Chantal's homemade lasagna and
their fresh goat cheese, and drink way too much of Gianni's
homemade *eau de vie*. After a lot of goat and liquor, Gianni's
thirteen-year-old son, David, would usually serenade the
diners with some ear-splitting Hendrix on his electric guitar, which was a little unnerving for Norton. Other than
that, it was a perfect place for a cat to feel as if he were very
much the rustic, French mountain *chat*.

The only unpleasant thing that had to be dealt with quickly
after we arrived in Provence was that Janis didn't know how
to drive a stick shift. Before coming over, I'd assured her
that it was no big deal and that I could teach her easily. She
was a good driver, I was a good teacher, what could be
easier? It turned out that climbing Mount Everest naked
while surrounded by a swarm of killer bees would have
been easier. A *lot* easier. There were a few elements of the
equation that I hadn't counted on. First of all, it's never a
good idea to teach one's mate how to drive. That's a lesson
I should have known just from watching sitcoms all my life,
but I chose to ignore it. The second warning sign I ignored
was that I'm not the most patient person in the world. If I
tell someone what to do, I expect them to do it perfectly.
I'm aware that that's an unreasonable expectation, but that
doesn't stop me from expecting it. The third thing that
made our driving lesson difficult was that I'd never quite
realized before that Janis was a total nut.

Norton and I took her out in our leased Citroën. Norton
hopped into his usual spot, perched on the shelf of the rear
windshield. He stretched out, expecting to whizz along to
another great lunch spot. Instead, he got taken down to the

soccer field below town, the only level place within thirty miles that wasn't a highway.

It had been a long time since I'd tried to teach someone how to shift and use a clutch, but I explained it plainly, simply, and calmly. After the explanation, Janis, who tends to be slightly negative in her approach to life, looked at me and said, "I will *never* be able to do this."

I took these words as a challenge and told her that within fifteen minutes she'd be speeding along the highway, confident as could be.

Two hours later, after lurching around the soccer field, nearly getting squashed by a truck at an intersection, and almost driving off a cliff, I would have told Janis that she was right, she'd never be able to drive a stick, except I couldn't tell her because we weren't speaking to each other.

Norton was not taking sides. Once, when she was trying to pull onto the highway and it looked as if there was a fifty-fifty chance we were going to die, Norton meowed a fairly firm meow. Janis turned and glowered at him, and he quickly decided that meowing was not the way to go. But by the third time I'd made her cry and said something along the lines of, "Even Norton would have learned to get up this hill by now!" Norton would have none of me either. Either I'd offended him by saying *even* he would have figured it out or else he was just fed up with all the lurching about and wanted to go someplace where there was peace and quiet.

The thing was, Janis *had* to learn how to drive. I couldn't be her chauffeur for the year and, despite my assertion, Norton was way too short to reach the car's pedals.

She came through, of course, with flying colors. Once we started speaking to each other again, I reassured her that no one could actually learn all this in fifteen minutes. It would take a few days, perhaps a week, but she would definitely learn. Janis is the type who doesn't like to learn: She likes to be perfect. Since learning, or at least the *process* of learning, is antithetical to short-term perfection, she tended to get rather cranky when doing things like stalling in the middle of a big intersection or coming to a stop at the top of the hill and then rolling half a mile backward before being able to get the car moving forward again. She had the same problem learning French. She didn't want to speak the language until she actually *knew* the language. This was not a very practical approach, not if she ever wanted to go anywhere or do anything. So she gritted her teeth and, not exactly happy but not completely miserable, learned how to drive a stick shift and how to speak French.

Another thing we never anticipated was the French mail system.

It can take two weeks for a letter or package to make its way from America to a small town in the south of France. One of the reasons, we eventually discovered, is because somewhere there is someone who has something to do with French mail delivery who is always on strike. After we'd been there a few weeks, we stopped getting mail. For three or four days straight we'd check the box at the back of the garden and *rien*. Zippo. Not even the *Herald Tribune*. We finally worked up the nerve to ask at the post office and they told us that the Avignon mailmen were on strike. Since Avignon was fifty kilometers away, you might ask yourself what that had to do with us. Well . . . we never quite got a satisfactory answer to that question. The nearest we could tell was (1) most mail had to go through the large Avignon post office before it was sent on to Goult's little, tiny post office and (2) because Avignon was more important than

Goult or any of its surrounding towns, the local Lubéron mailmen were being enlisted to deliver the Avignon mail.

That strike lasted two weeks. When it was over, we got our mail for three days in a row, then it stopped again. On the second day (of the second round) of no more mail, we went back to the post office to see what the story was. The story was that the Avignon mailmen had ended their strike in victory; they'd gotten raises and better benefits. Now the local Lubéron mailmen were striking because they were making less than the Avignon mailmen.

If the mailmen weren't striking, the truckers were striking, which meant no packages could be delivered. If the truckers weren't striking, the railroads were striking, which somehow still meant that no packages could be delivered. If the railroads weren't striking, then the farmers were protesting the horror that's known as EuroDisney and were blocking all the roads and railroads, so no packages could be delivered.

One day, after we'd been in Goult for several months, we noticed once again that the mail had stopped arriving. We trekked back to the post office (all of a two-block trek) to find out who was on strike. No strike, we were told. But our mailman had had an accident. He'd fallen off his scooter— a tiny motorbike, at least a foot too short for his long legs, with the world's loudest engine—and broken his collarbone.

"Oh, that's terrible," I sympathized. "Please send him my best. But what does that have to do with why we're not getting any mail?"

Which is when I realized that there was only one mailman for Goult. If he wasn't able to deliver mail, no one was. He was the only one who knew how to sort the letters, he was the only one who knew where everyone lived, and my guess is he was the only one available for the job who had a motor scooter.

It was two weeks before we got our mail again. And the mailman, a gangly, unhappy-looking man, looked even more solemn than usual as he chugged around town on his motorbike, his arm in an uncomfortable-looking sling.

Norton was, for a while, our only touch with regularity. He was awake and waiting by his food dish at the same time every morning, curled up in the same two or three spots every day, meowing hungrily for dinner at the same time every evening. Everything else in France seemed to us to operate on a whim.

One morning we woke up to find that someone had dumped approximately a ton of rocks in our backyard. This seemed quite mysterious to us, since we were positive we hadn't ordered a ton of rocks. We called our landlady, Elisabeth, in Paris, who was equally mystified. She said she'd get back to us. A week later, the mystery was solved. Several months before, she'd spoken to a *maçon* about rebuilding the stone wall at the back of her garden. She'd asked him to get back to her with a price. He never did. But he did wake up one day, remember that she'd wanted her wall fixed, so he thought he'd just get started. His start was to dump all the stones needed for the job in the yard and leave them there.

After Elisabeth figured out that he must be the culprit, she called him to say that we didn't appreciate the gesture. The next day, he came and gathered them all back up, I assume to dump in somebody else's yard.

Dumping clearly was a major activity in our new neighborhood (or *voisinage,* as I was now learning to call it).

As winter started to settle in, we realized we'd better

store up on our wood for the fireplace. We'd heard all sorts of horror stories of the Provençal wind and cold. When the *mistral* came whistling through the trees, word was that it gave new meaning to the words "when hell freezes over."

We followed a series of crude hand-made signs—WOOD FOR SALE: simple, straightforward, and effective advertising—that led us perhaps a mile away from Goult, to a small farmhouse. The owner shuffled out, smoking a cigarette, beret tipped at the jauntiest of angles over his head, and I couldn't help but notice a disturbing pattern: All small-town French men over the age of sixty-five reminded me of William Demarest.

It's worth bringing up here that there's such a thing as a Provençal accent. It is, in fact, so thick as to render normal French completely incomprehensible, until you get used to its twangs and blangs and various nasal inflections. A Provençal accent puts a "g" at the end of just about everything. The French word for tomorrow is *demain*. With a Provençal accent, it's *demaing*. The word for hand is *main*. With the southern accent, it becomes *maing*. By way of example, take a sentence in English: "When did the man ban guns, John?" An easy sentence, right? Well, pretend you're hearing it for the first time, and with the Provençal accent added to it. It becomes: "Wheng did the mang bang gungs, Jong?" It sounds more like Chinese than English. That's about what Provençalian sounded like to us when we first arrived: some strange tongue spoken only in places where you have to ask directions of Sherpas.

The man selling the wood had the thickest, most impenetrable accent I'd ever encountered. The only thing I was able to clearly understand was when he looked at Norton, who was busy poking around the man's garden, and said, *"Votre chat. Il est très sage."* Several French people made this comment about Norton when we were on our travels. Most Americans, when they meet the little guy, say, "Oh, he's so cute" or "Oh, he's so calm." I much prefer the French way and I think it's indicative of their true respect for cats as well as life: "Oh, he's so wise." *Il est très sage* indeed.

Aside from the flattery about Norton's sagaciousness, after half an hour of conversation this is what I'd learned about the winter wood situation: We either could or couldn't buy it from him. Either his son or his daughter would come visit us or we had to go visit them, although they seemed to live in Spain. If we could get wood at all, it would either come that night, the next week, or never. And it would either cost a million dollars or would be free. When we finally left, my head was spinning, but I was fairly sure I'd ordered a small amount of wood that would be reasonably inexpensive.

I was right about the inexpensive part; I was wrong about the small amount. Three days after our conversation, a dump truck backed up in front of our house, which was no mean feat in itself because the truck fit on our narrow street with perhaps half an inch to spare on each side. When it arrived, the son of the man I'd talked to pulled the lever inside the truck, the back began to rise, and in moments, enough wood to rebuild the Brazilian rain forests came tumbling out onto the street. It took perhaps three minutes for all the wood to empty out of the truck. It then took another two minutes for the truck to make its way back to the end of our street and hightail it out of there. And then it took six hours for me and Janis to carry it, stack it anywhere there was a spare inch—in the three outbuildings in the backyard, in the *cave,* in the kitchen, in the stone hallway by Norton's litter box—and then collapse in an exhausted heap on the floor.

In some odd way, we felt comfortable being in the midst

of such eccentricity. It made us feel a part of the town. And this feeling was magnified because we were accepted by the local Goultoise with surprising ease. We made friends with a French neighbor, who also became our French teacher. She in turn introduced us to another friend, who became our Goult version of Millie in "The Dick Van Dyke Show"—she would pop in at any hour of the day or night; we were free to do the same. She also spent a couple of hours a week teaching us French; we spent the same amount of time teaching her English. And from there, our circle of friends expanded until, by the time we left, we numbered as lifelong friends four French women, one Swedish woman, and two French guys (one of whom became my sports buddy; since I couldn't get my much needed football, basketball, or baseball fix, Norton and I would go to his house to watch the soccer matches. Olympic Marseille became, to me, nearly what the '86 Mets had once been).

We also fell into the extraordinarily interesting expatriate community that populated the Lubéron. Most were Brits, a few were American. Expatriates are usually running away from something. Some from work. Some from politics. Some from relationships. Almost all, in one way or another, are running away from themselves and feel that a new life in a new place, particularly a place like Provence, will help them re-create themselves. Sometimes they like to start from scratch, sometimes just partial replacements are needed.

Almost every expatriate we met had some sort of secret. There were messy divorces in their pasts. Some had left husbands for younger men. Some had left *wives* for younger men. There were vaguely sinister stories: violent ends to affairs; suicide attempts; the mysterious loss of millions of dollars. Everyone we became friends with had a vague shadow hanging over them—and that made them all the

more interesting. It made them appealing. Couple that with
the fact that they'd all made the same choice we'd made—to
leave one life behind and resettle in a French paradise—and
it created an instant bond, one not felt to this extent, from
my end, since I'd been given a certain six-week-old Scottish
Fold kitten.

We went with these people to the opera house in Avignon to see Mozart concerts and we practiced our French
reading from the *Provençal,* the local newspaper equivalent
of the *National Enquirer* (their favorite thing to write about
is how many people were killed and injured on the highway
during the week: 4 MORTS ET 7 BLESSÉS! is a typical head-
line of the *Provençal*). We went to harpsichord concerts in
local churches and trudged to Avignon to see English-language movies. We hiked for miles with them, exploring the
wonders of the mountains, and went on treasure hunts and
once, on a magical New Year's Day picnic, even danced
around in a circle, holding hands, singing the words to "Sur
le Pont d'Avignon" (although if you tell that to any of my
close, personal friends, I'll deny it). We stayed up late nurs-
ing them through broken hearts, we lived through their
affairs with married men, we ate in their homes and cooked
for them. We told jokes—in various languages—and made
one another laugh. And we slowly learned a lot about a
group of people—English, American, French, Swedish, you
name it—with whom, ostensibly, we had nothing in common, yet grew to treasure.

Not all of our treasured memories, however, revolve
around people. Or even cats, for that matter. Every so often
there were other—if you'll excuse the expression—catalysts
working their magic.

By far the strangest and, in some ways, the most delightful experience we had the entire time we were in Goult was
when Janis came running into the house late one afternoon.
Excited, she told me to hurry up, get Norton, and jump in
the car. She wouldn't tell me what was going on, she just
insisted I follow instructions.

She drove—she was becoming quite proficient with the
Citroën and by this time could almost get up a steep hill
without my head banging against the windshield thirty or
forty times—until we came to the town of Menerbes, another perfect Lubéron mountain village, ten minutes away
from Goult.

Just outside the town, Janis stopped the car to let an
animal cross the street in front of us. It was a goat. I was
about to say, "What's a goat doing in Menerbes?" when I
looked to the right of the car and saw two lions lounging
by the side of the road. Next to them was a friendly but
quite large elephant. Before I could get too disoriented,
Janis drove a little further and we came to a small tent that
had been set up. In front of the tent was a man in a clown
outfit and five or six small children running around in front
of him, giggling and yelling with pleasure.

"We're going to a circus?" I asked Janis in disbelief.

"We're going to a circus," she answered.

I would love to report that this charming country circus
was an artistic triumph, everything that the overdone and
overhyped Ringling Bros. type of show is not. Unfortunately, if I did report such a thing, I'd be lying through my
teeth. This little circus that Janis brought me and Norton to
was the cheesiest, most pathetic, most hilarious thing I'd
ever seen in my entire life:

The human troupe consisted of a ringmaster, two clowns,
and a woman acrobat who, every time she so much as did

a simple somersault, looked as if it was going to be her last act of life. She tripped and fell down *twice* while walking across the arena to encourage us to applaud the ringmaster. The clowns also were not of the highest possible caliber. One clown's wig kept falling off, and you could tell he wasn't happy about dressing up in the stupid-looking costume anyway. The other clown's sole job was keeping the bouncy music going, but the tape machine was on the old side, so the music wasn't all that bouncy because it was played somewhere around two speeds too slow. When it came time to bring the speakers inside—they'd been outside to help broadcast the exciting news that the circus was in town—the whole troupe chipped in. It was a struggle for all of them to lift the things—enough of a struggle that they almost knocked the entire tent over in the process.

Once the show started, things managed to get lots worse. The opening act was Minou the Dog Genius. Minou's trainer (the ringmaster) strode out into the middle of the ring, announced that we were about to see the smartest dog in the world, then, with a deep bow and a majestic wave of an arm, called for Minou to come running. No such luck. Minou was either asleep or hadn't been paid in a week, because there was nothing they could do to get that dog into the ring. The ringmaster kept calling him, but Minou never showed up. Finally, one of the clowns had to carry the pup into the tent and plop him down in the center. The ringmaster then told the genius dog to leap up onto a stool—and he announced to the audience that we were going to see the most amazing mental feat ever performed by a member of the canine race. It really wasn't as amazing as all that—because all Minou did was turn around and run out of the tent again.

The ringmaster began to realize that Minou was off his

performance that night, so he called for JoJo the Brilliant Horse. Norton enjoyed JoJo tremendously, especially when JoJo refused to do anything except trot around the ring. "Up, JoJo!" the ringmaster would thunder, and JoJo would trot some more. "JoJo! How much is two plus two?" the ringmaster asked. Unless I lost count and JoJo trotted around the entire ring four times, I don't think he had any idea how much two plus two were. That didn't stop the ringmaster from thanking everyone for watching JoJo the Brilliant Horse (*"Mes amis, messieurs, mesdames, les enfants, JoJo le cheval génie!"*), and then introducing The World's Most Intelligent Monkeys. Their entire act was to eat their dinner as fast and as messily as they could in front of the rapt crowd.

By the time of the monkey act, Norton was getting a little bored. I'm sure it was beginning to occur to him that if these animals were making a decent living, he could become a millionaire without too much trouble if he ran away to join a French circus.

That was when he got his moment in the sun.

There were not a lot of people in the audience. I'd say perhaps twenty small children, two or three mothers, and us. But when I heard the ringmaster say, into the mike, *"Monsieur! Monsieur, s'il vous plaît,"* I really didn't think anything of it. Not, that is, until Janis pointed out that he was talking to *me,* since I was the only adult *monsieur* in the joint.

"Monsieur," he repeated, when he finally caught my eye. "Come here," he said. *"Venez."*

If I knew what I was in for, I don't think I would have brought Norton into the ring, but I truly wasn't expecting anything other than semi-funny banter. Even if I did have to participate in something physical, I figured I could just eat some food quickly or jog around the ring twice when they asked me how much one plus one was. Even when they brought the camel center stage, I still didn't understand what I was supposed to do. Only when the camel knelt down and one of the clowns led me over to it, did I realize I was supposed to get up on the thing and ride it around the tent.

Norton was a real trouper, I'll say that for him. He let me hold him as the clown boosted us up onto the camel's back. I held on to the cat with one hand and on to the camel's hump with the other. As the *dromadaire* sped faster and faster around the ring, and Norton got more and more relaxed, the children in the audience went wilder and wilder. Out of the corner of my eye, I'm pretty sure I saw Janis laughing uncontrollably, though she swore to me later she was impressed with how well I'd maintained my dignity.

The main thing I remember is the ringmaster, who realized that with all his trained elephants and monkeys and horses and dogs, a nonprofessional cat was stealing his show. To his credit, he went with it. Standing off to the side, he began bellowing into his microphone as we rode past and the cheers grew louder and louder and Norton sat up straighter and straighter on the back of the camel. "Ladies and gentlemen, boys and girls," he was saying. *"Messieurs et mesdames, les enfants, mes amis! Je vous present le monsieur et son chat extraordinaire!"*

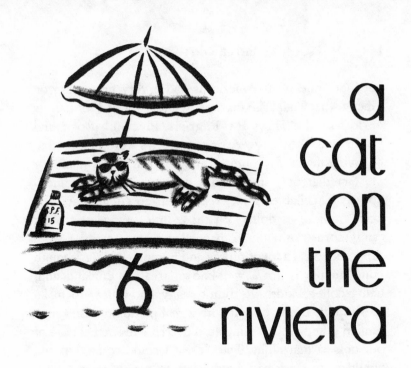

a cat on the riviera

One of the strangest things about living abroad is being away from home for holidays.

I'm fairly big on tradition. Every Christmas Eve I go to my friends Glen and Sharon's apartment for dinner. Every December, on the first weekend of the month, I throw a waffle and champagne party and make everyone I know watch *It's a Wonderful Life.* Thanksgiving is my favorite holiday of all and for ten years I've been going to other friends, Kathleen and Dominick (of the traumatic Search for Norton Day), to eat a major feast, drink many bottles of delicious port, and play a killer game of charades. In general, I'd have to say that Thanksgiving is my very favorite day of the year.

In France, Thanksgiving doesn't exist. I experienced this once before, when I went to college at the University of London. I gathered a few American students over at my flat, along with some newly acquired British friends. It turned

out that none of us Americans had a very firm grasp on
exactly what Thanksgiving was. We knew it had something
to do with the Three P's: Pilgrims, Plymouth Rock, and
Pocahontas. And we were pretty sure we were supposed to
be giving thanks for religious and political freedom and for
the fact that only in America could there be an official
holiday that enabled some creative entrepreneur to actually
make millions of dollars off those little orange and black
candy corns. Other than that, all we knew was we were
supposed to eat a lot of turkey and pumpkin pie. (Although
pumpkin pie is not a well-known treat in England and,
being college kids, we didn't really know how to make
one—so we tried doing it with a real pumpkin rather than
canned pumpkin. It's difficult to describe the actual taste of
our dessert that night. The closest I could come, I think,
would be to say it had the delicate texture of a terry-cloth
robe and the subtle taste of a whole lot of unsweetened
chocolate.) To this day, I think there are several English
people walking around London who think that every final
Thursday in November, Americans celebrate a bizarre Pil-
grim-Indian sex rite by eating terrible food.

We did slightly better in France, though not at first.

Two weeks before the big day, we went to one of the two
butchers in Goult—we'd settled on one we preferred,
though for no logical reason—and told him we'd like to
order a turkey *(un dinde)* for the end of November.

"You mean the end of December," he said.

"No," I said. "I mean the end of November."

"That's impossible," he told us.

"And why is that?" we wanted to know.

"Because the turkeys are not fat yet," he said.

It turns out that no one in the south of France ever eats
turkey except for Christmas. So, especially in such rural

areas as the Lubéron, November and December are months spent feeding the birds and getting them plump enough for *le dîner de Noël.*

"But it's a very important American holiday," I explained to Monsieur Isnard, our butcher of choice. "What if we order a pathetic thin turkey?"

Non.

We debated having a Thanksgiving feast of chicken and shallot tart, but we were spared such an agonizing break from tradition when our friends Nicholas and Linda called and told us to come up to Paris to have Thanksgiving with them.

Nicholas is French and Linda is American and they've been living in Paris for five years now. They also have twin five-year-old daughters, Naomi and Gala, possibly the most gorgeous, sweetest children who ever lived. At the time, they were refusing to speak so much as one word of English, even though Mom was American and they absolutely could understand anything spoken in English that they wanted to understand. Instead, they would look adorable and speak perfect French, saying such cute little *enfant-*like things as, when riding in the car on a cold winter day, *"Oh, maman, j'adore la musique et la chauffage!"* which means, "Oh, Mom, I adore music and the heating system." I know it doesn't sound nearly as good in English, but nothing does, and when they'd spew out these accented epigrams, my heart would melt so quickly it was pathetic. So we were in the mood to see Linda, Nicholas, and the kids anyway, and our choice was made easier yet when we took into consideration that Linda was a cook of the first degree. So it was on to Paris for Thanksgiving.

The TGV—*train de grande vitesse* ("train of great speed," or "big, really, really fast train," as I like to call it)—has changed everyone's life down in Provence. In the old days, it was a seven- or eight-hour train ride from Paris to Avignon. By the time you got to the train station, waited for the train, stopped a hundred times along the way, and got to your final destination, it was an all-day trip. Now, with the fast train, it takes three hours to get from Provence to Paris, and you get there in extremely luxurious fashion. The drawback is that wealthier and more annoying Parisians are now able to consider Provence something of a weekend retreat. On the other hand, it makes it awfully nice to live down there, knowing how simple and hassle-free it is to get up to the greatest city in the world.

Norton was a big TGV fan. Human seats need to be reserved but pet seats don't. And because the train is built for comfort as well as speed, there are thick, plush armrests which, when pushed down, make the perfect seating arrangement for Scottish Folds. Norton could stretch out on the armrests and do his favorite thing in the whole world: stare out the window at the countryside as the train sped along at a hundred miles an hour. Since it was only a three-hour trip, he didn't even need a litter box.

This was our first weekend in the big city since we'd moved down to Goult, and we decided to live it up. We stayed in L'Hôtel, a very beautiful hotel on the left bank on the rue des Beaux-Arts, celebrated because it's the house where Oscar Wilde died. It's even possible to stay in the very room—and bed—Oscar Wilde died in, although why anyone would want to do that I'm not exactly sure. The rooms are tiny (unless you take the suite on the top floor, which is huge and looks like a very classy nineteenth-century whorehouse; unfortunately, the cost is more like a twenty-first-century whorehouse) but are filled with antiques and decorated in lots of bright red and green velvet.

The colors somehow work, though they tend to be just a tad overpowering. In fact, as the bellman was opening the door to our room, he said softly, *"J'espère que vous aimez la couleur rouge"*—"I hope you like the color red." It was a fair question because *everything* in our small room was bright, shocking red. The wallpaper, the bedspread, the chairs, the towels. We got used to it in a few moments, but I must admit that for several days after we left, everything we saw looked rather drab and bland.

As usual, the hotel was totally taken with the cat. Within minutes of checking in, the concierge sent up a bowl of milk for Norton's cocktail hour. Just to be on the safe side, I checked to see whether Janis or I had gotten any fruit or chocolates, but as usual it was only *le chat* who received any complimentary calories.

The first day we were there, we did a lot of Christmas shopping at the antique stores along the nearby rue Jacob and, farther away, rue St. Paul in the Marais. One St. Paul store particularly impressed me. They remembered me from previous shopping sprees—usually to bring something back to Janis when I felt particularly guilty about being there without her—and even remembered most of the things I'd bought there over the years, which I have to admit made me feel about as sophisticated as I can feel. They clearly had no idea what my name was but they did remember my shopping companion. When I strolled in with a cloth bag on my shoulder and a gray cat poking his head out of the bag, they greeted us with the warm words, *"Bonjour, monsieur! Et bonjour, Monsieur Norton! Ça va?"* It never fails.

The night before Thanksgiving, Norton met his French *attaché de presse. The Cat Who Went to Paris* was being published in France before too long and the editor, an American woman named Nina Salter who was an editor at the Parisian publishing company Albin Michel, decided it would be wise if Norton met the woman who'd be doing the publicity for the book.

Janis, Norton, and I went to a restaurant called Le Square Trousseau, a smoky bistro populated with a lot of publishing and show-biz types, near to the Bastille. Nina and Kathy, the publicist, were regulars but the place was jampacked, so even at nine-thirty at night we had to have a drink at the bar before being seated. No problem for Norton. He took a stool at the end of the bar, his little head popping up over the brass railing. Kathy sat next to him, petted him, and clearly fell in love. What's not to love, I guess. Norton's a great date.

Dinner went smoothly as the relationship between Norton and his publicist proved to be the real thing. Norton sat in his own chair, and nothing going on around him disturbed him—not the noisy crowd, not the giant St. Bernard who camped under his chair almost the entire evening, not the patrons of the restaurant who, periodically, would come over and ask me if that was a real cat.

Kathy made his life a lot easier—and mine a lot harder—by giving Norton the full star treatment. She hand-fed him some of her foie gras, then some of her chicken. For dessert, she ordered him a plate of chocolate ice cream (it was far superior to that of Bistro d'Albert). As an after-dinner drink, she ordered him some milk and, since he is the world's sloppiest milk slurper, Kathy even wiped his mouth with her napkin after each session with the milk bowl. That was the final straw as far as Janis was concerned. For months afterward, she complained vociferously that no one ever wiped her mouth after she ate. I tried pointing out that perhaps someone would if she would agree to bend down and eat out of a bowl, but she never took my advice to heart, which was probably all for the best.

The next day, we were all slightly hung over. Janis and I from too much wine and *eau de vie,* Norton from too much spoon-fed foie gras. We were content to linger in our red velvet room for most of the morning. I was especially content because there was a TV in the room and I'd been having sports withdrawal down in Goult. Much to Janis's horror, I watched a Pistons-Pacers basketball game on an English cable station, then, much more to her horror, proved how desperate I really was by watching almost all of a Hulk Hogan versus The Undertaker wrestling match. Our only interruption came when two of the hotel maids knocked at the door. Janis told them we'd be out of the room in another hour or so, but they weren't there to clean—they were there to introduce themselves to Norton and play with him. We told them we'd leave him in the room for the afternoon so they could pet him to their heart's content.

That night was Thanksgiving dinner over at Linda and Nicholas's apartment. I believe this was Norton's first official Thanksgiving (he's never gone to Kathleen and Dominick's because they have two cats, Lulu and Zonker, who don't cotton to any feline competition in the annual charades game). He was made to feel welcome by the twins, Naomi and Gala, who crayoned little place settings for everyone. They drew a picture of me and set it in front of my plate on the table. They did the same for Janis and for their mom and dad. For Norton, they drew a lovely picture of him, complete with flattened ears, and put it on the floor, right next to my chair, along with a bowl which happened to be perfect for holding bite-sized morsels of turkey scraps.

The dinner was a grand success. In Paris it was not only

possible to get fattened turkeys at the end of November, it was possible to get everything needed for stuffing and sweet potatoes and mashed potatoes and all other Thanksgiving delicacies.

By the end of the weekend, we felt we'd had a touch of home, which we'd needed. Norton felt as if he'd had a *new* home since, when we checked out of L'Hôtel, I believe that every single employee came to say good-bye to him and wish him *bon chance*.

Norton, Janis, and I had the next several weeks to ourselves, during which we continued our Provençal explorations and our Provençal ritual of stuffing our faces at every possible moment. And then, right at Christmastime, a new ritual began: Company started arriving.

Our first guests were—and don't start any gossip, this was strictly a platonic arrangement—my friend Norm Stiles, the "Sesame Street" maven, and my friend and book agent, Esther Newberg, the well-known cranky person. Neither Esther nor Norm had ever been to Provence before and we were determined to show them how perfect life could be.

It wasn't as difficult as we thought.

It turns out it's not hard to convince people that life is perfect—not when they're in Goult for Christmas.

The lights in town are, of course, tasteful and elegant. Strings of colored lights ring the tower of the church in the lower part of the town; a strand of white lights sits over the thousand-year-old vaulted arch that leads to the town *château*. Along the main street, artfully decorated lights run, every ten yards or so, across the width of the street, from one building to another.

In our cozy house, we got two Christmas trees—a large

one for the living room and a small one for my third-floor (or second-floor, if you're French) office. Both trees were decorated Provençal-style: with various fruits (tiny tangerines, which are called *clementines,* small apples, and pears) and strands of nuts.

On Christmas Day, Janis, Norton, and I strode around Goult, enjoying the simple fact that we were there and nowhere else. Norton started out in his shoulder bag but before long hopped out and walked with us. The town was fairly empty—even the tiny caged birds were inside—so we had a relaxed cat on our hands, one who was ready to stroll anywhere.

We passed one house we'd admired since the day we'd arrived. It was off a small grassy triangle at the top of the main street, before one reached the castle. From the outside, Janis had picked this as her favorite place in town—it was quite old and at one time had been the Goult post office, but had obviously long ago been converted to a spectacular home. They'd been doing some work on the house, fixing up the courtyard, and I'd peeked my head through from time to time, admiring and envious. On Christmas Day, as we passed by, a grungy-looking workman in overalls was busy poking and scratching at the stone outside the house. The doorway leading to the courtyard was open, so I pulled Janis in to show her the work that had been done. The workman looked at us but didn't say anything, but after it was clear that we were so admiring of the place, he asked us if we wanted to see the rest of the house. Since looking in other people's houses is our favorite thing in the world, we immediately said yes. The workman started leading us through the entire home, which was much larger than it looked from the outside and even more spectacular. It was restored magnificently and furnished to the period, the late 1500s. After twenty minutes or so, we arrived at the kitchen. Sitting around the kitchen table were two women—clearly a mother and daughter—and two young children. The younger of the grown women looked at us—two strangers, a workman, and a cat—and asked the workman what he thought he was doing. The workman replied that we—the strangers and the cat—had admired the house and he thought we might like to see it. She sighed, they discussed the situation, and pretty soon Janis and I realized that the workman wasn't a workman—he was the owner of the house. We'd just managed to worm our way into his family's Christmas celebration.

We immediately apologized and tried to leave, but now the family would have none of it. They insisted we see the rest of the house, which got better and better with each room we toured, then they made us stay for a drink (okay, okay, they didn't *make* us, but it would have seemed inhospitable just to tour and run). The man who'd been showing us his place turned out to be a Belgian architect who lived, most of the time, in Algiers. This magnificent home was his weekend retreat, which he used only three or four weekends a year, plus Christmas week.

After our drink, we realized Norton had wandered off to examine the house on his own. I'm sorry to report that I panicked briefly; in that house he could have hid for days at a time and I had a sudden vision of not only ruining these people's Christmas but their New Year's as well. Luckily, he came the moment I called him, hopped into his shoulder bag, and Janis and I took him back to our house on rue St. Frusquin.

It was still relatively early, and we decided now it was time to open Christmas presents. Janis and I exchanged first. I got an ancient hanging oil lamp (I have a fetish for old lighting fixtures) as well as something I'd been looking to get for myself for over five years: a beautiful bowl and matching pitcher to go in a wooden dry sink I'd bought long ago. I'd never been able to find one I liked, but Janis had spotted this at the weekly antique mart in L'Isle-sur-la-Sorgue and hidden it away some weeks before. She received, in turn, an eighteenth-century iron (she has the same fetish for old irons that I have for lamps) and two nineteenth-century casserole dishes in the shape of hearts. Aaaaahhhhhhhh.

Norton did all right, too. He received several cans of Pounce (which I'd had someone send to me from New York; good cat treats are the one thing France seems to lack) and two fine catnip toys, one in the shape of a mouse, one in the shape of French bread.

For dinner that night, we did it up. We invited several Goultois to join us and devoured our very own fat turkey, chestnut stuffing, *patate douce avec cognac* (sweet potatoes drowned in brandy, to you), and some of the old toothless crone's killer goat cheese.

All in all, it was a perfect French Christmas and we were now ready to face Americans.

The next morning, we drove down to the Marseille airport, an hour away, to pick up Esther and Norm. They are both very dear friends and we were thrilled that they were our first guests, but, to be fair, I've got to paint a realistic picture. Neither of them had ever been in the European countryside before. This was Norm's very first trip to France. Within moments, he was so overjoyed at being there, he was speaking "like zees: I luf ze French. Zay are ze best. Oui!" and thinking that he was already able to communicate with the French on their own level. Esther, on the other hand, is not a person who's very comfortable when she's away from her office (picture a small, tightly wound Ethel Merman and you'll have the picture—I won't have an agent, but you'll have the picture). By the time we got back to Goult, she had three faxes waiting and two urgent calls to return. So while we showed them their rooms and helped them get settled, Esther spent an hour on the phone negotiating various deals and Norm walked all over the garden, speaking to the trees and stray cats in some language he was convinced was French. "Allo, leetle tree, 'ow aire yew? Et bonjour, Monsieur Bird. Eet ees very nice tew see yew. *Oui?*"

Our rule of thumb with jet-lagged arrivals was that they had to stay up until ten P.M. That way they'd be exhausted, would sleep through the night, and would wake up refreshed and back on a regular schedule at nine or ten the next morning.

That afternoon we took them to a cocktail party at our neighbor's (she was English; it was a Boxing Day party). Then we took them up into the mountains to Auberge de la Loube. We were the only people in the restaurant that night, so they moved a big table right in front of the fireplace. Norm toasted everybody and everything, while Esther dozed off in her chair (in addition to jet lag, she was also carsick from going up the winding road to the restaurant). Norton was now on such friendly terms with the three dogs that he hopped into their hiding place under the hearth with them for much of dinner.

We had a few days to be tourists with our guests and we enjoyed every moment of it. The next day, we began running them around to all our favorite places. We made them climb to the top of Oppede-le-vieux, a medieval village dominated by wonderful ruins at its peak. There is a straight drop from the cliff when you get to the top of the town. I, myself, never ventured too close, but Janis liked to teeter on the edge and drive me crazy. Once, while she was doing that, a private airplane flew by *below* her. The passengers waved while I held on to a tree, getting dizzy just thinking about it.

After Oppede, we had lunch at an amazing *routier* called Bistrot du Paradou in the very small town of Paradou. The restaurant is a four- or five-hundred-year-old stone house divided into two dining rooms. The front room has an enormous bar, usually surrounded by local truck drivers swigging wine and *pastis* and telling stories. The back room is perhaps twenty tables along with a fireplace, which usually has a *rôti* going, with lamb or chicken or rabbit on it. In wintertime, the Bistrot is only open for lunch, and only during the week, and each day they serve only one thing. You call up and ask what their menu is that day and they'll tell you they're having a *pot-au-feu* or an *aïoli* (which they have every Friday) or a *coq au vin* and then you decide if that's what you feel like eating that day. They also serve a delicious salad and as much red wine as you wish to drink (the bottle's waiting for you on your table when you sit down; it's produced directly for the restaurant and is *biologique*—organic—which means there are no sulfites or other nasty chemicals). The owner was a successful advertising executive who decided one day he'd had enough of selling Perrier or whatever it was he was selling, so he opened up the perfect fantasy of a French restaurant.

The Bistrot du Paradou is one of Norton's top three Provençal restaurants as well as ours. I think this is due to a combination of the fact that one particular waitress there likes him very much and is always telling him how much smarter he is than her dog, and the fact that the hearth is so large, Norton can sit almost anywhere in the whole restaurant and be warmed by the blazing fire.

After lunch, we went several miles down the road to the best olive oil mill in all of France, the cooperative mill in the town of Maussane. Maussane happens to be Janis's favorite town in the south of France, with the possible exception of St. Remy. It's built right onto the road, is small and charming yet extremely sophisticated, and looks exactly like the kind of place where Sergeant Saunders always used to get wounded in the show "Combat." More to the point, their olive oil is so delicious that we have personally risked lengthy prison terms smuggling many liters of the stuff back to New York.

After watching them crush olives, then buying enough oil to pan-fry half of Western Europe, we drove back to Goult. That afternoon, we had a party of our own, a cocktail party from five until whenever, so all our new friends could meet our two old friends. We had about thirty people in all, some Brits, one expatriate American, a couple of Swedes, and mostly French. We served leftover turkey and a giant ham and lots and lots of delicious cold *champagnoise* from the *cave* in Coustellet, but the biggest hit was the bagels and cream cheese that Norm and Esther brought from New York. The French people thought this was the most delicious thing since the invention of the croissant and gobbled down the onion bagels like there was no tomorrow.

The biggest surprise of the party was not that all our friends got along so well. It was that Norton, for the very first time in his life, not only spent most of the evening attending a party, he let all the children there come up and pet him.

I have not discussed the dark side of Norton's personality, mostly because there really isn't one. If he has a flaw at all, it's that he doesn't much like children. Small children, to be exact. I suppose it's understandable. Children are very volatile and loud and move in sudden herky-jerky motions. As a grown-up, I find them scary enough, so I really can see why Norton has always shied away from them. If we're in public, which we often are, Norton doesn't hiss or scratch them or anything like that. He simply gets very passive and withdraws into a shell, or else, if he's able, he'll make sure to just stay out of their way. At our first major Goult cocktail party, however, we had many children underfoot. They ranged from five years old to twelve, and somewhere around eight at night, I saw Norton calmly sprawled on the living-room floor, letting one of the five-year-olds try to crayon the top of his head.

France was clearly having its effect on the star of my family. And I must say I approved.

The next couple of days went by in a blur of tourism.

We all went to Arles and tried to find some semblance of Van Gogh but, except for the ultramodern Van Gogh Café and a Van Gogh gas station, hardly a trace remains. It is a beautiful town, however, and Norton was fascinated by the bullfighting school that practices in the town's Roman coliseum. We also went to Avignon, a truly great city. I don't know if Norton was able to appreciate the Palais du Papes or the spectacular wall that rings the town or even the Utopia, the only English-language movie theater south of Paris. I do know he definitely appreciated the *manège,* the merry-go-round, that sits in front of the opera house, gloriously lit, and spins around all night. Norton would have been happy to sit there with it, watching it go until dawn.

We took our visitors to the market at L'Isle-sur-la-Sorgue, of course, where we bumped into every single person we knew in Provence. By the end of the shopping trip, I'm sure Esther and Norm thought we'd bribed total strangers to pretend that they knew us and fake our guests into thinking we were popular. After buying our weekly supplies, we then took a wine tasting trip to Châteauneuf-du-Pape, which was only forty minutes from Goult. (In case no one seems to be making the connection between all these places with the word *pape* in them, here's a very brief and probably inaccurate history lesson: When the French government was trying to, more or less, take over the Vatican, they wound up installing their own Pope and luring the Catholic Church headquarters over to France. When you tour Avignon and Châteauneuf, it's not really hard to see why they came running. The palaces are awe-inspiring and the wine is, arguably, the best in the world. When the corrupt French Pope finally died, he was replaced by a corrupt Italian Pope who went back to Italy, but the palaces and the wines remain, with Avignon as their approximate center. End of lesson.) Janis and I had made several trips out Châteauneuf way and even knew some of the owners of the smaller vineyards (we're easy to remember: There aren't many American couples who come wine-tasting with a Scottish Fold). Typical of the Provençal French—of their class, their warmth, and their style—one of the *cave* owners we'd previously spent time talking to about wine gave a half bottle of his newest vintage to Esther and one to Norm as presents. He also offered one to Norton, but I decided my cat had already picked up enough bad habits and, since Norton was technically a minor, I declined for him.

By the time Monday rolled around, Esther and Norm

were fairly convinced that we were living in paradise. And then we decided to *really* go wild.

One of the best things about Goult was its location. Not only was it in the heart of the magnificent Lubéron, it was a two-and-a-half-hour drive from skiing in the Alps, it was two and a half hours down to Barcelona, it was two hours from Nice and Cannes, and it was two and a half hours to Italy. So we decided to have an adventure and go visiting foreign lands.

Norton had already spent lots of time in Italy and down on the Riviera. Nice (which is pronounced Neese; trust me: This will come into play later) was one of his favorite towns in France. He liked the accommodations, the food, and found the Niçoise particularly friendly. We'd been down there often, partly for business, mostly because we had friends living there.

An old friend of mine was Joel Douglas (Kirk's son, Michael's brother, a successful film producer in his own right). I'd known Joel and Michael when we were youths and had kept in touch over the years. Michael, of course, went on to become a zillionaire movie star and Oscar winner and even see Sharon Stone naked (for which I would happily give up the zillions and the Oscar). Joel wound up living the perfect life, moving to Monaco, marrying a terrifically nice woman from Nice (or neese woman from Nice; uh-oh, don't get me started), and was running the oldest working film studio in Europe, which he and Michael were in the process of buying. (Just to clarify: They were buying the studio, not Europe, although I have a feeling Michael could afford to actually buy the Continent if he so desired.) I was talking to them about doing some work out of the studio, so after we'd been in Goult a few weeks, we went down to talk some new business as well as catch up on old times.

Norton, Janis, and I met Joel and his wife, Paddy, at the commissary at the old Victorine Studios. After a very tasty lunch and even tastier conversation—we hadn't seen each other for years and had a lot to catch up on: brothers, parents, work, ex-girlfriends or ex-wives as the case may have been—Joel took the three of us on a tour of the studio. I was in heaven, because Victorine is like an old Hollywood studio from the twenties and thirties. It's got all the atmosphere and magic and romance that studios used to have (they still have them in L.A. to a certain extent, but it's all tempered by the fact that Sam Goldwyn and Harry Cohn have been replaced by either agents, morons, or corporate Japanese people). On the lot we saw the places where they filmed Truffaut's *Day for Night* and Hitchcock's *To Catch a Thief,* and the greatest French movie of them all, *Children of Paradise.* Joel also showed us a rough cut of a promotional film they were putting together about the history of the studio. It was put together by the studio projectionist (whose father was the studio projectionist, as was his grandfather. This guy *lives* for the studio). Unfortunately, despite the best of intentions, it was a *very* rough cut—dominated by a lot of unknown actors in period wigs—but the screening room was very luxurious. After half an hour or so of the film, Norton stretched out on the chair next to mine and took a little cat nap.

That night, we had dinner at a fish restaurant with Joel and Paddy and their small, very friendly if somewhat overactive dog. Norton and the hyper pup got along quite well, though Norton spent a little more time on my lap than he usually does.

The next day, we strolled around Old Nice, where I

could happily live. The new part of Nice couldn't be uglier (actually, that's not true, it could be Cannes, which is perhaps the ugliest beach city in the world), but Vieux Nice is full of cobblestone streets and ancient churches and wonderful little shops and restaurants. Since it's so close to the border, only fifteen or twenty minutes away, Nice is as much an Italian city as it is a French one, and the combination definitely works.

Norton made several trips to Nice while we were in France and, while that may be his city of choice on the Riviera, I think he found St.-Jean-Cap-Ferrat a close second.

The day we went to Cap-Ferrat—or as I like to think of it, "The Village That Only Donald Trump Can Afford to Live In"—we were visiting Nina Salter, the editor of the French edition of *The Cat Who Went to Paris* (the translated title: *Le Chat Qui Dînait Chez Maxim's*). It's not that French publishers pay their editors so much more money than American publishers do, it's that Nina was visiting a childhood friend of hers, whose parents had a nice little mansion in Cap-Ferrat, right on the sea.

Norton took to it immediately, ignoring the scrumptious repast that was set before us when we arrived, preferring to stroll the grounds and sniff out the new surroundings. After lunch, he came for a walk with us, along the boardwalk and up into the rocky crags of the shoreline. Norton was not as foolhardy as Nina, who dove into the sea and took a lengthy swim (this was in early March, when the temperature was all of forty degrees). My little cat much preferred the dry rocks and, while various swimmers trembled and turned blue, Norton found the only ray of sun to luxuriate in.

It really *is* hard to argue when someone says that cats are a lot smarter than people.

Norton also spent some time in the ultra-chic town of Ramatuelle, just outside of St. Tropez. An author and friend of mine, Edward Behr, was based in Paris but had bought a house in Ramatuelle in 1966, for something like forty dollars. It was a modest little joint: a one-time hotel with six or seven bedrooms, a professional kitchen (including walk-in freezer), an uncountable number of dens and offices, a balcony overlooking St. Tropez and the Mediterranean, and, surrounding the swimming pool, sloping gardens that rivaled those at Versailles. That's all.

Norton, jet-setter that he is, liked Ramatuelle fine, but he really took to St. Tropez, where he got to sit on the bay and sip—or, more accurately, slurp—a *café liegois,* a fancy name for a cross between an iced coffee and a coffee sundae, the first nonchocolate concoction I've ever seen my cat flip over.

All of this is by way of pointing out that Norton was a far more experienced traveler in the south of France than either of our Christmas Week human guests.

The first thing we decided to do with Esther and Norm was to stop off in Nice to walk them through the old town. This we did, and all went smoothly, except for the moment when Norm, forgetting once again that he couldn't speak French, got into a conversation with a shopkeeper. He was buying a few presents for people back home, and the woman at the store asked him a question in her native tongue. Norm, still refusing to acknowledge that he didn't understand the language, nodded and responded, *"Oui. Un peu."* (Yes. A little.) This confused the woman no end, since the question she'd asked was, "Would you like this gift-wrapped?"

You try gift-wrapping something just "a little."

Being the ultrasophisticates that we were, we decided to

venture into Italy for lunch. We also decided that spontaneity was the way to go for this brief two-day trip—we would just do whatever the hell we felt like for thirty-six hours. Naturally, the first thing we felt like doing was eating. So we drove half an hour to the town of Ventimiglia, the Italian/French equivalent of Tijuana.

Janis, Norton, and I had done this trip several times. Nothing made us appreciate our year more than saying, spur of the moment, "Let's drive to Italy for lunch." And Ventimiglia happens to be a perfectly nice town. It's not Rome or Verona or Venice, but it *is* Italy, so what could be bad?

We had a delicious lunch right on the sea. Norton got his own plate of scampi and the restaurant made him feel so at home, he did a little wandering, checking out a few of the other diners, moseying into the kitchen to see what else he could dig up in the way of antipasto. After lunch, we did what people seem to do in Italy: We spent two hours waiting in line at a bank trying to change our francs into lira, and then we went to an open-air market to buy yet more food. The only hitch in this part of the operation was that Norton single-handedly almost started World War III.

As we walked into the market, the little guy was in his usual position, sitting up with his head swiveling out of his shoulder bag. The Italians feel just as warmly toward cats and dogs as the French do—they see nothing even remotely strange about a cat visiting a restaurant or a market—so as soon as we stepped inside, one of the vendors sprang into action and offered Norton a fresh sardine. Norton looked at him as if he was insane, sniffed at the fish rather rudely, and turned his attention elsewhere—mostly toward the *gelato* stand.

"What's the matter with him?" he asked me. "He's too good for my fish?"

"No, no, no," I hurriedly assured him. "He just doesn't *like* fish."

"He's a cat, isn't he?" the fish vendor wanted to know.

"Sure, he's a cat," I agreed.

"Then he should eat fish."

"I know he should"—and here I shrugged very philosophically; that usually worked with French people—"but he seems to be more of a meat eater."

I should point out here that what I was speaking was NormLanguage. I don't speak a word of Italian, so I was mixing in a little French with a little English, and a lot of a Vito Scotti–like Italian accent.

"This is a *fish* market," the guy now pointed out to me. By this time, several other vendors had gathered around to see what the commotion was. No one was happy to see it was a cat who didn't eat fish.

"Yeah," another one grumbled. "Why bring a cat who hates fish into a fish market?"

Smiling at all of them, I mumbled to my cat under my breath, "Norton, sweet little cat, *please* eat the sardine."

No chance. My sweet little cat simply doesn't eat fish. But the vendor held it out in front of him again and Norton practically gagged. Before there was a full-scale riot, Janis wandered over, took me and Norton by the arm (and paw), and led us back out into sunlight and safety.

"*What* was that all about?" she demanded.

"He's got fussy eating habits," I said, pointing to our gray companion. "It's not his fault."

"No, it's not *his* fault," she said and rolled her eyes, leaving no doubt whose fault she thought it was.

Full and now feisty—and still living on spontaneity—we

all piled back in the car and decided to keep forging further into Italy.

"What about the French Riviera?" Esther wanted to know.

"Italy's great," I told her. "It'll be fun. We'll just drive until we get to someplace nice and then we'll find a hotel."

"What about a reservation?" she asked, and we all explained to her, once again, this whole concept of spontaneity. Reluctantly, Esther agreed to go along with the crowd.

And the crowd proceeded to drive into five hours of hell.

We checked a map and decided we'd go on to San Remo, a supposedly nice resort town, supposedly only another hour or so further into Italy. Note the key repetition of the word *supposedly.*

The first part of the drive went smoothly. Then, as we approached San Remo, we noticed that traffic was slowing down. The last mile or so into town took a little longer to travel than it should have—by about an hour. The next thing we knew, we were on the outskirts of San Remo stuck in the worst traffic jam in history. The first half hour, we were all calm. The second half hour, Janis went to sleep. We had now progressed about a hundred feet into town. The third half hour, Esther started to whine. The fourth half hour, Janis woke up again and she joined in the whining. We were now all of a hundred and ten feet into town. Somewhere in there, Norm snapped. He began talking in a thick Italian accent, pretending he was a native of San Remo. "Excusa me," he said, tapping on the window as if he were outside the car. "I'ma liva here an' Ia been inna my car fora fourteen years. The radio no work—hassa anything happened?" I started giggling, which was a bad sign, and only egged him on. The Italian accent continued. "Excusa

me. I justa bringa my new son homa from the hospital. It
taka me eighteen years and now I have to finda the college." By the time Norm was through with his riff, we
learned that no one in the town of San Remo had ever been
out of their cars, no one in town knew how to walk, and that
forty-two percent of the town's population had the first
name of Fiat. This went on for nearly an hour (or another
hundred and fifty feet). Janis and Esther were in a total
panic by this point. They not only hated being in traffic, they
hated me and Norm, who were laughing so hard as to be
near some strange form of mental illness. Norton was the
only one keeping his head, but I maintain it's because he
was in the backseat with Esther and Janis and simply didn't
want to face their wrath if he started laughing along
with us.

In addition to his take on San Remo, Norman also explained a word game he'd invented several years before
when the Ayatollah Khomeini was first popping up in the
news. Norm was obsessed with the whole Ayatollah/Sal-
man Rushdie business ever since he found out that Salman
Rushdie had gotten engaged. Norm figured that he, Norm,
went out almost every night in search of the perfect
woman—or even a date who'd see him a second time—and
had never been able to find her. Now, here was a guy who
was in hiding, under the threat of death, and he was getting
married! My pal Norm didn't think this was fair or just. So
he created a game about the Ayatollah hoping perhaps an
entire religion would put a price on his head and he'd get
to meet an attractive woman.

The game he invented was that you had to come up with
a new type of Ayatollah, defined by his job or his attitude,
but one who rhymed with Khomeini. For instance: The
Ayatollah who loves dogs is the Ayatollah Great Daney.

The Ayatollah mystery writer is the Ayatollah Ed McBainy. The weird Ayatollah is the Ayatollah Insaney. Okay, granted that on paper it might not look like much, but after hours of being stuck in the car with crazy Italian drivers honking their horns every fifteen seconds, it was the greatest thing that had happened to me since I was twenty-one years old in St. Tropez and saw a gorgeous blond woman walking along the beach wearing nothing but sunglasses, a thong bikini bottom, and white cowboy boots. For the rest of our trip—which at the time seemed as though it would probably be spent on the not-all-that-attractive road leading to San Remo—I became obsessed with rhyming Ayatollahs. Some of the better ones: The accordion-playing Ayatollah (the Ayatollah Lady of Spainy), the mogul Ayatollah (the Ayatollah Citizen Kaney), and the spitfire-singing Ayatollah (the Ayatollah Abbe Laney). My guess is, if I keep this up much longer, my editor will cut all the rest of them out anyway, so I think I'll stop here with the Ayatollahs.

We did finally get out of San Remo, at which point Esther seized control of the situation. We stopped at a not-fancy-looking hotel, desperate for accommodations. It wasn't seedy but it also wasn't the Ritz. Esther strode in and asked if they knew of a nice hotel anywhere in the vicinity that had a room. They asked if she wanted a room there and she said no: She wanted a *nice* hotel. (Okay: Here's where that whole Nice pronunciation comes in handy. The same way I overdid the Thanksgiving jokes when Janis and I were once in Turkey, I became a little too vigorous about switching the uses of Nice, the city, and nice, the adjective. I can't tell you how many times one of us would say, "That looks like a nice restaurant," and I would respond, "Do you mean a nice restaurant or a Nice restaurant?" I can't really defend myself on this matter, but I found it funny every single time this came up in conversation, until Janis told me that if I said "Nice" for "nice" one more time, she'd kill me.) Anyway, despite Esther's insult in the roadside hotel, she did find out that we were never going to be able to stay anywhere on the coast of Italy that week. It turns out that the whole country has Christmas Week off for vacation and, apparently, everybody *in* the whole country comes down to the coast. What was causing the traffic jam is that there is exactly *one* coast road. That's right. If you want to get anywhere on the Italian (or French, for that matter) Riviera and you don't use the highway, there is one tiny, winding road and that's it.

It didn't take us long to change our plans. We turned around immediately and headed back to Nice (which seemed like it would be nice). There we decided to treat ourselves to a magnificent evening, since our day had been so completely miserable. Instead of staying at the nice (sorry! I can't help myself) but small and moderately priced hotel Janis, Norton, and I usually stayed at, we checked into the Negresco. And we didn't just check into the Negresco—we checked into the most expensive, luxurious, over-the-top two-bedroom suite they had. For you prudes in the reading audience, don't worry; Esther checked into a third room far down the hall. She didn't want to be anywhere near any of us.

We went to a lovely restaurant, Coco Beach, right on the water, and had a perfect fish dinner. The owner—I know you'll think I'm making this up, but he really did remind me of a French William Demarest—prepared a few grilled shrimp for Norton when he got word that the cat wasn't wild about regular fish. The shrimp seemed to do the trick. As a matter of fact, ever since Coco Beach, Norton has been willing to chow down on all shellfish as well as the occasional bite of salmon. Tuna, however, remains out of the question, as do sardines.

After dinner, we went to the Nice casino. (Don't worry: My lips are sealed. I will make no comment on whether the casino was . . . ummm . . . pleasant or not.) Norm was the big winner. Not only did he pocket several hundred dollars, he came up with the world's stupidest Ayatollah (the Ayatollah No Brainy).

The next morning, we drove back to France along the glorious Mediterranean, stopping off in Eze, probably the most touristy village of its type but nonetheless a spectacular medieval town that cannot be missed. We had lunch at the Grill du Château at the very top of the town, where the waiter went crazy over Norton.

"Vôtre chat," he told me. *"Il est superb!"* He was the first cat, the waiter gushed, he'd ever seen behave like a human being.

That night was New Year's Eve and we spent it back in the Lubéron in fine style. We had a few French friends come over for some champagne—no *champagnoise* that night!— then the five of us went to Auberge de la Loube for their special New Year's dinner.

I've already described the delectable appetizers at the Auberge, but on New Year's Eve Maurice puts on a special spread. It starts with a truffle omelet—two or three eggs scrambled with the scrapings of wild, black French truffles, mushrooms so strong and delicious they are considered one of the great delicacies in the world (and priced accordingly, although Maurice doesn't charge for this dish—it's his gift to his regular clients). I don't think Maurice was all that thrilled when I gave Norton a taste, but he softened when he saw how much Norton enjoyed it.

The rest of the dinner was on a par with the *truffes,* then exactly at midnight, Maurice poured champagne for everyone and we all toasted and hugged and meowed appropriately, welcoming in the New Year.

Thursday was Esther's and Norm's last night in Provence, so naturally we had to eat even more food by way of a fond farewell.

I'd lost a bet to Esther before leaving for France—I'd said that Clarence Thomas wouldn't be confirmed; she told me I was a naive ignoramus and, of course, she turned out to be right—so my payment was to take her to Oustau de Baumanière, the legendary restaurant which is the best and most famous in this area of Provence.

Janis and I had been there before. The owner and chef, Jean André Charial, is a friend of Wolfgang Puck's and so I'd heard about this place for years and years. In fact, it's thanks to Baumanière that Janis and I really wound up in Goult. Several years before, we had stayed at the hotel (it's not just a restaurant; it's one of the great hotels in the world, too). As if the feather beds and down comforters aren't enough of an enticement, the town of Les Baux is spectacularly set into white Bauxite mountains. When you first see the town, and the hotel right outside of town, it's as if you're Ronald Colman in *Lost Horizon* and have just found Shangri-la. Over the years, we'd stayed and/or eaten there several times. Since we'd been in Goult, we'd made the forty-five-minute drive a couple of times to worship at the feet of the two-star chef. More important, Baumanière was, no question about it, Norton's favorite restaurant. The staff loved him and usually greeted him with affection and a bit of wonderment. He was automatically given his own chair when we were seated at a table, and often had a special dinner prepared for him.

This night, the restaurant outdid themselves, both for humans and for cat. Esther agreed she'd never eaten a meal like that, even in her dreams. Norm could barely say he'd had a Nice time. Janis, as usual, kept her dignity until the huge cheese cart arrived, then she lost any sense of propriety and basically just kept screaming out, "More! More! More!" to the server. Norton was served a small dish with three separate specialties—duck, scallops, and fish. At Baumanière, even Norton will eat the fish.

The *pièce de résistance,* as usual, was the dessert.

Each of the humans had ordered a specialty of the house—a hot soufflé, covered in *crème fraîche* and the appropriate sauce (if a raspberry soufflé, raspberry sauce; if chocolate soufflé, chocolate sauce; if gingerbread soufflé, their newest and possibly greatest creation, gingerbread sauce). Each of the soufflés is presented on a covered silver dish. The soufflé is brought before the diner, placed on the table, and then with a flamboyant but spritely motion, the cover is whisked away and the customer usually goes something like "Oh my God!" or "Ooooooooohhhhhhhh!" or, if you're our friend Dominick, "Is that all?!"

Four times we witnessed this ritual, first for Janis, then Esther, then Norm, then me. Then we realized there was a fifth silver dish and it was placed directly in front of Norton.

Before I really had time to ponder what they could have possibly made for my cat—a Pounce soufflé??? a Whiskas Chopped Chicken and Cheese soufflé????—the waiter whisked off the silver cover to reveal a small, gray, marzipan mouse, complete with tail, pink eyes, gray whiskers, and black marzipan nose.

The creation drew well-deserved applause—not just

from us, from other appreciative diners as well—and the pastry chef received Norton's permanent and undying gratitude.

Deep down, despite all the proof to the contrary, I know that Esther, my own agent, thinks I make all this stuff up about Norton. This night, I made a special point of watching her as she stared at the cat, who was calmly taking a few licks of his mouse on a silver tray in a two-star French restaurant as if this were something he was used to every night of the week. The look in Esther's eyes at that moment told me it was almost worth having Clarence Thomas on the Supreme Court. Not quite but almost.

The next day, my gourmet cat was most sorry to see Norm and Esther go back to New York. It meant that life, for him, was going to return to normal.

Or as normal as Norton's life ever gets.

a cat in spain

For the month of February, my old pal and writing partner, David, came to pay us a visit. It was not entirely social; we were writing a screenplay together and we decided there was no better place to write together than in my temporary office on the third (or second) floor overlooking the Lubéron valley.

In a sense, history was repeating itself as far as David and I were concerned.

So many years ago it's a little depressing, we went to the south of France together for our first collaboration. He had just graduated from journalism school and was taking a year off to travel in Europe with his girlfriend. I had just finished writing my first novel and was certain it was only a matter of time before I would be rich, famous, and a celebrated literary man about town. I was young and headstrong and thought I could do anything. One of the things I thought I could do was to quit my first real job at a publishing

company and my $135 a week salary and go off and spend
a year in the south of France. This was a concept carefully
planned and maturely thought out in the manner of most
of my plans in those years: David and I got extraordinarily
drunk and stoned on a train ride from Boston to New York
and at some point during the five-hour trip, we decided
we'd rendezvous in Europe and write a movie together.
This was in 1976.

Several terrific things came out of that train trip. We
actually did write a movie together, which was flat-out horrible, but which eventually was sold as a television pilot,
helping us to break into that charming business. We're still
writing partners, after all these years, which was another
nice result of that fifth or sixth Jack Daniel's on wheels. The
best thing that happened, of course, was that we wound up
rendezvousing just north of the Spanish border halfway in
between the towns of Collioure and Port Vendres, which
was about as close to heaven as two young, broke, would-
be-screenwriters and novelists could possibly come. We had
a dirt-cheap apartment and we could actually jump from our
balcony into the clear, blue Mediterranean (we never did,
but we *could* have, if we were really the Ernest Hemingway
clones we thought we were instead of two fairly cautious
Jews who didn't want to have to learn the French phrase for
"Excuse me, do you have a very large bottle of iodine and
several hundred yards of bandages?"). We shopped at the
open-air market, which magically appeared in the Port Vendres square every Saturday, and bought fresh fish direct
from the fishermen during the week (Port Vendres was still
a mainstream fishing village in those days). Wine was
twenty-five cents a bottle and we were too young to have
ever heard about cholesterol, so we basically spread cheese

on anything or anyone we possibly could. Nobody in town spoke a word of English, the temperature seemed to be eighty degrees every single day, and there was one great café in Collioure, an amazing place called the Templiers, which astonishingly had original Picassos on the wall because old Pablo and Braque and Matisse used to trade paintings for food when they were mere pups (or *petits chiens,* if you want to be technical) and lived down there. We went into the Templiers every single day after we were done writing, for a cognac or a *pastis* or just a cold beer, and when the eighty-year-old owner of the Templiers actually deigned to shake our hand one day when we came in—the ultimate sign that we were considered regulars and were now accepted by the town—we knew that, indeed, life was a very, very good thing.

We were young and even though we ran out of money in several months and had to return to New York—my novel had indeed sold to a publisher, but I learned the harsh truth that while an advance paid for a first novel does allow one to actually buy meat once in a while, it doesn't allow one to lead a Scott Fitzgerald–like lifestyle—I was under the impression that this was the way my life would be lived from then on. I did not appreciate that the daily handshakes at the Templiers and the Brigadoon-like fog of perfection surrounding Collioure were not things simply handed over on a regular basis to anyone who thinks he deserves it. It was the zenith, the goal that one strives for throughout one's life. It was, in a sense, a dream, but it was a dream I had actually experienced—and one I would not and could not forget.

Clearly, since I was now, sixteen years later, doing my best to repeat it.

I'd even gotten my old buddy Dave to repeat it with me. And what better way to do this than by returning to our old stomping grounds? With Janis and Norton, no less.

~~~

Janis had heard our romantic rhapsodizing and seen several million photos of Collioure over the years. She also knew me and David too well, and was aware that as soon as we were back in the town for a weekend, we'd be laughing our heads off over things unexplainable and want to see places that had no interest for anyone who wasn't personally involved in the sightseeing. So she decided that Collioure could not be our one and only destination. After a brief discussion, we all agreed to stop off in Collioure Friday night, spend some time there Saturday, then drive on down into Spain for the rest of the weekend. We settled on Barcelona as our final destination, as neither Janis, David, nor Norton had ever been there.

France has changed quite a bit since David and I first discovered what it was like to live there. French people now use English words like *parking* (as in "Make ze first right and zen go to ze parkeeng") and *fax* has actually been given a gender (it's male, in case you're interested—*le* fax). Plenty of McDonald's do, indeed, dot the landscape, and French politicians are now more or less as corrupt as their American equivalents. (They probably were always corrupt but it seemed as if the corruption always revolved around sex and food. Now French corruption has been Washingtonized and the scandals have become financial.) Even so, we were not prepared for our first look at the 1990s version of Collioure.

It looked a lot like Miami Beach.

When we'd lived there, it had been a sleepy village. It

was a resort town but was not considered chic or hip and was known mostly to French people who lived in the southwest part of the country. We lived in one of the few modern apartment buildings; it was on the southern outskirts of town and was one of perhaps five or six buildings in the complex. Now, as we pulled up in our Citroën, it was almost impossible to see the village, which was completely hidden behind a skyline of giant condominiums. It was a lot like the scene in *It's a Wonderful Life* where Clarence the Angel takes Jimmy Stewart back to Bedford Falls to see what it would have been like if he'd never lived—and sleepy, all-American Bedford Falls has turned into Pottersville, where every other store is a nasty-looking saloon and naked dancing girls are everywhere you turn. Perhaps Collioure wasn't *that* bad, but it *was* a shock to the system. Everything was new and everything was ugly. Janis had that look in her eye, the one that said, *"This* is the place you've been telling me about all this time?!"

I didn't panic, however, and my patience was rewarded once we made it into the old part of town. The French may put up truly ugly new structures, but at least they don't tear down the old beautiful ones in the process. The old village was left untouched and was exactly as David and I remembered it. Once we were safely ensconced within the medieval walls of Collioure, everything was fine.

We had booked rooms at the hotel Templiers. This was not a coincidence—the Templiers was the place with the Picassos and Braques and Matisses, our old watering hole. When we lived in Collioure, we had never been able to afford to eat there, much less stay there, though the old man, Monsieur Pous, had once shown us through the whole building, pointing out some of the famous artists whose paintings also adorned the hotel walls and corridors.

The restaurant was Norton's kind of place. Very casual, very friendly, a little bit of sawdust on the floor. An excellent eatery for a cat to wander through and poke around in.

David and I were thrilled to be eating there. It was as if we'd been in there drinking our *kirs* just the day before. Some of the old-timers sitting playing cards at the back table even looked familiar. Exactly as we remembered, every inch of the walls were covered with paintings and sketches. Some of them were awful, some of them were wonderful. Some were done by absolute nobodies—if *I* gave the owner a drawing or painting, he'd put it up; and, believe me, my artistic ability stops at stick figures—but some were, incredibly, original Picassos. Right in the middle of the room was a large photo of Monsieur Pous, the owner, with his arm around Pablo himself. Framed with the photo was a Picasso line drawing of a reclining nude.

One thing had changed, sadly, in the years since we'd last been there: The old man, Monsieur Pous, had died. But his sons now ran the place, and they obviously had a keen sense of tradition. We were glad we'd had the opportunity to shake Monsieur Pous's hand back when we were young, and we'd seen enough of the way he'd run his place to know he'd approve of the way his family was carrying on.

The meal was exquisite. Norton came back from his tour just in time to share my plate of grilled squid and garlic, and stuck around long enough to have a reasonable amount of my bouillabaise. He didn't taste any of the local wine, which was very dry and very good. (In fact, the wine from Collioure is now the latest "hot" wine in France. It's still fairly inexpensive and really is delicious. It makes me proud to realize that many years ago I used to practically bathe in the stuff.)

The next day, David and I took Janis and Norton on a

nostalgic trip through our past. I sensed that Janis was a little bored but Norton seemed interested. His head was out of the shoulder bag the entire trek. I think he was glad to find that I'd actually lived a life before he'd arrived on the scene.

We took them first around the old village. We went into the *pâtisserie* I used to go into every morning to buy breakfast. Every single day for three months, I'd go in and ask for *"deux pains au chocolat"*—two chocolate croissants. Unfortunately, my *"deux"*—two—sounded like *"du"*—some. So five days a week, four weeks a month, for three full months, I'd ask for *two pains au chocolat,* and each one of those days the woman behind the counter would smile and say, "Very well, monsieur. And how many would you like?" It didn't matter how I pronounced the *"deux,"* it didn't matter that I sometimes repeated it three times, as in, *"Je voudrais deux, deux, deux pains au chocolat"* and hold two fingers up in front of me. Every single time she would ask me how many I wanted and every single time I'd want to kill myself because I couldn't make her understand my French. Years later, a dear friend of ours in Goult, Danie, showed me how to distinctly differ my pronunciation when saying *"du"* and *"deux."* Still psychologically scarred after all that time, I worked up my nerve, went into the Goult *pâtisserie,* and asked for *"deux pains au chocolat."* "Very well, monsieur," the woman behind the Goult counter said. "And how many would you like?" Crushed and humiliated, I went running to Danie for consolation. She told me how to avoid this problem forever after: I should, from here on in, order *trois pains au chocolat!*

We walked out to the old stone lighthouse and in and out of the town's alleyways and cobblestone paths. In these sections, nothing had changed at all and that stability was, to me, remarkably reassuring and exhilarating.

After we got through walking Janis and Norton all over town, we drove out to see our old apartment building. This was the worst change of all. It was no longer one small ugly building surrounded by four or five other small ugly buildings. It had turned into a giant and horrendous apartment complex. There were probably a hundred and fifty hideous condos built at the spot. We still were excited to see it— although Janis couldn't understand why we'd get excited visiting the ugliest place she'd ever seen in France.

By late Saturday morning, we'd gotten the past out of our system and were now ready to head to Spain.

Collioure is only a few miles north of the border. We drove past Port Vendres, which was just as lovely as we remembered, past the towns of Banyul and Corbere, and then we were in Spain. Or nearly in Spain.

Going from France to Italy with a cat is no problem. In fact, the Italian border guards never even look at Norton when we drive there. The same for Switzerland. Luckily, I'd brought Norton's papers along, because it turns out the Spanish are very strict about bringing pets into their country.

"You have a cat," one of the six border guards told me.

"*Si,*" I said. (Spanish is one of the many languages I also don't speak. I tried French and English and even a word or two of Italian, hoping one of those would work. They didn't.)

"He has a cat," the guard now said to another guard. Why they needed six border guards when clearly ours was the only car that had passed through all day was beyond me. But I didn't want to ask. I was already in enough of a jam.

"*Si, si,*" one of the guards now chimed in. "*Uno gato!*"

"Do you have the papers for the cat?" I was now asked.

It turned out I *didn't* have the papers for the cat. I had

papers, but not the right papers. In Spain, you need some special permission from the embassy or some such place. But, happily, the guards didn't really have any idea what the right papers were either.

"He has papers," one of them announced.

"Are they the right papers?" another one asked.

"I don't know. They're in English."

"Ask him if they're the right papers."

"*Señor,*" the first guard now asked me. "Are these the right papers for the cat?"

"Yes," I lied and nodded very convincingly.

The guards relaxed and smiled—all six of them—and waved us through.

Now we were in Spain.

Our first stop was Cadeques, one-time home of Salvador Dali as well as a lovely northern beach town. The drive there was fairly uneventful, except that the road was particularly winding and curving and both Janis and David got kind of woozy. They wound up in the backseat feeling sorry for themselves. Norton sat happily beside me, the perfect passenger.

After lunch in Cadeques, we took the *péage*—the high-speed toll highway—to Barcelona.

Barcelona may be the perfect European city. It's small, stunningly beautiful, very sophisticated. The people are friendly and the food is delicious. And they like cats. As I said: perfect.

Norton toured the city with us from morning till night. He saw the spot from which Columbus set sail for America, he took a walking tour of the Barri Gòtic (the Gothic Quarter), he visited several Gaudi buildings, including the still-being-constructed Sagrada Famillia cathedral, he ate a special Catalanes paella for dinner at the restaurant La Cuineta.

Then, to top it off, he—and we—saw one of the great sights of the western world.

In front of the cathedral, which dominates the square in the center of the majestic Gothic Quarter, we witnessed a hundred Barcelonians dancing the official dance of Barcelona—the almost indescribable "sardana."

Night had just arrived, candles were flickering on the tables in the outdoor cafés, there was mystery and romance in the darkness and shadows. Suddenly ten circles formed, rings of ten people each. Every member of the circle held hands, the hands raised triumphantly above their heads, and all had replaced their regular shoes with white espadrilles. The ritual had begun. They stood like this, motionless, for perhaps thirty seconds, then an orchestra, tucked into a corner of the massive square, began playing lively, sensual, exquisite Spanish music—and then a hundred grown-ups began spinning and dancing and flailing exactly like Jerry Lewis on the bandstand in *You're Never Too Young*. It was the scariest, most inane sight I've *ever* seen. If a hundred people did this in New York, I guarantee they'd be beaten to a pulp and then arrested—and deservedly so. Forget the ritualized beauty and power everyone talks about. Forget all that passionate blood coursing through Spanish veins. I'm telling you, this was worse than the clog dancers on the Labor Day telethon.

That more or less ended Norton's first visit to Spain. I believe a statue was later erected after our weekend trip, commemorating the very spot on the square where an American tourist actually laughed so hard, he almost passed out.

We did stop for lunch on the way back, at a tiny café on the coast. The sun was shining, so we sat outside and drank sangria while Norton ate to his heart's content off an enormous plate of grilled shrimp.

The waiter came by at some point; he stood over our table without saying anything, watching the cat. Finally, he turned to me and said, "Your *gato*. He is Spanish?"

"No," I told him. "American. By way of Scotland."

The waiter stayed by our table for another few minutes, watching Norton munch on the *gambas*. Before he turned to go back to the kitchen, the waiter tapped me on the shoulder, then pointed at Norton.

"He is handsome enough to be Spanish," he announced.

We finished our sangria, gathered the cat up, and headed back for the car and for France.

"You are handsome enough," I said to my little gray pal. "Just don't try puttin' on those espadrilles. Even *I* have my limits."

Forty-five minutes later we were back on French soil, where the border guards didn't ask to see Norton's papers, only welcomed him into the country with a very polite *"Bonjour, Monsieur le chat. Ça va?"*

It felt a lot like coming home.

a cat in Italy

8

At some point, before we settled on Provence, there was a very good chance that Norton was going to have to learn Italian.

I think he would have adjusted with few qualms. For one thing, he's very happy with Italian cat food. He still won't eat Petreet's *Tonno con Riso* (although I definitely would, in a pinch; it looks *good*), but the Gioie di Miao version of *Pranzo Regale con Gamberetti* is, judging from the way Norton attacks it, as good as anything he's had in the finest restaurants. He even enjoys, when the mood strikes, the Italian dry food, the Brekkies *con pollo* and *con manzo*. And Norton usually feels about dry food the way I feel about movies where Barbra Streisand plays the sex object.

Norton's spent a lot of time in Italy over the years, as have Janis and I. Since Goult was so close to the border, and since all three of us had travel in our blood, we spent a lot of time in Pastaland during our year abroad.

Our first foray came only a few weeks after we'd arrived in France. We went down to Nice to visit our friends the Douglases, and the next morning, instead of turning back and heading home, we ventured twenty minutes further away and went to Italy for lunch.

The moment you cross the border, everything changes. The French plant in straight, orderly rows. Their vineyards are organized and perfectly manicured. In Italy, nothing is straight or orderly. Everything looks as if it's been planted by Foster Brooks. Five minutes away from France, the cheese is completely different, the vegetables are different, the whole way of life is as if it's another planet.

This was always difficult to explain to our Goult friends, who usually thought we were nuts when we'd tell them we went to Italy for lunch or drove to Barcelona for the weekend. That's not something they ever would have done. We would explain that in America you can drive for three days straight, and still be in the same country and the same basic culture. If you start in Goult and drive for three days straight, you're in a completely new world.

So we would pop over to the border town Ventimiglia for lunch on occasion, usually to the *ristorantes* La Caravella (on the water) or Cuneo (right in town; very near the market where Norton refused to scarf down a sardine). At Cuneo, the proprietors, Beraudo and Figli, were particularly nice to Norton. By the end of our first visit, it was clear he was free to wander through the restaurant; what was theirs was his. One thing I'll never know is how or why cats pick their favorite spots, but pick them they do, and at Cuneo Norton's favorite spot was underneath a large, elaborately carved wooden hutch. That's where he'd eat and that's where he'd stay until we'd polished off every last drop of our Chianti.

The first time we made this sojourn to Italy, we had a little surprise waiting for us back in Goult.

We left Ventimiglia soon after lunch, at three-thirty or so, and arrived in Goult at six P.M. As we pulled into town, we were a little startled to find somewhere around two hundred and fifty people—approximately a quarter of the town—marching around the streets, up, over, and down, starting and ending at the Salle des Fêtes (literally, the Holiday Room, but what it is is the town meeting place, where they have everything from political rap sessions to the weekly bingo festivities). As if it weren't strange enough to find the whole town on parade, they were being led by twenty guys dressed like Richard Burton at the end of *Beckett*. They had on red and green robes, pointy hats, and were wearing religious-looking insignia and necklaces. As if *that* weren't enough, they would stop walking every ten feet or so and blow into long trumpets, blaring something vaguely heraldic. Every time they stopped and blew, the whole town would cheer wildly.

Needless to say, we parked our car and joined the rally, curious to see what could possibly be going on. I assumed Goult had won the French version of the World Series or else it was Bridget Bardot's birthday, which I'm sure must be a national holiday over there. It turns out I was wrong on both counts. The guys in the red and green robes were The Brotherhood of Wine Growers (those religious necklaces weren't religious or necklaces, it turned out: They were silver wine-tasting cups), and this was the annual march to celebrate the new vintage Côtes du Ventoux wine. They didn't just march, either. They gathered the whole town in the Salle des Fêtes and handed out free glasses of red, rosé, and white to anyone who wanted to taste it. We followed the parade from beginning to end, went into the

Salle des Fêtes, happily drank our glasses of wine, shook hands with the silly-looking guys in the robes (there were also two silly-looking women in robes, to show how far the French have progressed), then we went home, wondering if this is what would happen every time we went off to Italy for a day.

It wasn't. But that didn't stop us from going there. And we did venture further than Ventimiglia on several occasions.

My mother came over from Los Angeles to visit us for a while. We decided, on the semi-spur of the moment, to take a few days off and head toward Tuscany, which, unbelievably to us, was only a five-hour drive away. Going there is like driving from New York to Boston, except when you arrive you don't have to listen to Red Sox fans feel sorry for themselves. Plus the food's a lot better.

Our first stop was the town of Levanto, in the provence of Liguria, and the hotel Stella Maris (Roger's wife—and yes, I did say that at the time, and yes, Janis did swat me on the arm). The hotel is really nothing more than a bed and breakfast, slightly run-down but very cozy, and only a block from the beach, which is nice in season. But what really makes it special is that there are huge and spectacular sixteenth-century frescoes all over the ceilings, and the people who run the hotel make you feel as if you're a member of their family. Norton was the first cat who'd ever stayed there and at first they didn't know what to do for him. They kept knocking on our door and offering food, then milk, then they knocked just to see if he was content and comfortable.

We'd had a bit of trouble finding the Stella Maris the night we pulled into town. After driving aimlessly for a few minutes, we decided to stop at a café and see if we could figure out how to ask directions. The café we stopped at had nothing but Italian men standing around swigging down beer and anisette. Norton and I went in to see what was what. At first, the guys in the café stared at me as if I were from Mars. Not because I had a cat on my shoulder, but because I kept asking for a street called the via Marconi. After a while, one of the grizzled regulars came over to me and said, "Via *Mar*coni?" "Sì, sì," I said. "Via *Mar*coni." They all got a major laugh about the fact that I thought such a street might have been pronounced via Mar*co*ni, and then the real laughs started when they tried to give me directions. At some point, the same grizzler took me by the arm, put his hand on Norton's head, and yanked me out of the bar and into my car. He then shoved Janis over, climbed in, and began barking out orders that we interpreted, sometimes correctly, sometimes not, as things like "Go!" and "Right!" and "Left!" After fifteen minutes, he said something we were pretty sure meant "Stop!" and when I did, he hopped out of the car, disappeared around a corner, and we found our car parked right in front of the hotel Stella Maris.

Our second night in Italy, we stayed in the truly extraordinary town of Lucca and in the even more extraordinary hotel (a misnomer; it really is a castle), Villa S. Michele.

Villa S. Michele was originally built in the fourteenth century, added on to in the seventeenth century, and has been magnificently restored by the owner, whose name actually was Giuseppe, an Italian charmer in his late fifties or early sixties.

We spent the day touring Lucca, an old walled city that has to be seen to be believed. After many months in the small and relatively unsophisticated environs of Goult, we were surprised at how sophisticated and stylish the Italian version of the Lubéron really was. The chicest thing one could buy at the L'isle-sur-la-Sorgue market was a fancy apron. In Lucca, built into the ancient stone and rock, were row after row of designer clothing stores. Even Norton seemed to get a little bit of a lift spending the day around so many gorgeous and well-turned-out people.

At lunchtime, at another superb Italian restaurant, Bucadisantantonio, Norton was paid the supreme compliment. The four of us were quietly making oohing and ahhing noises over our pastas (or our small ashtray full of diced-up grilled chicken, depending on whom we're talking about), when I noticed a man at a nearby table doing nothing but staring at Norton, who, as usual, was sitting next to me on his own chair, eating and minding his own business. I smiled at the man but he didn't smile back—he just kept staring. Finally, after he and his wife paid their check and stood up to leave, he hesitated, then approached our table. He said something to me in Italian and when I indicated that I didn't understand, he asked whether I spoke French. When I nodded, he said, as solemnly as could be, *"Votre chat, monsieur. Il est très sage."*

Your cat, sir. He is very wise.

Yes, I agreed. I'd been told that before. Very wise. And the man, content to have paid homage, turned and left the restaurant.

We got back to the hotel, exhausted, having covered every inch of Lucca on foot (Norton was sound asleep in his shoulder bag long before we made it back to the hotel). When we arrived, the owner/restorer was behind the desk. He was a friendly sort, so when we asked for our key, he started talking, asking us what we'd done all day, etc., etc. As we were starting to trudge upstairs to our rooms, for some reason he stopped us and said the magical words, "Do you like to eat?"

I don't know what made him ask that. Perhaps it was the strands of pasta that were still dangling from my mouth, several hours after lunch. Perhaps we just had that lean and hungry look (well, hungry look, anyway). Either way, his eyes lit up when I said to him that yes, not only did we like to eat but that my mother was a fairly well-known cook and cookbook writer back in the United States.

Our new best friend got incredibly excited.

"Where are you going for dinner tonight?" he asked, and when I told him, he shook his head and said, "No, no, no." Then he paused and asked, "Do you like truffles?"

We all looked at one another, shrugged, and went, "Sure." (By the way, this conversation was not as easy as it looked—our new pal didn't speak a word of English; we compromised on a fairly rocky bastardization of French.) "I will take care of you," he announced and immediately went to the phone, dialed, waited a few seconds, then spoke rapid Italian for several seconds and hung up. He turned to us proudly and said, "I called the best restaurant in the region, told them a famous chef was coming, and told them to prepare a masterpiece for you!" He then insisted that we come down an hour before dinner, so he could serve us a drink and some cheese.

After a brief nap, we rendezvoused back in the lobby and met our new protector. He took us downstairs to his private bar, in the hotel's *cave,* where he poured an ice-cold local white wine for an aperitif. Just in case we weren't going to eat enough food at the restaurant he was sending us to, he also cut some slabs of fresh Parmesan cheese and homemade sausage (which Norton thought was the single most delicious thing he'd ever eaten).

Our host, Giuseppe, had thinning white-yellow hair, thick black-framed glasses, and wore a black turtleneck. He looked like a worker; his hands were rough and strong when he slapped you on the back (as he was wont to do) or clasped your hands in friendship. He was extremely energetic, full of life and lust (I'm fairly sure I caught him batting his eyes at dear old Mom once or twice). He also loved to talk, and thus told us his entire life story. He spoke French because he'd learned it in school. While studying, his teacher had given him the name of a girl in Paris—a countess. They exchanged letters (supposedly as language practice) and he fell in love, going back and forth between Rome and Paris to see her for eighteen years. (I don't know what happened after the eighteen years. At that point in the story, I started to be able to think of nothing else but how delicious that cheese was and concentrated on eating as much as possible before we had to leave for the restaurant.) He used to run a modern hotel on the island of Elba, then decided to come to Tuscany, where he renovated S. Michele over a period of three and a half years (it had just opened a few months before we'd accidentally stumbled in there).

By the time we'd polished off his bottle of wine—for which he refused to charge us—it was time to leave for our truffle extravaganza. It turned out to be far more than we had bargained for.

The restaurant Solferino, just outside of Lucca, was nothing fancy. Quite the contrary. It was a family-run joint, divided up into seven or eight small rooms. The bar was filled, as so many Italian places are, with locals playing cards and arguing over something or other. But we did happen to have the best dinner I've ever had in my life.

Nobody in the restaurant spoke a word of English. Or French, for that matter. So we were helpless captives. One of the waiters recognized us as the Americans they had been told about, so he ushered us to a table and just started bringing food over. Since our friend at the hotel had told them we liked truffles, it was truffles we were served. The first dish was sliced raw beef topped with thinly sliced truffles and olive oil. Then came a pasta dish—ravioli stuffed with truffles and topped with truffle cream. Then came another pasta dish—gnocchi in red-pepper truffle sauce. Then came *another* pasta—ravioli stuffed with roast pheasant and, you guessed it, truffles.

Before we came into the restaurant, Janis had made a point of saying that she wanted to pay for dinner; she hadn't been allowed to pay for anything on the trip so far. My mother agreed to keep her hands off the check, as did I (Norton's only flaw is that he *never* picks up the check, so we didn't bother to clear it with him). However, at this point in the meal, as we realized there was more food still to come, I pointed out to Janis that, with all the truffles we were getting, this meal was likely to cost several million dollars (or several billion lira, as the case may be). That certainly didn't stop us from eating, however. We were then served a guinea hen roasted with truffles—that was the highlight, for me—and then, believe it or not, we were each served a small beefsteak topped with truffles and grated fresh Parmesan cheese. At this point, I thought there was a fifty-fifty chance I was going to explode.

Even Norton had had enough by this time. Still exhausted from his tour of Lucca, he even decided he'd get off his own chair and snuggle up onto my lap for a while. He figured he deserved a soft lap and some petting while we were waiting for dessert.

All during dinner, there was a man sitting at the table behind us. He had a loud, gravelly voice; he sounded as if Lucca Brazi had, some years earlier, removed his vocal chords with a fork. The entire time we were there, he would point over at Norton, pound the table, laugh incredibly loudly, and scream out to the entire restaurant, *"Il gatto! Incredibile!"* This went on for hours.

The incredible *gatto* was now sound asleep on my lap, but the humans were still going. The waiter brought out some chocolate-covered grapes and three round custard-filled doughy pastries, with miniature American flags stuck into them.

Finally, when we were finished stuffing our faces, the owner of the restaurant made an appearance. He sat down with us and we did our best to converse, although there really was a serious language barrier. We got him to understand that my mother worked with some famous chefs back in Los Angeles, and he got all excited, ran back into another room somewhere, then returned with his scrapbook. As we were flipping through it, admiring his various clippings and credentials, we realized that many of the chefs my mother was friendly with had come to study under or work with this guy. Suddenly she was looking at pictures of her L.A. cooking pals, all with their arms around Mr. Truffle. Needless to say, this lent a whole new air of excitement to our evening. Everyone started talking loudly and waving their hands, even though no one had any idea what anyone else was saying. After we'd gone through all the clippings, he took us on a tour of the kitchen and the rest of the restaurant and then introduced us to his mother—who was eighty-three years old and was still the chef for the restaurant. She'd done all the cooking that night—and did all the cooking six nights a week. We learned that it was her father who'd started the restaurant sixty years earlier.

The check came—and it was embarrassingly low after my snide comment; he hardly charged us for anything, much less for the truffles—and with it came a complimentary bottle of *grappa*. Even for us, that was just too much. We told him we couldn't possibly eat or drink one more thing, so our host and new pal wrapped up the bottle and told us to take it back to France, which of course we did.

As we left, we got hugged and kissed by the old mother, and we were hugging and kissing anyone else who got in our way. Norton had revived himself, so he came in for some heavy petting, too. As we stepped out the door, we were told that we—all four of us—would be welcome back whenever we happened to be in the neighborhood.

a cat
in sicily

(and
other places)

One of the things Janis most wanted to do on her year's sabbatical was travel. Unlike me, who left to my own devices would have been content to plop down in Goult and plop up a year later when it was time to leave, Janis wanted to visit as many places and see as many new things as possible.

Having positions that couldn't be more polar opposites, we compromised. We would travel and visit and see as much as we could until I got too cranky and started complaining. At that point, we'd either return to Goult or find a nice, quiet beach somewhere where the most active moment would be turning over from back to stomach to tan another side of the body.

We wound up moving around quite a bit and, of course, wherever we moved, Norton moved. We and he would have it no other way.

One of my fantasies in life is to, one of these days, spend a month or two being a ski bum. I don't actually ski very often or very well, although I can get down a not-too-difficult slope without killing myself. But I enjoy it and it seems like something worth mastering. The idea of paralleling down a mountain at breakneck speed is extraordinarily appealing to me, although I know if I really went at it, there's a good chance I'd wind up in a Swiss emergency room looking a lot like the Boris Karloff version of *The Mummy*.

Norton had been cross-country skiing in Vermont, where I must confess he spent most of the trek on my shoulder, though he did run around in the bushes, following the trail for part of the time. I decided he'd like to see the Alps, so we drove up into the mountains for a weekend.

Janis's idea of fun, in case you were ever in doubt, does not include skiing. It does not, in fact, include any activity where it's possible to break a bone, scrape skin off the body, or ever possibly see one's own blood. But even she was charmed by Aix-les-Bains, on the French side of the Alps.

She got her hopes up as we pulled into town, when she saw there was no snow on the ground. I pointed out to her, however, that the skiing—and thus the snow—was several miles higher. We would stay in Les Bains for two nights, but most of our activities would take place up by the ski slopes.

At this point in the narrative, I would like to interrupt to give a free lesson to everyone reading this book: Don't, under any circumstances, ever try to teach your spouse to ski. It's much, *much* worse than teaching the proper way to drive a stick shift.

I think it sufficient to say that Janis fell down fourteen times in the first three minutes of our lesson. Most of those were directly in front of the ski shop where we rented our equipment. She never even made it to the beginners' slope. Within seconds of her final tumble, her skis were off and she was sitting in the warm restaurant trying to decide which she hated more, skiing or me.

Even Norton deserted me on this occasion. He just wasn't in the mood to frolic in the snow, so he joined Janis for the cat equivalent of a hot toddy.

By the time I'd gotten in my ski time, both girlfriend and cat were, luckily for me, warm and relaxed. They liked the *raclette* dinner I took them to much more than they liked battling nature.

A *raclette* is a very special Alps experience. *Raclette* is a type of cheese that comes in a large brick. When it's served up in the mountains, it's placed on a special *raclette* oven that gets extremely hot and melts the cheese down layer by layer. As it melts, people at the table reach over and use everything from bread to *vinaigred* onions to *cornichons* to tiny baked potatoes to scoop the now-gooey cheese up and eat it. Add some good beer or a cold bottle of white wine, plus a stunning view of the snow-covered Alps, and you've got a memorable dining experience.

Norton was quite pleased with his first *raclette* experience. He was also pleased with the owner of the restaurant, who kept wagging his finger at Norton and enticing him through the swinging door into the kitchen. Every few minutes, we'd hear a "Psssttt" and turn to see the owner, visible through the small porthole in the kitchen door, motioning for the cat to join him. Norton would hop off his chair, disappear for a few moments, then return happily licking his lips.

～～～

As our year abroad was drawing to a close, *The Cat Who Went to Paris* began to be published in various countries around the world. Several of those countries wanted Norton to come do publicity.

England was the one country Norton couldn't visit, since they still have that horrendous six-month quarantine for all animals. But at least the Brits could understand the language and most of the references made in the book. The Japanese translator had a few problems.

While we were in Goult, she wrote me the following note:

Dear Mr. Gethers,

  It was my great pleasure to translate your book. I can't believe there is such an amazing cat as Norton. I have been a dog lover and afraid of cats since my childhood, but through the translation of this book, I have changed greatly. Now I can walk up to a cat, say hello, and scratch under his (or her) chin. I am surprised to know how beautiful and elegant the felines are.

  While translating Norton's story into Japanese, I came across a lot of phrases and a lot of proper nouns which I couldn't understand. I will be very happy if you kindly answer the following questions.

She then proceeded to list all the things she couldn't understand. By the time I got to the end of the list, I was not only amazed that she liked it, I was shocked she had any idea at all what I was writing about. Plus, when I saw the particular references she was questioning, I became a little worried about my own sensibility.

Her first question was: "Is Eric your older brother or younger brother? I have to know which, because in Japan we use a different word for each of them." (More than anything, this made me happy I was only learning French, not Japanese.) Her next question was: "Tarte tatin. What is this? How do you pronounce these words?" (This also made me happy I was living in France rather than Japan.) The list went on: "P. 20. Willie Davis, Willie Wilson, Willie Mays. Who are they? Please explain about them." "P. 20: Who is Roger 'the Dodger' Staubach? Is 'the Dodger' his nickname?" "Grand High Exalted Wizard. What is this?" "What is kibble? Cat food?" "Ted Bundy. Please explain." "Who are the Seven Santini Brothers?" "Who is John Gotti? A real man or an imaginary one?" "What are the Rams? And why do they stink? Please explain." "What kind of shop is Victoria's Secret?" "What is the Liberace Museum in Las Vegas?" "I do not understand the phrase 'Jack La Lanne's personal hell.' Who is Jack La Lanne?"

It went on, but you get the idea. More than anything else, I wondered if there was any other book ever published that had references to Willie Mays, Ted Bundy, kibble, Victoria's Secret, and the Seven Santini Brothers. Probably not. And that was probably a good thing.

The Dutch had a few problems, too. They didn't know the reference to The Grand High Exalted Wizard either, which, of course, is from "The Honeymooners," from whence Norton derives his memorable moniker. They also didn't know who Laura Petrie or Oscar the Grouch were. They did know who Willie Mays was, which made me feel somewhat better. I never heard from the Italian, German, or Swedish translators, so I assume those countries all watch old Seven Santini Brothers movies and shop mail order at Victoria's Secret.

The Dutch publisher invited us to come up from Provence for the publication in Holland. In Amsterdam—where, several years before, Norton had taken the town by storm when we went there with Polanski—my cat picked up exactly where he left off.

The afternoon we arrived, the publisher, a delightful woman named Hanca Leppink, who ran the firm of Luitingh Sijthoff (don't worry: I can't come close to pronouncing it either), had a pub party for Norton up in her conference room. The entire staff turned up to shake hands (or paws) with *De kat die naar Parijs gin.* The humans all drank champagne and munched on Dutch hors d'oeuvres while the star of the party, a certain Scottish Fold, sat in the center of the room munching on his own special plate of herring while everyone at the company took turns petting him.

After the party, Hanca and a few other people from the office took Janis, Norton, and me out to dinner. Norton, still a bit full from all that raw herring, barely nibbled at his share of the *rijstaffel,* though he enjoyed the evening immensely.

The next two days in Amsterdam were spent being interviewed and photographed by Dutch and Belgian newspapers and magazines. The interviews proved to be remarkably similar to the American interviews we'd done—with one exception. There was one question that all Americans stayed away from. But every single Dutch journalist made a point of bringing this up: They wanted to know what I would do when Norton died.

I was so startled by the question and the topic that the first time I had to give an answer, I fumbled and stumbled through some complete piece of pap. By the third or fourth time this came up, I was at least composed, though I never was able to come up with anything satisfactory, much less glib. Basically, what I said is exactly what I felt: This was something I would have great difficulty dealing with and I didn't think I had to begin dealing with it yet. There was a good chance Norton would live for another ten years, at least. Who knew what would happen in ten years? Who knew if *I'd* be alive in ten years?

To be honest, Norton's death is something I'm not able to think about. I know it happens to the best of us; I've certainly been through it with humans, with those closest to me, those whom I've loved the most. Yet, somehow, it's different with my cat. Maybe it's because there's no formal language with which to directly communicate caring or sorrow. When a parent is old or dying, it's easy (unless you're British) to say the words "I love you." And once those words are said, it makes everything less difficult, even the pain of a final separation. Perhaps that kind of verbal communication assuages guilt. Perhaps it's merely a soothing way to release emotions. But with an animal, words are meaningless. It's actions that count (which, strangely enough since I'm a writer, I prefer. I don't really trust words. They can be used to manipulate too easily). In a sense, there's no way to finalize and communicate grief to an animal. And somehow that makes grief all the more difficult to comprehend and come to grips with.

There's no real point to this diatribe except to say that, after my morbid grilling by the Dutch, I think I've become even more solicitous of Norton. When it does finally come time to say good-bye to him, I want to be sure he knows how much he's meant to me.

I may not be able to *tell* him I love him, but I sure can *show* him.

Our brief trip to Amsterdam was notable for a few other memorable moments. I don't know whether I'm responsible for this great cultural leap forward, but I do know that the week Norton and I were there promoting our book, "The Honeymooners" made its first ever appearance on Dutch TV. In the television listings, under the heading for 7 P.M. on the channel Nederland 3, it read: *"Honeymooners. Is een in 1955 opgenomen komische Amerikaanse serie over twee echtparen. De opschepperige bus-chauffeur Ralph Kramden en zign vrouw Alice, en hun buren Ed en Trixie Norton."* I have absolutely no idea what that means, but I desperately hope *opgenomen komische* is the Dutch translation for "Raccoon Lodge."

I'd been to Amsterdam for the first time twenty years before. What I mostly remembered from that trip was that hashish was legal and that, if you took the boat trip up and down the canals, you heard the single most annoying phrase in the world over and over and *over* again. On those trips, the tour guides repeat everything in four languages: English, French, German, and Dutch. So, near the beginning of the tour, when they tell you the history of how Amsterdam got its name, you hear this, in a lilting, lovely accented English: "First the town was built around the Amstel River. And the dams were what made the river function. So you see? Amstel . . . dam . . . Ams*tel*dam . . . *Amster*dam!" Then, once the English version is finished, a couple of minutes later, you hear the guide, blabbing away in German. You don't understand anything you hear until the guide comes to the phrase "Amstel . . . dam . . . Ams*tel*dam . . . *Amster*dam!" A few minutes after that, the French begins and you can maybe pick out one or two phrases, and then comes "Amstel . . . dam . . . Ams*tel*dam . . . *Amster*dam!" And there's still one more to go. There's some guttural Dutch, then some more guttural Dutch, then even more guttural Dutch, then, that's right: "Amstel . . . dam . . . Ams*tel*-

dam . . . *Amster* dam!'' Believe me, this is not something you can get out of your mind easily. Twenty years later, if someone orders an Amstel Light, I find myself going, ''Amstel . . . light . . . Amstellight . . . Amster Light!''

I'm almost over the fixation now, and I suppose I should get serious psychiatric help, but I did refuse to take another canal tour with Norton and Janis. I didn't want to be repeating that phrase over and over to myself when I'm eighty years old and living in the home for aged cat owners.

One thing I did revisit while in Amsterdam was the Anne Frank house.

Janis and I walked to the famed hiding place with Norton on my shoulder. Two blocks away, Janis suddenly went sprawling in the middle of the street. I helped her up, concerned but certainly not overly concerned, figuring she'd merely tripped. But when she was back on her feet, tears were streaming down her cheeks and she grabbed me, bordering on hysteria. Astonished, I asked her what the hell was going on.

''You don't understand,'' she sobbed. ''I sprain my ankle almost every week! My ankles are so weak I can hardly walk and it hurts so *much!*''

''Don't cry,'' I tried to soothe. ''It's not the worst thing in the world.''

That only made her sob harder. ''It *is* the worst thing in the world. I can't walk without hurting myself! And I look like an idiot, falling down all the time! *What could be worse!!!*''

''Well,'' I said slowly, holding her in my arms and thinking about where we were headed, ''how about being forced to hide in an attic for three years and then being killed by Nazis?''

That ended the ankle problem and any ensuing complaints. We then walked—slowly—to the museum and, with a subdued cat, saw where the tragic story had all transpired.

Afterward, we walked back to our hotel in silence—it's almost impossible to talk after being enveloped by the sadness of that house. Janis didn't mention her ankle and, for the first time in months, Norton didn't meow repeatedly to let me know it was past his feeding time.

~~~

Our last major trip of the year was to Sicily, a place I'd desperately wanted to visit after sitting through *Godfather I* and *II* forty-seven times each.

We were particularly excited about going. It seemed more exotic than our other travels yet not at all intimidating. It promised to be luxurious yet still mysterious. There was Italian food, but even better than normal because it was *garlicy* Italian food. And we knew Norton would be accepted. He'd seen *The Godfather* at least as many times as I had.

Getting there was your basic nightmare, unfortunately. This is the worst thing about traveling with a cat: If a plane's late, a person can relax in the bar, go to the bathroom, do whatever he wants. But it's extremely difficult for a cat to cope when takeoff is delayed by an hour or two. I do everything possible to keep things under control for Norton. He has access to his litter box until the last possible moment. He's free to roam around at all times except for when airline officials tell me he must be in his traveling kennel. And, of course, Norton is an experienced traveler, so he rarely panics. But it's not fair to keep a cat away from a litter box too long (even Norton has his limits), and though I try to make traveling as comfortable as possible for him, it has to be faced that he must go through some inconveniences if he wants to come along.

The plane leaving for Rome was an hour and a half late. Luckily the plane was fairly empty and, having learned my lesson from a couple of accidents early in our traveling experiences, I brought a portable litter box on board. I didn't fill it up with litter—that would have been a little much—but I did unfold it and put it under the seat in front of me. Every twenty minutes or so, I'd put Norton in the box until he got the urge to use it. Then I was able to get rid of the box in the bathroom—and no one on the plane was ever bothered.

The airline officials in Italy are even more relaxed than in France. For both takeoffs and landings (from Marseille to Rome, then from Rome to Catania in Sicily), the stewards let Norton sit calmly on my lap. I think he reminded them a little bit of Marcello Mastroianni, so they just decided to leave him be.

Supposedly, our hotel was about an hour's drive from the Catania airport. There was one small problem, however: It's not possible to get *out* of Catania. We picked up our rental car (and immediately put a litter box *with* litter on the floor in the back), took a look at our instructions, drove away—and got hopelessly lost. We were told to leave the airport and look for signs that lead to the autostrade, then take that in the direction of the town of Enna. We left the airport—and there were no signs. Not one. Not even a stop sign at the intersection. We took a guess and made a right, heading down a road that looked like something out of *Mad Max.* After fifteen minutes of aimless driving through slums

and totally deserted, burnt-out areas, we stopped and motioned to a pedestrian. "Autostrade?" we said pathetically.
"Enna?"

We got directions promptly (and loudly)—but they were
the wrong directions. After another bewildering fifteen
minutes, we stopped and asked somebody else. This person
shook his head gravely, started doing "tsk tsk" with his
tongue, and told us we were lost. Thanks a lot, pal. He then
gave us long, complicated *new* directions, which also
proved to be completely wrong. Eventually we struck out
on our own again and found the autostrade, although we
never saw a sign that said anything even remotely resem-
bling ENNA. However, we did see something that pointed
us toward Messina, which the map showed was approximately the right direction. The miracle of it all was that we
were told it would take us an hour to get to Taormina,
where we were staying, and when we pulled up to our
hotel, the trip had taken exactly an hour. The moral of that
story is that normal directions in Sicily seem to be, "First
you pull out of the airport. Then you get lost for half an
hour and feel like an idiot . . ."

I don't want to turn this section into a travelogue. Let's
just leave it that Norton did all the usual touring. He went
to the Villa Romana, near the Piazza Armerina, which has
incredible Roman tiles (Janis liked the ones of the birds
with bright plumage; I preferred the bikini-clad women
dancing arm in arm). We went up to Castlemodo, a little
town that overlooks what seems to be the entire world.
Norton got lugged to Siracusa, which once was the center
of the world and, judging from everything I've seen, probably should be again. He went with us to Noto, an eighteenth-century village which is entirely gold-hewed. Even
the white wine has a bronze tint to it. He also went to

Agricento and the extraordinary Valley of the Temples and to the town of Sciacca, a city of thermal baths (I'm sure this doesn't need to be said, but yes, I did drive Janis crazy doing a lot of Sciacca Therapy jokes). We had dinner one night in a total nontouristy town called Forza d'Agro. We ate at a small café as farmers walked by, carrying on their heads baskets of grain and fruit and even chickens, on their way home from the fields. Wild cats kept coming up to our table to beg for food, which I think made Norton feel a little guilty. Also somewhat thankful that he was with us, rather than out on his own.

The only place Norton didn't go with us was to see Mount Etna—while it was exploding. We went at night and it was an awesome sight, beautiful and terrible at the same time. Everywhere we looked there was molten red lava flowing down the mountain toward small besieged villages. I figured Norton was better off in the hotel. I didn't know if he'd be feeling adventurous, but I didn't particularly want to deal with having a Scottish Fold Red Adair on my hands.

Of the places we stayed, Norton much preferred Taormina. We stayed in a fifteenth-century castle that stood on a cliff, looming several hundred feet over the sea. And when I say looming, I mean *looming*. The first thing Norton did when we checked in was to dash out onto our balcony and go racing—much too fast to do my heart much good—across the very narrow ledge, the entire length of the hotel. Practically every minute we were in our room, Norton spent on that ledge, staring out over the water far below. If he wasn't there, he was outside by the pool, which was also located high above the sea. He liked it there, too, mostly because the waitresses would bring him little strips of chicken while he sat on his chaise longue.

The highlight of our Sicilian trip, without question, was

discovering an inn and restaurant in the middle of nowhere (or near the town of Gangivecchia, to be more precise, absolutely smack dab in the middle of the island). The restaurant is called The ex-Convento di Gangivecchia. It's called that, cleverly enough, because it's an ex-convent, dating from the thirteenth century.

It's a giant and magnificent structure, over forty rooms, surrounded by two hundred acres of gardens and farm-land—everything served there is grown or slaughtered there, too—and it's run by two women, a mother and daughter, the Baroness Wanda Tornabene and Giovanna Tornabene. We made so many pleasurable groaning noises while we were eating the asparagus fritter, the fresh *tape-nade,* the homemade gnocchi in eggplant and tomato sauce, and the homemade cannolis and hot lemon-curd fritters, that the Baroness came over to our table to talk (I think she was just happy to get us to stop eating). She admired Nor-ton right off, which endeared her to us, and told us that the last such distinguished visitor at the ex-Convento was Prince Charles. Personally, I think Norton could have held on to Di if he'd had the chance, so I didn't think much of the comparison, but I thanked her for the compliment anyway.

Despite the fact that the ex-Convento was three hours from anywhere a normal person might be in Sicily, the three of us drove back there four days later—when I told Janis that I might kill someone if I saw another Roman temple. Since it was his second visit, Norton felt right at home and made himself comfortable while he explored various rooms supposedly off-limits to customers. But the Tornabenes didn't mind. In fact, when we left, we discov-ered there was no check.

They felt honored to be able to treat Signore Norton to a good lunch, they said.

Touched, I told them that Signore Norton was equally honored. I, however, was happy the next day when it was time for the gray Signore to return to France. If he spent much more time in Sicily, I believe his little folded ears might just have been overwhelmed by his ever-larger swelled head.

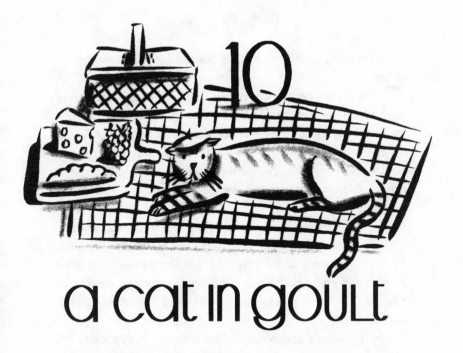

a cat in goult

On New Year's Day of last year, our French friends gave
us a present: They provided us with the most wonderful day
I've ever spent. In so many ways it's what our entire year
was all about.

Our friends in Goult had a tradition. For ten years, they'd
hiked up into the mountains on New Year's Day. The hike
was a relatively easy one, beginning just above the town of
St. Saturnin d'Apt. Each year, they started at the same spot
and hiked about an hour until they reached an old deserted
stone village, abandoned over a hundred years ago when
the town's water supply ran out. Everyone who hiked had
to bring some form of good food or drink; when they
arrived at the abandoned village—called Travignon—everyone then ate and drank, napped in the sun, celebrated
another year of good living, wished for a new year with
more of the same, then hiked back home, happy, tired, a

little bit drunk, and more than a little bit filled with good
cheer.

A few weeks before Christmas, Janis, Norton, and I were
invited on their hike. Touched and honored, we agreed
immediately, though we warned them that two other Americans would also be with us—that was the week Norm and
Esther came visiting. No problem, we were told. We were
official Goultoise now and we could invite whomever we
wanted.

The day before New Year's Day was cold and wintry.
The day after New Year's Day was even colder and rainy.
But our *bons amis* had assured us that the weather for their
New Year's hike was always perfect—and when we awoke
that day, the sun was shining down and the sky was blue
and clear.

I had crudités and wine stuffed into my backpack and a
curious cat stuffed into my shoulder bag as we hiked up into
the hills. We all bounced along, chattering in bizarre pi-
geon-English and pseudo-French, everyone being ultrasen-
sitive to everyone else's inability to communicate properly.
We took in the glory of the countryside until we reached
Travignon, situated at the top of the mountain. It was a kind
of hippie camp now. In the structures that still had roofs,
there were mattresses, tattered sleeping bags, and crude
tables made out of large rocks. There was also a nice tradition: In some of the ruins, there were full bottles of wine,
left by the last person to sleep there, waiting to greet the
next camper.

The sun was shining and warm (the official weather word
on Provence from the locals: a cold climate with a hot
sun—and that's the perfect description) and it was now time
to eat. Blankets were spread on the ground. Cheese and
fruit and bread were spread out; wine was opened. We

gathered kindling to build a campfire, on which was cooked delicious homemade sausages.

After lunch, some of the group went off hiking and prowling. Two American pseudo-Goultoise lay down on a large, surprisingly comfortable rock and took naps in the sun. The smallest, grayest, flattest-earred member of the hike did his best to poke through the campfire and eat as many leftover sausage bits as he could find before joining his dad in the midday snooze.

Years of tradition broke on the hike back. We all realized we weren't ready for the day to end, so we went back to one of the hikers' houses to prolong the warmth and good cheer. We ate pasta and sat around until one in the morning listening to our friend Jean-Guy, a musician, play the guitar and sing his own, romantic compositions. Norton was having such a good time, I'm sure that if only Jean-Guy knew any tunes in English, one member of the hike would have happily meowed out the words to "Michael Row the Boat Ashore."

By the time we made it back to our house, the day had become a dreamlike experience. Friendships were cemented, new traditions were established, new levels of communication had been reached. Sometimes when I'm lecturing about the wonders of my cat, I do feel a little guilty and feel as if I should add a P.S., which I will add here, that occasionally people—even relative strangers—can also provide an awful lot of the good things in life.

There is a New Year's superstition in France. It is believed that the first twelve days of the year are crucial to one's happiness. If the first day is a good one, you will have a good month of January. If day two goes well, so will February. If day three is fine, March will be a lucky month, and so on. I don't remember all the details of our first twelve days of last year, but it's certain we were living under a lucky star. Or perhaps it's easier to make your own luck when surrounded by true friends, Monsieur Bonnelly's wine, and a cat who appreciates the splendor and glory of the hot Provençal sun.

~~~

As all good things must, our year abroad did end.

Duty, not to mention the need to make a living, called.

In our last weeks, we went from town to town—from nontouristy Jucas and Murs to the magnificent red cliffs of Roussillon to the chilly ruins of Oppede-le-vieux—soaking it all in, trying to sere into our brains not only the magnificent sights but the European attitude and the feeling of appreciation for life which we hoped to carry back to America. We lunched in the wonderful villages of Manosque, stuffed ourselves with desserts from the *pâtisserie* in Cabrieres, toured the beauteous St.-Rémy and the rest of the region known as Les Alpilles, and often just sat in our house in Goult, sipping a glass of cold rosé wine and marveling at the splendor we could find in our own backyard.

Our last night in Goult, our friend Anne had a small dinner party. Just our close circle of French friends (though one woman, Anette, was Swedish, she was considered honorary French, having lived in Goult for years).

We sat around Anne's dining table—Janis, Norton, myself, our new friends—talking easily and eating well, of course, and, naturally, drinking a lot of good red wine. And during the evening, our sense of sadness lifted. We somehow knew we'd be back. Or these new people in our lives would visit us in New York. Or that, even if we never saw them again, they'd all somehow be with us for the rest of our lives.

At midnight, we knew it was finally time to say good-bye. Everyone kissed and hugged and exchanged small gifts of farewell and of thanks. Then Janis, Norton, and I strolled the two or three streets back to our house. When we rounded the corner across from the restaurant Le Tonneau, walking along the front of Goult's thousand-year-old castle, we found ourselves at the very spot of the dread outdoor bird cage. But the birds were not there; for some reason they'd been taken inside. Norton, not believing his good fortune but wanting to take advantage of it, hesitated, then walked to the front door of the house and sniffed cautiously. Proudly, he turned toward us and took one strutting step forward. At that moment, we heard the loud chirp of a bird from somewhere within the house. A final farewell.

Norton led the way, of course, but Janis and I sprinted after him the best we could, running and laughing—and meowing—all the way back to our three-hundred-year-old home.

And the next morning, we were still laughing—and meowing—as we left Goult and headed back to America.

PART THREE

a cat returns

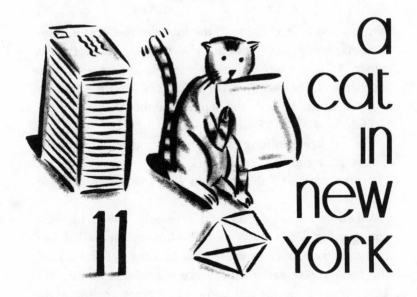

a cat in new york

11

Janis and I returned home wondering exactly how we were going to resume our previous lives. Our careers were up in the air—her sabbatical was over and she had to find out what, if indeed any, job was waiting for her; I had to decide whether or not to return to corporate life—as were our living arrangements, our relationship, and all sorts of other loose ends.

Norton had none of those questions to resolve. He returned to find himself a changed man (I know that's not exactly right, but it sounds a lot better than "a changed cat"). He returned to find himself a celebrity.

Soon after arriving back in New York, Norton and I were on the road again, traveling to Los Angeles for business and venturing around the country for the paperback publicity tour for *The Cat Who Went to Paris.*

The first indication I had that, in the year we were away, fame had found a certain Scottish Fold, came in Boston.

Norton and I were sitting in the lobby of the Boston Four Seasons, being interviewed by a reporter for a Boston paper. All of a sudden, three women walked by—a fiftyish mother and her two thirtyish daughters—and the mother stopped short, turned, and stared straight at us.

"Oh my god!" she said slowly. "Is that *him?*"

For one brief, shining moment, I, of course, thought she was referring to me. Yeah, *right.*

"Is that *Norton?!*" she squealed and came rushing over to pet him.

When I acknowledged that the creature now on his back and purring loudly was indeed Norton, she called her two daughters over to meet him. It turns out she'd read the book a year earlier and, since she traveled a lot, had kept her eye open for you-know-who whenever she was on the road.

"I *knew* I'd run into him one of these days," she gushed. "Do you think he'd ever want to come up and visit us on the Cape?"

This was by no means his only brush with Fold groupies. When I—excuse me, we—appeared at Books & Company in Dayton, Ohio, one woman came up and shyly told me she'd driven over a hundred miles just to meet Norton. Since she'd come so far, I introduced the two of them and left them alone for several minutes. When their chat was over, the woman didn't seem at all disappointed. In fact, she had a big smile on her face. I have no idea what they discussed and decided I was better off not knowing.

In Detroit he was recognized in the airport. As we were boarding the plane, a woman came over and asked whether that was that strange cat who went to Paris. When I said yes, she asked if she could have his autograph. I tried to explain to her that even though he was a very smart cat, he couldn't

actually hold a pen and write. So she wouldn't be too disillu-
sioned, I told her I was sure he could spell his name, but
the problem was a lack of opposable thumbs. That seemed
to satisfy her.

In Los Angeles, a bellman at the Four Seasons told me a
great story. He said he was helping two women up to their
rooms and he overheard them talking about a book they'd
read about a most amazing cat.

"Ladies," he said to them. "Excuse me for kibitzing
your conversation, but are you talking about Norton
Gethers?"

Astonished, they said that they were. "But how did you
know?" one of them asked him.

"Because he stays here," the bellman told the women. "I
know him. This is Norton's hotel of choice."

Norton and I were in L.A. that trip to talk about selling
the movie rights to our book. Initially, quite a few producers and directors were interested. There was a lot of talk
about Mel Gibson as me (a natural, I figured) and Michelle
Pfeiffer as Janis (a natural, she figured). Norton was tough
casting—I thought maybe they'd get a dog who was an
impressionist—but that wasn't really my problem. We narrowed the list down to five producers, then those five took
it to their respective film studios. That's when we ran into
a bit of trouble.

The first executive called me from 20th Century-Fox. "I
like it," she said. "But I think it's a little soft. Explain to me
how you'd turn it into a movie." So I did. I went through
Act One, Act Two, and Act Three. I told how I'd develop
the characters and I told exactly what role the cat would
play. "I still like it," she said when I was finished. "But I
still think it's a little soft. Is it possible that we can add some
sort of thriller element?"

"Like a Cat-Meets-Clint-Eastwood-kind-of-a-thing?" I said. *"Dirty Norton?"*

"That's interesting," she said. "That's a very interesting way to go."

"Not for me," I told her and hung up.

The next executive I had to go through was at Warner Brothers. She, too, felt it was a little soft for a movie. So I went through the same pitch, told her how it would work, and she said, "I like it. But do you think it would be possible to have the cat talk?"

"You mean like *Look Who's Meowing?*"

"Exactly," she said.

"I'm hanging up now," I said.

The third person worked at the Imagine film studio. We went through the usual exchange—Her: too soft; Me: here's how to do it—and then when I was all finished, we had this memorable exchange:

"I love it," she told me. "I really do." (Important Aside: The phrase "I love it" is totally meaningless. Studio executives want you to like them, so they never tell you face-to-face that they think anything is bad. Afterward, they just refuse to take your phone calls, so you get the hint that they don't want to do your project.) "But," she went on, "you have to help me with one thing."

"Anything," I promised.

"What do I do when my boss comes into my office and says, 'How is this different from *Turner and Hootch?*' "

"You mean the Tom Hanks police thriller about a cop and his dog?" I asked.

"Uh-huh," she said.

"Welllll . . . that's a tough one," I agreed. "How about telling him this *isn't* a police thriller, there's *no* cop and *no* dog?"

"I don't know if that'll do it," she said.

That's when I called my agent and told him I didn't want to have any more conversations about turning the book into a movie. So Norton wouldn't ever get his paw prints in front of Mann's Chinese Theater—we could live with that. At least I could.

This isn't to say that he was ignored by his adoring public. I would guess that, over time, we've received a thousand letters from people who've read *The Cat Who Went to Paris*. Every so often, someone mentions that they liked the book. Mostly, people ask questions about Norton. Or just praise him. Some people send him presents. Norton has received his own Feline Passport (a popular new product, so I'm told), he got a self-published book of poetry that was dedicated to him, and he was sent several inspirational poems, framed quite nicely. One woman sent him a package that included a couple of cans of Pounce, a lovely salt shaker (don't ask me—I just report the facts!), a Christmas tree ornament, and a photo of her car, which she thought he'd be interested in seeing.

Many people send photos of their cats. I'm glad to report they usually preface these with the words "Dear Norton, I know my little [fill in the blank: Daffodil, Sarge, or Ezekial] isn't as handsome as you are but . . ."

Most of the letters are actually wonderful. A lot of people were moved by the story of the death of my father and wanted to let me know that by sharing my grief I'd helped them with theirs. Many letters began with phrases like "Dear Peter and Norton, Excuse the familiarity of the greeting, but I feel like I know you both so well now. You seem like old pals." Many letters, amazingly enough, were simply addressed to Norton, Sag Harbor, New York. Don't ask me how the post office knew to deliver them, but they arrived.

Norton and I got letters from ninety-year-old people letting me know that my book inspired them to get one last cat before they died; women who sent semi-suggestive photos or suggestions along with invitations to visit anytime (my favorite enticement was from one woman who ended her letter with: "I keep a can of Pounce handy at all times. One in the kitchen, one in the bedroom. You're welcome to use either one." I don't know about you, but a can of shrimp Pounce by the bed turns *me* on!); letters from people with AIDS who told me their cats provided them with enormous solace and comfort; and one extraordinarily moving call from a woman who had a retarded daughter and wanted to tell me that the only thing that made her daughter smile was when she looked at the photo of Norton on the cover of our book.

Some people wrote eloquently of being touched by my relationship with Norton and by his unique personality. Others wrote simply to tell me that my feelings about Norton made them realize how much they loved their own cats.

I got several angry letters and calls, too. Several people worried that I placed my cat in too many dangerous situations (which I don't—honest), and one man wrote me an extremely nasty letter, telling me that just because my life was so interesting was no reason to write a book shoving his face in the fact that his life was so boring.

The ASPCA got in touch with me. They were putting out a book of photographs of famous animals. Would Norton agree to be included? It was for a good cause, so I agreed. Then they called back and said that the person in charge of the project had just read my book—and he was shocked to find that I let Norton eat ice cream and jelly doughnuts. He found that so offensive, he wouldn't allow Norton to be associated with his work.

And people wonder why organizations have trouble getting donations.

My two very favorite letters came from young girls (get your mind out of the gutter!).

One was from a thirteen-year-old in Greater Manchester, England. After telling me that *The Cat Who Went to Paris* was her favorite book ever, she added such gems as: "We have a cat named Floyd and he is just like Norton except (1) he has blue eyes, (2) he is not a Scottish Fold and (3) he is not very smart." Other than that, exactly alike. My English fan also told me that she "ranked the book as one of the greatest modern books ever written." Ah, yes. *The Brothers Karamazov, The Great Gatsby,* and *The Cat Who Went to Paris,* not necessarily in that order.

The best of them all, however, came from an eleven-year-old girl in Colorado. Here's how her letter began: "Dear Mr. Gethers, I just want to tell you that your book is one of the *absolute best* books I have *ever* read (and believe me I read almost everything). I'm in love with Norton!" She also had this to say, which I liked quite a lot: "To tell you the truth, when I first got your book (for Christmas) I thought it was going to be another hummdrumm book (like us kids so commonly get). But it definitely wasn't!" What made her letter so memorable, however, was her spelling. Among the misspelled words: seems (seams), believe (belive), commonly (comenly), commonly (comonly), definitely (defenetly), wasn't (wasen't), perfect (perfict), writing (writeing), and please (pelease). At the end, she added these two wonderful addendums: "P.S. I admire your work because I want to be a author also and I hope I can be as good as you. P.P.S. Sorry my spelling isn't grate."

~~~

One of the most amazing side effects of writing about my cat is how interested people are in Norton. They've taken to him as if he's a member of their own family. The nice thing is, people seem to appreciate him. They "get" what it is that makes him so special. Another amazing thing to me is how interested people became in *my* life. It's a strange sensation to open yourself up to a hundred thousand people or so, telling very personal stories about everything from idiotically talking aloud to a cat to coping with the death of a parent. But all of a sudden, I find that Norton and I have this kind of odd (sometimes very odd!) extended family all over the country. All over the world, in fact. When we're on the road or via letters or even in the occasional stray phone call, people tend to want answers to the same questions. I think it might not be a bad idea to answer them all here. Not only will this save you the twenty-nine cents for a stamp, it'll keep me from losing my voice on the next tour.

The single most common question—usually asked by women with thirty-year-old unmarried daughters—is: "Are you and Janis married yet?" The answer is no. We lived together for the year we were in France and, except for the several moments per week when we wanted to kill each other (especially when she refuses to put the open milk back in the refrigerator), we did okay. But I don't seem to be the marrying (or even the living together) kind and neither does she. We're also both children of the sixties and we share the same view of marriage: It's only a piece of paper and a relationship doesn't have to be made legal for it to be a good one. To top that all off (since you're so nosy), and I realize this is a character flaw, I figure there is a reasonable chance I'll one day meet either Sarah Jessica Parker, Michelle Pfeiffer, Katie Couric, Uma Thurman, or Sandra Day O'Connor (okay, okay, I don't *really* think she belongs on this list of sexy women, but I don't want people to think I'm shallow) and if I do, I just don't think I could bring myself to say the words "Hi. Meet the wife."

The second most asked question: "How old is Norton?" Here are all of his vital statistics: By the time this book comes out, he will be ten years old. I'm expecting him to be around at least ten more years (and every time I see an item in a newspaper or magazine about a twenty-two-year-old cat, I make sure I read it aloud to him). He weighs nine and a half pounds, is still pretty trim, is in excellent health (he's been sick twice that I can think of, both times with a touch of the flu), and yes, he does like traveling with me. I am starting to think of getting another cat. I think it would be good for him; it would help keep him young. But I'm still too selfish to do so. Traveling with two cats would be too difficult. Perhaps in another few years, when Norton really starts to slow down and traveling becomes less fun for him.

In descending order, these are the other questions I'm usually bombarded with:

3. *Do cats need passports?* No. When traveling internationally, all they need is a health certificate. They need to have their shots within a week of leaving for Europe—and be sure to keep the record because, to return to America, you have to prove that those shots were received within a year of your return. Any vet knows exactly what shots to give and what papers are needed.

4. *How's your mom?* She's great. I just threw her a surprise seventieth birthday party at Spago (Norton didn't go but he

did send a telegram). She's writing two new cookbooks, travels constantly, is so busy it's hard to get her to sit still for more than two minutes, and generally is quite happy.

5. *Will you publish my cat book?* No.

6. *Will you read my cat book?* Not unless I have to.

7. *Do cats get jet lag?* Think about it. Cats sleep *all* the time. They're not awake long enough to get jet lag!

8. *Why won't my cat act like Norton?* I have no idea. Do you talk to him constantly, pet him incessantly, give him whatever he wants whenever he wants it, and pamper him at first-class hotels all around the world? This may have something to do with it.

9. *Is* The Cat Who Went to Paris *ever going to be a movie? And is Norton going to play himself?* Believe it or not, after the nightmare of trying to sell the book when it first came out, it looks like things worked out after all. The book has been bought by Paramount and the screenplay is in the works. Norton is definitely *not* going to play himself. That's where I drew the line and demanded a stunt cat. However, we did have to go to L.A. recently for a movie pow-wow. Norton and I went onto the studio back lot for our meeting. (The best thing about going to the Paramount back lot are the names of the buildings. You can sit around a conference table in the Bob Hope Building or stroll by the Edith Head Wardrobe Building. If you prefer, you can also rendezvous at the Ernst Lubitsch Annex, at the corner of Rudolph Valentino Place, in the Mary Pickford Wing, or my favorite—and this is where I got to have my meeting—in the Jerry Lewis Building.) We met with the studio executive in charge of the project and the producers of the film. When we walked in, I think they were all a little nervous that Norton would turn out to be somewhat of a letdown. But, as usual, he was anything but. He sat on the couch next to

me for the first part of the meeting, then as he got a little bored hearing all the stories about his life repeated for the umpteenth time, he began to explore. First he sized up the producer's gigantic office, sniffing at the various cupboards, shelves, and tables. Then he hopped up onto the desk and snooped around there, probably trying to catch a glimpse of the contract to see if he had script approval. Then, while we story-conferenced the movie, Norton went out into the hallway and introduced himself to the various secretaries and story editors in their nearby offices. By the time he came back, the script was ready to be written and I think the Paramount executive was thinking of starring Norton in a remake of *Gone With the Wind*. The producer also had a vision of screening the movie, if it's actually made, at the White House. I think he figures we can get a good quote from Socks. My hope is merely that Norton is the first cat invited to a state dinner. Or that he receives some kind of official post (even if it's only a Scratching Post).

10. *Will you write another book about Norton?* No. I think this is it. It's time for me to reclaim my own life as a human being able to stand on my own two feet (or nearly) and to let my cat return to his anonymous, if still extraordinary, ways.

~~~

The first book I wrote about Norton ended with the death of my father. Luckily for me, this book does not end with anything nearly so dramatic or traumatic. However, that doesn't mean that life has and will continue to sail a smooth course.

The Cat Who Went to Paris ended with everyone living happily ever after. But, of course, nobody *really* lives happily ever after. Things happen.

Things change.

That's what makes life interesting, if not always sane.

But, to steal from a fairly respectable poetic voice, most things change with a whimper rather than a bang.

My father's been dead three and a half years now and the pain has certainly subsided, but it's a very strange thing: His death has left me with a perpetual sadness. There is a great poem by Gerard Manley Hopkins called "Margaret Are You Grieving?" It's ostensibly about the grief one feels for a loved one who dies, but it's *really* about the fact that what we're feeling is grief for *ourselves.* That what we're all crying about is our own mortality. While I can honestly say I miss my dad every single day in all sorts of little ways—I con-stantly think how he would have loved a particular movie or book, or how I'd like to get his opinion on something, or how happy he'd have been that Clinton won the elec-tion—I know that some of that sadness I'm feeling is for myself. I remember how upset I was when my grandfather died. Then, of course, the pain of my father's death is still a wound, perhaps not so raw anymore but certainly still tender. And then I think, Uh-oh—guess who's next in line?

So, happily, there are no recent deaths to deal with these days, but there is still grief nonetheless. I find myself crying at movies I never would have cried at in the past. Every so often, I'll even find myself crying at bad sitcoms that deal with the subject of loss (and believe me, something's a little screwy when you cry at the rerun of "Family Ties" when Alex goes off to college). There's nothing to do about this. It doesn't affect my life. I have as much fun as I've always had. I laugh just as much as always. It's just that, as one gets older, life gets slightly and irreversibly sadder.

Relationships change, too.

I am, of course, still crazy about my mom. She's as cool

as a mother can be. But, though she's coping wonderfully well with widowhood, she's more nervous about things than she used to be. She spent her whole life taking care of my father. Now there's a void: She needs something and someone else to take care of. I find I'm a lot less patient around her, that I get irritated over practically nothing. This has nothing to do with her. She's still great. It has everything to do with my reaction to the fact that she, too, is getting older and isn't—and couldn't be—the same person she was in the past.

I guess I don't like when things change, although I have yet to discover any way to stop them from doing so.

My brother, Eric—the one who's responsible for giving me Norton—and I don't speak anymore. I thought he was screwing up his life and made the mistake of telling him so, in no uncertain terms. He was equally certain I was wrong. Also that it was none of my business, which in retrospect is hard to argue with. So in a particularly painful conversation, he made it clear that, though at one point when we were younger we were very, very friendly, our lives are no longer entwined.

I've come from a family that was extremely close and loving. And we've been close my entire life. That foundation has always been a big part of my identity. But somehow, inexorably it seems, that family and foundation has eroded. The family no longer exists. It's gone, and that is a change most difficult and painful to adjust to.

Friendships, too, alter themselves. It was interesting to see the reactions when Janis and I left for France. Many of my relationships are professional ones. As a publisher, I buy books from agents, I work closely with authors. Once I stepped down as the head of a company, it was extraordinary to see which agents stopped calling because they decided I was no longer useful, and which authors suddenly realized there might be someone who could be a more beneficial dinner companion. Some people, I think, were resentful that I was actually trying to make my life better. Some didn't give it nearly that much thought and simply moved on to someone else who could help them more.

Even more personal friendships went through changes. Some very close friends resented our leaving, didn't understand why we'd want new friendships and new experiences. They felt that our leaving was some form of rejection. So, much to my surprise, certain relationships were altered, some subtly, some not, for reasons that were beyond my control as well as my comprehension.

One big change, of my own doing, is that I have made my escape from corporate life a long-lasting one. Recently, I was offered the chance to get back on the publishing fast track and run a very large company. This would have meant quite a bit of prestige and more money than I'd ever thought I'd make. But after an agonizing week of worrying about my future and dreaming of a large house in Provence that would now be affordable, I turned the job down. I decided to follow my cat on this one and stay as independent as possible. I may regret it—and already have, on occasion—but when I finally rejected the offer, it was as if a five-hundred-pound weight was lifted from my back. This is one instance where change might be for the better.

Janis and I haven't changed very much. We still have our separate apartments and our separate lives, yet we still have our life together. We both seem to like it this way. Is it permanent? Is it unchangeable? I don't have the foggiest. But we've been through too much together and care about each other way too much to even conceive of anything else. I like our chances.

However, as life shows us over and over again, things do change.

Except for one.

I've spent a lot of time thinking about what it is that makes cats and our relationships to cats so special. Yes, they are extraordinary in their wisdom and their independence and their beauty. Yes, they provide comfort and company and, of course, fun. But it's more than that. I think cats provide permanence.

Cats don't change.

Certainly they get older and certainly they die, but while they're here they are what they are and that's *all* that they are.

Yes, Norton has a tiny touch of arthritis now and can't jump quite as nimbly onto the kitchen cabinet as he used to. And yes, occasionally he will not make the jump at all because he doesn't think he'll make it—which pretty near breaks my heart. And I think he sleeps a bit more than usual and he's no longer quite so eager to go on walks with me—he'd rather stay home and conserve his energy.

But he *is* under my cheek every morning when I wake up.

He meows for breakfast every single day the moment I swing out of bed and my feet touch the floor.

When I come home at night, he's waiting by the front door as soon as my key turns the lock.

When I'm home working, I know that all I have to do is turn slightly to my left and he'll be stretched out on the back of the couch, basking in any sun that might be streaming through the living-room window.

There is absolutely nothing I could do—or ever would do—that could stop him from loving me. And vice versa. There is not much else in life you can say that about.

I'm not old and neither is he, but we're getting older. Just recently I turned forty and Norton turned ten. To celebrate, Janis and I went to New Orleans with some of our closest and dearest friends. We ate *beignets* and oyster po' boys and obscene amounts of crayfish and drank a whole bunch of spicy Cajun martinis and celebrated what's been a pretty damn good life, which is going to, I hope, get even better. We stayed at a beautiful small hotel in the French Quarter called The Lamothe House. When I called to make the reservation, I asked the manager, whose name was Brant, if I could bring my cat.

"I'm terribly sorry," he told me, "but we don't allow pets."

"See, it's my birthday," I started to explain. "And Norton, my cat, kind of goes everywhere I go and this is going to be a big celebration and—"

"Your cat's *Norton?*" Brant asked over the phone.

"Yes," I said, a little taken aback.

"Oh, Norton can come," he then told me matter-of-factly. "Norton's different."

So Norton came. He basked in the sun in the hotel's courtyard, got powdered sugar all over himself eating *beignets* at Café du Monde, charmed the hotel maid, and generally had a good time as we both eased into the next stage of our lives.

And while the older I get, it seems the less I know, I *do* know one thing: For the next important day of my life, whatever and wherever it is, Norton will be there also—to celebrate, to participate, to do whatever it is he decides to do. But he'll be there.

That will never change.

afterword

Janis and I learned all sorts of things from our year living in France.

We learned about wine. We learned how to cook and how to speak a different language. We learned how to balance work with life. We learned how to put a lot of different things in perspective.

Norton learned something, too, which we just discovered.

In our house in Sag Harbor, our bedroom door locks in two ways. It's really two doors that close and meet in the middle of the doorway. On one of them there's a small hook, waist-high, that flips over and catches onto the other door, keeping the doors closed but somewhat flimsily. Then, on the bottom of one of the doors is a latch that slips down and fits into a notch in the floor. This secures both doors as well as our privacy.

We don't usually lock or even close the bedroom door

except when we have overnight guests, because our second bedroom is very nearby. I don't mind being behind closed doors and neither does Janis. Norton, however, doesn't care for it one iota.

He must have a touch of claustrophobia. He almost always spends the entire night in bed with us, but I guess he likes it to be his option because as soon as the door is locked, Norton hops out of bed and decides he has to escape the confines of the room. This is one of the few times in his life he doesn't get his way. When the door's locked, it stays locked. His litter box is upstairs, he's got water upstairs—there's no need for him to leave. So he stays, even if it's against his will.

Until recently, that is.

Before we left for France, Norton could not solve the system of the two locks. Soon after we got back, however, he did something that even I found a little scary.

We had guests one night, so the door was locked. Somewhere around two in the morning, I heard a scratching noise. I tried my best to ignore it, but after a minute or two that proved impossible, so I leaned over the bed to see what the hell was going on.

What was going on was that Norton was trying to lift the latch on the floor with his paw. I watched him claw at it once, twice, three times. Around the sixth or seventh time, he caught it and lifted it out of its notch. He then jumped straight up four or five times until he managed to swat at the waist-high hook that held both doors shut and unlatch that, too. With all the hard work done, Norton gently butted his head into one of the doors, swinging it wide open, then stepped nonchalantly out into the hallway and disappeared.

By this time, Janis was also wide awake and staring down at our little cat.

"You don't think . . ." she started to say to me.

"I *do* think," I told her, in a hushed tone.

We didn't have to say more than that. We were both remembering a moment in France. In the town of Sancerre, at a vineyard. It was the moment Norton saw that amazing dog stand on his hind legs, turn the doorknob, and open the door when he wanted to come in and out. That was the one thing in France that had seemed to overwhelm my cat. It was the only time he'd seen an animal do something he himself couldn't do.

"I don't believe it," Janis sputtered. "He couldn't still remember that. And even if he could, he couldn't make the connection . . . I mean, he just couldn't see that dog and . . . *Could he?*"

"Trust me," I said, nodding as her voice trailed off. "I know my cat."

About the Author

Peter Gethers is—in addition to being his cat's Boswell—a novelist, publisher, and writer for TV and movies. Under the pseudonym Russell Andrews, he is the author of the bestselling thrillers *Gideon* and *Icarus*. He lives in New York City, Sag Harbor, and luckily for him, Sicily (where he was taken by Norton).